Towards an Alternative for Central America and the Caribbean

Edited by
George Irvin and Xabier Gorostiaga

Published in co-operation with
The Institute of Social Studies at The Hague

London
GEORGE ALLEN & UNWIN
Boston   Sydney

© Institute of Social Studies, The Hague, 1985

George Allen & Unwin (Publishers) Ltd,
40 Museum Street, London WC1A 1LU, UK

George Allen & Unwin (Publishers) Ltd,
Park Lane, Hemel Hempstead, Herts HP2 4TE, UK

Allen & Unwin, Inc.,
Fifty Cross Street, Winchester, Mass. 01890, USA

George Allen & Unwin Australia Pty Ltd,
8 Napier Street, North Sydney, NSW 2060, Australia

First published in 1985

British Library Cataloguing in Publication Data

Towards an alternative for Central America and the Caribbean.
1. Central America—Social conditions
I. Irvin, George II. Gorostiaga, Xabier
III. Institute of Social Studies
972.8'053   HN122.5

ISBN 0-04-320172-5
ISBN 0-04-320173-3 pbk

Library of Congress Cataloging in Publication Data

Towards an alternative for Central America and the Caribbean.

"Published in co-operation with the Institute of
Social Studies at The Hague."
  Bibliography: p.
  Includes index.
  1. Central America—Politics and government—1979
—Addresses, essays, lectures. 2. Geopolitics—Central
America—Addresses, essays, lectures. 3. Central America
—Economic policy—Addresses, essays, lectures.
4. Central America—Social policy—Addresses, essays.'
lectures. I. Irvin, George. II. Gorostiaga, Xabier.
III. Institute of Social Studies (Netherlands)

F1439.5.T68 1985   320.9728   84-28228
ISBN 0-04-320172-5 (alk. paper)
ISBN 0-04-320173-3 (pbk. ; alk. paper)

Typeset by Mathematical Composition Setters Ltd
7 Ivy Street, Salisbury, Wilts
and printed in Great Britain by Mackays of Chatham.

CONTENTS

ACKNOWLEDGEMENTS

The papers published in this volume are the revised versions of some of those presented at a Policy Workshop on Central America and the Caribbean held in June 1983 at the Institute of Social Studies, The Hague, in cooperation with the Nicaraguan Institute of Economic and Social Research (INIES) and the Regional Coordinating Body for Research on Central America and the Caribbean (CRIES). That Policy Workshop and the Seminar that followed were financed by the Ministry of Foreign Affairs, Department of Technical Cooperation, of the Government of the Netherlands, and indirectly by all the institutions involved. I am grateful for all that assistance, without which the venture would not have been possible.

I am also grateful to the academic and administrative staff of the Institute of Social Studies for their willing assistance and cooperation, to the Publications Committee of the Institute for agreeing to help finance the publication of this book, and to Jean Sanders for her final editing of the manuscript.

George Irvin
Institute of Social Studies
October 1984

PREFACE

The purpose of this book is to make available to an English-speaking readership a set of critical essays on Central America and the Caribbean written mainly by academics from the region itself. The book is neither conventionally disciplinary nor primarily academic. It is a contribution to a political debate at a time of acute, if uneven, regional crisis which in Central America has taken the form of protracted insurrectionary struggle in which the United States is now directly involved. The debate over the future of the region, for this reason, may prove to be as decisive to international politics in the 1980s as that over Vietnam was in the 1960s.

Although the Vietnam analogy must be treated with care it does serve to illuminate at least one area of our concern. The debate over Vietnam was dominated by the logic of East-West conflict and, in the end, its resolution turned on growing public awareness of the political and financial cost of continued US military presence in South East Asia. Even at the end of the war, detailed knowledge of the economics and politics of Vietnam remained a specialist preserve. Today, by contrast, the debate over the Caribbean Basin is more informed by North-South considerations and by the need to locate revolutionary struggles within a specific historical and social context. This is why the book is both an attempt to analyse the roots of the current crisis and to shift the terrain of debate towards outlining perspectives for an alternative model of development. It is this vision of a region, still desperately poor but with an enormous development potential given its combined population and resources, which lies at the heart of the present work.

The book grows out of a Policy Workshop, held in June 1983, at the Institute of Social Studies in The Hague in co-operation with the Nicaraguan Institute of Economic and Social Research (INIES) and the Regional Co-ordinating Body for Research on Central America and the Caribbean (CRIES). The Workshop brought together nearly fifty academics from the region, from Western Europe and North America, and of the score of papers sent or presented, thirteen have been chosen for publication in this volume. Readers familiar with the summary document issued at the close of the Workshop (*The Hague Declaration*, ISS,

1983) will find the same themes developed here in greater detail and rigour. Particular acknowledgement is due to Dr Joop den Uyl, leader of the *Partij van de Arbeid* (Dutch Labour Party), whose address to the closing session of the Workshop appears at the start of the volume.

One problem with editing a book based on a seminar is that the range and theoretical coherence of themes covered must be set off against the need to present a representative cross-section of papers. Hence, the book is weighted in favour of Central America (as was the composition of the Workshop), and fails to do justice to the diversity of economic structure, colonial heritage and political tradition to be found in the Caribbean Basin. The finer points of argument for an alternative have undoubtedly suffered, and the reader will need to be aware of this shortcoming at the outset.

ORGANISATION AND CONTENT

The book is divided into three sections: the first deals with the regional geopolitical crisis and its possible resolution; the second with local and international dimensions of the region's ecnomic structure and how this might be altered to achieve more balanced and equitable development, and the third with selected aspects of political change in the region.

Of the five papers contained in Part One, the introductory piece by Gorostiaga sets out the main principles informing an alternative geopolitical view of the region's future. Drawing upon a growing body of literature, particularly from within the Caribbean Basin, Gorostiaga spells out the sorts of social and economic change which would be required to achieve long-term political stability and economic development based, in his phrase, on the 'logic of the majority'. At the same time, the author is aware of the danger of providing a single 'blueprint' for so heterogeneous a region; he stresses the need for a plurality of economic and geopolitical relations. It is the inability of successive US Administrations to accommodate any model of reform within the region, he argues, which has given rise to the present impasse. The article by Torres Rivas focuses on Central America and succinctly restates his pioneering work on the political contradictions inherent in the region's particular mode of capitalist development, though warning against overly mechanistic models of political change and stressing the distinct situations facing revolutionary movements in Nicaragua, El Salvador and Guatemala. The newly strengthened alliance between the US and the region's oligarchies, he argues, makes it unlikely that the Nicaraguan experience can be repeated, though this alliance is giving rise to new contradictions tending to undermine the coherence of traditional ruling groups.

The closely argued piece of Jiminez traces the different phases and changing options faced by US policy makers and provides a detailed account of the interplay of US diplomatic and military strategy towards the region. Jiminez argues that, despite changes in emphases, there is an overarching continuity of policy designed to preserve traditional US hegemony; current military intervention cannot be seen as a temporary aberration. The paper by Hertogs considers the importance of Western Europe as a 'new political actor' in the region and, while documenting the increasingly independent stance of some European (particularly social democratic) political currents, reserves judgement on whether this factor can be decisive. The note by Olga Pellicer, which closes Part One, argues that although Mexico's progressive role in regional politics will not change under the present Government of President de la Madrid, the limits of that role must be clearly understood.

The central section of the book is taken up by a collection of essays on key aspects of economics, and while the discussion focuses on policy options, it is informed by a strong element of theory. FitzGerald's opening contribution attempts to theorise, in the tradition of Kalecki, the 'planning problem' for a small, open economy, drawing upon the experience of Nicaragua. In such a situation, he argues, the 'classical' Soviet accumulation model which depends on squeezing the peasantry is unhelpful; the piece concentrates on clarifying key planning relationships (i.e. between promoting food production, restructuring domestic manufacturing to meet basic needs and increasing foreign exchange generating capacity, the latter ultimately 'determining' the rate of growth) from which decisive areas of state control can be identified.

The vital importance of the external sector is brought out, albeit from a somewhat different theoretical perspective, in the two articles on the island Caribbean by Bernal and Watson respectively. Bernal's piece provides a detailed empirical account of Jamaica's external vulnerability both before and during the Manley government. He argues that Jamaican growth in the 1960s was fuelled largely by private capital inflows and tourist receipts at the expense of an improved distribution of income and employment necessary to sustain internal accumulation. Unable to control the external sector, Manley's attempt to redistribute income via public sector expansion led directly to IMF intervention, thus undercutting the basis of reform and setting the stage for the PNP's defeat. Watson's contribution documents the growing role of transnational banks in the Caribbean and their impact on domestic investment and consumption patterns; more generally, he argues that the changing nature of the world financial market and the growing role of the IMF under conditions of world recession is tending to 'lock' small, peripheral economies into a 'perverse' model of growth without development.

The piece by Barraclough and Marchetti argues for a 'food first' development strategy and provides impressive statistical evidence showing that the Caribbean Basin, and particularly Central America which has more arable land *per capita* than many Western European countries, is increasingly less able to guarantee 'food security' for the majority of its inhabitants. If, traditionally, the growth of export agriculture has been at the expense of food agriculture, a more sensible strategy would reverse this relationship, reducing dependency on US food imports and taking advantage of intra-regional complementarities. Priority to transforming domestic food agriculture would mean drastic changes in land tenure, improved domestic linkages and more diversified trade patterns, thus laying the basis for a new model of accumulation. Nicaragua is used to illustrate the inherent possibilities (and tensions) of such a strategy. Finally, Bulmer-Thomas looks at Central American trade relations with the rest of the world, concentrating on the region's main commodities. While agreeing that domestic use agriculture (food) should be given overall priority, he argues that an expansion and diversification of export-agriculture will be necessary. This could be achieved more easily through a reduction in commodity concentration rather than in geographical concentration since world trade in the region's main exports (coffee, sugar, bananas, cotton, minerals) is largely regulated by quotas while reviving intra-regional trade depends on political change.

The concluding section of the book contains three articles of particular topicality in Central America though relevant to the rest of the Caribbean Basin. The contribution by Richard is an historical analysis of the changing role of the Church in Latin American political life and, in particular, provides a lucid analysis of the relationship between Central American political and social structures and the rise of the 'Popular Church' inspired by the Theology of Liberation. Equally, revolutionary ferment is accompanied by a growing awareness of the region's indigenous heritage, the historical role and present political significance of which are examined by Roxanne Dunbar Ortiz; her piece includes a brief discussion of the Miskitu question in Nicaragua. Together, the articles are suggestive of the impact of cultural issues on traditional revolutionary discourse. The final article by Coraggio and Irvin considers the meaning of 'political pluralism' in the Nicaraguan context and its implications for Third World revolutions. The authors argue that elections and democracy tend to be viewed unproblematically by both the Right (for whom the two concepts are interchangeable) and sections of the Left (for whom 'bourgeois' elections are irrelevant); such views, they say, miss the real point that, under revolutionary regimes, building independent workers'organisations and enhancing democratic traditions within civil society are preconditions to democratising state power. This is particularly true where, as in much of Central America, there exists a long history of stage-managed elections under military tutelage and where the majority of the population has, in practice, been excluded from meaningful political choice.

The above provides a sequential outline of the book's contents. At the same time, cutting across the book are a number of contending issues and positions which can best be summarised under three main headings.

GEO-POLITICAL CONTEXT AND SCOPE FOR A REGIONAL SOLUTION

If the central theme of the book is the need to conceptualise alternative policies at the level of the region as a whole, one must be realistic about the limitations imposed by both regional fragmentation and external pressures. Indeed, current usage of the term 'Caribbean Basin' is more a product of US strategic debate than of debate within the region itself (Gorostiaga). Hence, while countries of the region may possess certain common features — small, open economies and fragmented cultures moulded by the experience of colonialism — which argue for 'strength through unity', it is clear that far more work is needed on the political and economic instrumentalities of such unity. It would be simplistic to suggest (and no author has done so) that change in the region can only come about through simultaneous revolution. Even where internal conditions exist, the proximity of the US constrains revolutionary prospects, though it is also true that revolutionary governments and movements will play a growing role in shaping the region's future. This is not a conjunctural phenomenon; just as revolutionary struggles in the region have deep historical roots (Torres Rivas), so the logic of current US policies can be traced back over several decades (Jimenez).

What is true is that Western perceptions of US policies have changed substantially in the past two decades. This in part reflects growing social-democratic awareness of the importance of North-South relations (den Uyl), more particularly the emergence of independent Western European policies towards the region (Hertogs) and the growing influence of the larger Latin American countries of which Mexico is the obvious example (Pellicer). Equally, the region's internal politics are changing and older forms of 'populism' under national-bourgeois tutelage are gradually giving way to social-democratic experiments, as in Jamaica (Bernal) or, as in Nicaragua, El Salvador and Guatemala, to broadly-based revolutionary movements under 'popular hegemony' (Torres Rivas). At the same time, the regional confluence of these tendencies, while opening new possibilities for change (Gorostiaga), brings counter-forces into play. Hence any simple generalised model of regional change is impossible; instead, the dialectics of change require detailed analysis of specific countries (Torres Rivas) and forms of political praxis (Richard). It seems preferable to speak of gradually building a 'distinctive regional vision' of an alternative (Gorostiaga) than to slip into any 'triumphalist' vision of inevitable revolutionary victory. Equally, one must recognise that US policy is not 'determined' in any simple sense by economic interests, but by strategic considerations rooted in the ideology of the cold war. Just as in the case of the Vietnam war, the future of revolutionary struggles in the Caribbean Basin will be strongly conditioned by the evolution of politics in the United States (Gorostiaga).

NEW MODELS OF DEVELOPMENT

If the long recession in the West has exacerbated poverty in the region, the ubiquitous nature of poverty is symptomatic of an underlying model which in the 1960s produced growth for the few and at present produces no growth at all. While contributors to the economics section agree on the distinct logic of the small open economy (even allowing for the qualitative difference between an economy the size of Nicaragua and, say, Grenada) at least two lines of tension emerge from the discussion. One is evident from the treatment of the island Caribbean (Bernal, Watson) in which echoes of the 'dependency debate' are still present, though this need not detain us here. The other is between the 'food first' strategy (Barraclough and Marchetti) and what might be termed the 'food-constrained accumulation strategy' (FitzGerald). The problem, or more precisely the dilemma, can be stated in the following manner. Throughout the region, export-led growth has taken place very largely at the expense of food agriculture leading to a structure of income and employment inadequate to sustain domestic-use investment beyond simple first-stage import substitution (Bulmer-Thomas); i.e. such economies possess no proper internal dynamic of growth and are largely at the mercy of world market fluctuations. Food agriculture must be given priority (Barraclough and Marchetti), which is quite the opposite of the 'classical' notion of primitive socialist accumulation (FitzGerald), but to do so requires foreign exchange which can only be obtained by assigning priority to modernizing the export sector and restructuring domestic manufacturing to meet basic needs (FitzGerald).

In short, contributors agree that growth can only be achieved through a state-led accumulation process requiring a decisive shift in the balance between private and public economic power, though eschewing the bureaucratic 'state-socialist' model. Agreement also exists that accumulation cannot take place at the expense of the peasantry, though there is disagreement over the balance to be struck between food, other consumption goods and exportables. At one level, this appears to be the familiar problem of the trade-off between present and future consumption, but at another level this problem has crucial implications both for the scope and nature of state planning efforts and for the politics of the model (Coraggio and Irvin). That any model of 'democratic socialism' which stresses public consumption but disregards the external and accumulation balances is doomed to failure seems clear from the account of Jamaica (Bernal), or indeed any country where both internal and external savings are under foreign control (Watson). However, it is not clear that a food-first strategy (even where the state exercises control of all crucial economic levers) is the answer either, as the experience of Cuba in the early 1960s suggests. On the other hand, to argue for an accumulation-first strategy, which in effect means 'determining' the wage bill (and thus the food requirement) compatible with a given growth target (and hence the foreign exchange requirement and its allocation between investment and consumption), may be decisively constrained by international markets (Bulmer-Thomas) implying the need for a drastic restructuring of trade relations. This, of course, was the 'Cuban dilemma' though whether it need be repeated in the case of Nicaragua or other revolutions in the Caribbean Basin does not depend so much on what particular theories inform policy choice as on whether 'new international actors', particularly Western Europe, can provide more favourable trading arrangements and sources of finance.

REVOLUTION AND DEMOCRACY

The relationship between democracy and revolutionary transformation is a sensitive theme, particularly in a region saturated by anti-communist slogans. The 'political problem' of the region is not so much the absence of formal democracy as the 'transparency' with which electoral politics has been used to serve the interests of ruling elites. In many (if not most) countries, the mass of ordinary people have remained unincorporated into formal politics which remains the preserve of contending fractions of the ruling class (Torres Rivas). Populism (the reformist alliance between sections of the national bourgeoisie, workers and peasants) has emerged weakly and sporadically in Central America and, where limited reforms have been achieved, they have usually been quickly reversed. In the island Caribbean, populism has advanced more easily to fill the vacuum of colonial withdrawal, though its reformist impact has been generally minimal and uneven — in some cases, such as Haiti and Guyana, degenerating into dictatorship (Watson). Meanwhile, the region's form of capitalist development has tended to exacerbate inequality, leading both to the radicalisation of popular demands for change and growing divisions within ruling elites, now increasingly mediated by local armed forces under US tutelage which, in Central America, have become the main guarantors of the *status quo* (Gorostiaga). The central contradiction of current US policy can be traced back to the Alliance for Progress which sought to pre-empt revolutionary change through a combination of military aid and limited structural change. Such aid not only strengthened the region's oligarchies, further reducing the scope for reform, but ultimately undermined electoral processes as a means of legitimating state power (Jimenez, Torres Rivas).

It is against this background that the problem of combining democracy and social transformation in the region must be seen. The construction of democratic institutions within civil society, understood as the self-activity of an historically oppressed majority, is argued (Coraggio and Irvin) to be a precondition for the effective democratisation of the state and meaningful electoral politics. Indeed, the revolutionary transformation of political culture must involve the extension of political discourse beyond mechanical models of class struggle to include religious, ethnic and gender dimensions (Richard, Dunbar Ortiz). At the same time, there is an unavoidable tension between this position, and the more traditional position which sees the degree of economic centralisation required for effective planning as leading to authoritarian politics; i.e. under conditions of 'under-developed socialism' economic necessity leaves little space for the 'relative autonomy' of politics, particularly when faced by the permanent threat of US-backed counter-revolution.

We conclude this preface with the familiar *caveat* covering errors and omissions, though if the former is our responsibility the latter is not entirely. Limited space and choice of material have been an important constraint. Papers on Cuba and Costa Rica would have been useful in helping to illustrate more clearly some of the main issues outlined above. Papers on foreign policy as seen from the US, or on the development of the Contadora initiative, have not been included because the ground is well covered elsewhere. Equally important, the speed at which events have unfolded in the Caribbean Basin since the Policy Workshop has created further gaps, the obvious example being that of Grenada. Suffice it to say that while a descriptive article could have been included, our view was that only a careful analysis of the rise and fall of the Grenadian revolution would have been worth publishing. The issues raised by the US invasion are clear enough; those raised by problems of organisation and ideology which split the NJM, and their ultimate impact on Caribbean politics, are not. That the many positive achievements of that revolution now seem consigned, for a time at least, to obscurity is one more reason for reflecting on the manner in which the superimposition of the East-West conflict on the region's internal politics obscures a long, painful struggle for social justice and institutional change.

George Irvin
Institute of Social Studies
August 1984

I

ADDRESS TO THE ISS POLICY WORKSHOP ON CENTRAL AMERICA AND THE CARIBBEAN (25 JUNE 1983)

Joop den Uyl

'The Role of Social Democracy in Lessening the Tensions between East and West in Central America and the Caribbean', is the title of the paper I have been asked to deliver. I am much honoured to do so, because there certainly is a role for social democracy in promoting the search for peace in Central America and the Caribbean and in easing tensions between East and West. We in Europe live far from the political theatre you have been discussing here. The Mexican maxim, *Tan lejos de Dios, tan cerca de los Estados Unidos* (so far from God, so close to the United States), does not apply to European Social Democrats. In any event, the distance to God is difficult to measure for Democratic Socialists. Those of you from the Region know more about that than do Europeans. We Social Democrats are an independent force in a continent divided into two blocs, locked into a sometimes uneasy coalition with the USA because of the geographical and political situation on the continent of Europe. Warsaw is as far from The Hague as Managua is from Miami; in the past many Social Democrats or Democratic Socialists have neglected this fact.

As a result of the historical development of the workers' movement in industrialised countries and as a result of the rift between Communist and Social Democratic parties which has existed since the Russian revolution, some of us have been tempted to export a European model of Social Democracy to Latin America. In fact, I do not believe that this is possible. Latin American peoples have to look for their own models of development, models based on democracy, independence and social justice.

The Socialist International, the loose confederation of all the Democratic Socialist parties of the world, is still excessively dominated by European parties. This is regrettable, but it is understandable given the respective power positions of the parties. The Socialist International does not want to export a model of development; on the contrary, since the Geneva Conference in 1976 and under the presidency of Willy Brandt, the Socialist International has increasingly fostered initiatives designed to bring real sovereignty to the peoples of Latin America and the Caribbean. But before going into more detail about developments in Latin America and the Caribbean, let me first look at the role played by Social Democracy on the major East-West issues in the post-war period.

Generally speaking, social democracy has supported the movement for decolonisation, the struggle of the peoples of the Third World to achieve independence and freedom in the post-war period. But the record of social democracy is an uneven one. To give an example, following the Second World War, the French Socialist party was deeply divided over Indo-China and, in the mid-1950s, over Algeria. Those divisions weakened the party and contributed to the decay of the IV Republic and to the triumph of Gaullism at the end of the 1950s. When one looks at the 1960s, one has to acknowledge that, for example, the British Labour Government (1964–1970) broadly supported US policy on Vietnam despite Labour's previously important achievements in decolonisation. These are examples of the political reality of social democracy in Europe. One should add, however, that in this same period the Socialist International and many of its member parties became more outspoken in pressing for the decolonisation of Rhodesia and of Angola and Mozambique, the former Portuguese colonies, and in opposing the Fascist regime in South Africa. On the other hand, the decline of social democratic influence in Asia, where it played some role ideologically and politically during the 1940s and 1950s, is in my view largely due to the hesitant, dubious and divisive role played by many Socialist Parties in regard to the Vietnam war.

Another issue of major importance in the post-war period is the development of aid and cooperation with developing countries. In this respect, the Socialist International and social democratic parties have a better record. Since the beginning of the 1950s, the parties of the Socialist International have shown great interest in strengthening the position of developing nations. When I look at the acceptance of the concept of the New International Economic Order by the General Assembly of the United Nations in 1975, I would say that it cannot be understood without taking into account the ideas and activities of many social democratic parties, in particular those of Scandinavia, of my own country, and of other European countries, in promoting and supporting the idea of a new distribution of power between the industrialised and the developing nations. Moreover, if today the position of social democracy is better understood and appreciated in the Third World, this is largely due to the efforts and contributions of individuals such as Gunnar Myrdal, Jan Tinbergen, Judith Hart, Michael Manley, E. Epler, Jan Pronk, Edgard Pisani, to mention just a few social democrats who have accepted their responsibility as representatives of their parties in strengthening development cooperation. Again, when one looks at the two reports of the Brandt Commission, a great many of the ideas in those reports are attributable to new thinking and activities inside the social democratic movement. Broadly speaking, social democracy in the post-war period has increasingly sought to define an alternative policy, one which is neither capitalist not communist, a policy calling for the replacement of the present international capitalist order by a new order characterised by democratic planning, limiting the power of free market forces, limiting the power of multinational corporations and concentrating on aid programmes for the poorest parts of the population in developing areas.

Perhaps the most important contribution that social democracy has made to lessening the East-West tension in the post-war period has been to promote the concept of 'detente' in the 1960s and 1970s. Obviously, I would not claim that detente is a purely democratic socialist concept. But social democrats have played a major role in replacing the language of the cold war by the language of detente. When, in 1967, NATO accepted the Harmel Report (produced by the then Foreign Minister of Belgium, a Christian Democrat) it marked a major change in policy. In that report, the goals of military defence and detente were given at least equal significance in maintaining peace. It was the Social Democrat, Willy Brandt, who first as Foreign Minister and later as Chancellor of the Federal Republic, served as the architect of *Ost Politik* which was meant to replace confrontation by cooperation and mutual acceptance. This led to the treaties of Moscow and Warsaw and laid the foundations for peaceful developments which, I would say, are still essential for the maintenance of peace in the world. I cannot think of the world today without Ost Politik, without the treaties of Moscow and Warsaw, and again I do not claim these achievements for social democracy alone. On the other hand, I refuse to accept that for all the failures of social democracy, it did not play a decisive role in altering the very dangerous course of further confrontation on which the world was set and in reducing the risks of 'hot' war. And I do not accept the many attacks, from both left and right, which seek to characterise social democracy as being powerless. It is precisely in this area of decisive importance that social democracy has shown the power it can have if it formulates its goals clearly.

With the Helsinki Declaration of 1975, European co-operation and security may be considered to have 'peaked', marking the provisional end of that period of detente. Since then, social democratic policy in East-West relations has concentrated on measures to prevent the continuation of the nuclear arms race, to reduce the arsenals of nuclear weapons, and successfully to conclude negotiations in Geneva on intermediate and strategic nuclear weapons. The concept of common East-

West security and the fundamental rejection of the strategy of deterrence are central to the Palme Report and express the main line of thought on development of international relations among social democrats today.

Nevertheless, I do not want to paint too rosy an image of social democracy. Its history is one of successes and failures, and perhaps too many failures. The Socialist International, I repeat, is ony a loose grouping of the world's social democratic parties. And when speaking of Latin America and the Caribbean, I am aware that the image of social democracy in the world today is determined much more by the policies of socialist parties in power, mainly in Scandinavia and Southern Europe, than by theoretical declarations. Nevertheless, the struggle for sovereignty can take many forms. It is not up to Social Democrats to express a general preference for a given form of struggle or style of development. In that sense, the dichotomy 'revolution or evolution' is a false one. It is the particular situation and historical context in each given country which defines the political and social prerequisites for change. Therefore, Social Democrats support the Nicaraguan regime and Salvadorian liberation movement just as we have supported non-violent forms of struggle in Brazil and Argentina.

If we do not always accept armed struggle, neither do we reject it in certain situations. In some cases, armed struggle is the only means of fighting against exploitation and injustice. In my view, the Nicaraguan revolution of 1979 was just such a case. In what manner other than through armed insurrection could the *Sandinista* movement have toppled Somoza? The support by Social Democrats for this revolutionary process was an expression of the political line defined by the Geneva Congress of the Socialist International in 1976. It does not mean that we subscribe to a Marxist–Leninist view of revolution. Bloodshed and human misery are always the companions of armed struggle and one must never forget that. Prolonged conflict always aggravates international situations but, I repeat, there are situations of oppression and confrontation where there is no other way. Often the question is asked: but how far do you go in support of the revolutionary change? Do you put any limits on your measure of support? Well, the answer is that we support the Nicaraguan revolution in its quest for pluralism, non-alignment and a mixed economy. Those are the self-proclaimed aims of the Nicaraguan revolution, not our own. We accept their aims, and furthermore, it is in the interests of the Left in Europe and of Europe as a whole that countries like Nicaragua should have a wider choice in looking for reliable partners; that they should not have to choose simply between Washington and Moscow. As Hans Jurgen Wisnewski (foreign policy expert of the German Social Democratic Party) recently said during a visit to Nicaragua: 'We are friends of the revolution; this does not prevent us from criticising, but as a friend there is no problem in voicing criticism.'

So in my view, Europe has a definite role to play in facilitating genuine non-alignment, in the political, social and economic sense. A substantial increase in aid programmes and better access to European markets for countries like Nicaragua are practical matters on which European countries should act. But most importantly, we oppose confrontation in the region because present policies will not bring security to the region, not even for the USA. It would appear that today it is the USA that stands in the way of a political solution in Central America and the Caribbean, and though the situation is bleak, it is not hopeless. In the USA itself, there are a growing number of people, including many responsible figures, who are increasingly vocal in their criticism of the military interventionist policies of the present administration. I refer, for example, to ex-President Jimmy Carter who in a recent speech urged a change in policies, a way back to reason. Perhaps the United States is a victim of the 'Vietnam syndrome' and will continue to pursue its present fatal course. That the US wants to block Soviet influence in the region, given its own security interests, is understandable. But it is a big mistake to construe Cuban aid purely as an extension of Soviet influence. Cuban aid reflects the position of one country in the region, a country that gives aid where others are absent. Nobody can deny that Nicaragua, faced with a well-orchestrated effort of destabilisation, has the right to turn to other countries for military and humanitarian aid. If only a very few countries are willing to give such aid, Nicaragua's response is quite understandable, even if it entails more direct Soviet influence in this area of the world.

In the case of El Salvador, I want to be precise about what is happening there. Even the Ambassador of the United States, Mr Hinton, was convinced of the urgent need for a political settlement, as was Under-Secretary Thomas Enders. But both have now been fired. An ex-lobbyist for the Guatemalan military regime, Democratic Representative Stone, has been appointed Ambassador-at-large by the USA. I am afraid that, as long as Washington does not want to negotiate, he will be no more successful than his predecessor. On the other hand, whether from the Christian Democrats in Venezuela, or from the conservative President of Colombia, Señor Betancurt, or from the PRI in Mexico, the message is always the same. Please let us handle our own affairs; please give us the chance to exercise sovereignty. That in itself is not yet a concept of change, but it is a prerequisite for any real development in the region. That is why Felipe Gonzales spoke in the name of all Democratic Socialists when he asked President Reagan to stop interventionist policies and to support the latest peace initiative, that of the *Contadora* group. The Contadora initiative is far from ideal, but we in Europe will defend and support it wholeheartedly because it offers a possibility of ending the CIA-sponsored destabilisation of Nicaragua, of achieving a political solution in El Salvador and of isolating the oppressive regime in Guatemala,which has a despicable record of human rights violations, especially with respect to the indigenous Indian population. And I feel, just as at the time of the Vietnam war, that we in Europe should raise our voices and say to the American people and to the American government: 'Change your policy in Central America, it is the wrong policy and it will not even improve your own security in the region!' We in Europe have a special responsibility because of our relationship with the USA; we are in alliance with the USA and I have to represent and defend that alliance. But as a Social Democrat, I feel it necessary to speak critically when I see Washington defending the notion that what is at stake on the Nicaraguan border is a battle against Communism.

When I see what is happening in Central America now, I think back many times to an experience that I had in 1953 when I was visiting the USA and listened to a speech of Hubert Humphrey, at that time a US Senator who worked closely with the trade union movement. He was addressing the CIO congress in Cleveland, Ohio, and in speaking about Asia, he said: 'the war against communism is not won on the battlefields but in the ricefields'. Some years later in the 1960s, I reminded Humphrey, a very fine person incidentally, of what he had said. And he was very moved and very much concerned about his own position with respect to the war in Vietnam. In the USA, just as there is a long tradition of supporting the fight for freedom, there are also many people who understand that the fight against poverty cannot be won by arming right-wing regimes. I do very much hope that it is not a lost cause; we will continue to try to influence the American Administration and the American people in order to bring about a change in policies.

However, one should not over-estimate the manoeuvring room for Social Democracy to affirm itself as a more independent force in Europe and elsewhere. The quest for a political solution in Central America and the role of social democracy in opposing the politics of confrontation between the USA and USSR in Europe is an urgent one. This confrontation takes place in the context of a frustrating debate about the strategic balance of nuclear weapons in Europe, a debate which heightens tensions instead of alleviating them. This explains the reluctance of socialist and social democratic parties to agree to the introduction of new missiles on European soil. Moreover, the Soviet Union tends to revert to an old-fashioned superpower role when it refuses to dismantle a considerable number of its SS-20s to reduce tensions. Unfortunately, the ongoing debate in Europe about the missile question has tended to divert attention that should be given here to the politics of Central America and the Caribbean.

The new wave of conservatism in Europe tends to reduce the problems of economic crisis to a question of cutting public expenditure in the industrialised countries. The Williamsburg Economic Summit and the European Summit in Stuttgart did not produce genuine measures to reduce unemployment and alleviate the debt crisis which threatens the financial stability of the world. Thus, I would say, Europe is becoming increasingly 'egoistic' in its thinking and increasingly unwilling to adopt a development approach to the problems of regions in crisis, such as Central America. What is required is that development efforts be divorced from power politics, as illustrated by the case of the European Caribbean proposal which became a casualty of the bickering between European countries over aid policy towards Central America. This is the wrong way to proceed. The only positive result from Stuttgart was the support given to the Contadora initiative by the European community. This in itself is good, but it is not enough. Europe, especially the Social Democrats, must develop a political and economic programme of assistance to the region.

I understand that the present gathering has not only dealt with the alternative political models for the region but also with economic ones. In political terms, Europe should help the region to be less dependent on the superpowers. It has already been said here that this is in the interest of Europe, particularly of the Left in Europe. It implies closer European cooperation with all countries of the Region, except the blatantly oppressive ones like Guatemala and El Salvador. It means working to bring about better relations between Central American states like Nicaragua, Costa Rica, Cuba and the Dominican Republic, to take but a few examples. It would entail wider political cooperation encompassing ex-British colonies like Jamaica. Economically, emphasis should be placed on aid to countries under strain, like Nicaragua, and increased access should be provided to European markets. A re-activation of former internal common markets of the region should be sought, irrespective of political differences among countries, with the exception of the blatantly oppressive ones.

The struggle against the deep-rooted inequality brought about by decades of colonial rule and capitalist development will not easily be won. On the other hand, relations between Europe and the English and Spanish-speaking countries concerned are much closer than with many other regions of the world. Europeans identify strongly with the peoples of Latin and Central America. The lessening of international tensions demands a specific programme for Central America, a phase of independent development without interference of the USA. Genuine political non-alignment must include a partnership with Europe, and Europe must make a distinction between the Atlantic Alliance on the one hand, and its own interests on the other in promoting political and military non-alignment in the Central American and Caribbean region. Support must be given to all political movements seeking change and democratisation with the content of democracy determined by the peoples themselves, and not by their self-proclaimed leaders or by military dictators. One must also understand the mistrust that exists in the region for neo-capitalist models of development which too often in the past have been heralded as part of an alliance for progress and the struggle for democracy. It is time for each country concerned to find its own model based on its own characteristics.

I am grateful to have been given this opportunity to explain my conception of the role of Social Democracy which is, and should be, something far more than merely to serve as the weakest link in the chain of capitalist conspiracy. We do not deny our co-responsibility of belonging to the western world. Social Democracy has been a product of the particular philosophy and political and economic tradition of the western world, a world that is still predominantly capitalist. I cannot deny that, but on the other hand I do not think that Social Democracy can be considered merely a mild reformist current which does not challenge the capitalist world order. Social democracy is, it is true, fundamentally different from the communist concept as it exists in the Soviet Union. Social democracy is an independent political force, and a genuine vehicle for the change we need so much. It does not set limits nor does it impose conditions on its relations with the region and, in particular, with progressive forces in Central America. It struggles step-by-step along the road to social change. For some it goes too fast, for others too slow. But we have learned from experience that in times of crisis we can muster our forces against enormous odds, and that is what we want to do in Central America.

We will not be diverted from the political road we have chosen to follow since the Geneva meeting of the International in 1976. Democracy and Socialism are one and the same, but individual people have the right to choose their own road. We do not want to export a specific model of socialism; that would simply mean a new Social Democratic Comintern based in Bonn or Paris. That is a mistake we shall not make. We have learnt lessons from our own experience and that of others. We know well enough that you would not accept it and rightly so.

In closing, let us consider the situation of this moment in Latin America. The copper miners in Chile are organising a general strike. The Argentinians are on their way to freeing themselves from a shameful, murderous dictatorship. In Bolivia, a new government is struggling to achieve social justice. In Costa Rica, a social democratic government, much criticised I know, tries to lessen its dependence on the USA as far as its economic debts will permit. In Nicaragua, the Sandinistas will hold elections and, I trust and dearly hope, will achieve a decent standard of living for their fellow countrymen. In El Salvador, if there is the political will, a political solution is within reach. What I would like to say is that we must assist you from the Rio Grande to the Rio Plate, from (so to speak) the Bay of Pigs to Contadora. There are different ways of achieving these goals but the message is the same. As we say in Dutch, there is *een wereld te winnen* (a world to win), and as a born Calvinist I would add *aan het werk* (get to work) and we will work alongside you in your struggle for genuine independence and sovereignty, for development and for social justice, even where it means making sacrifices.

PART ONE

THE PRESENT GEOPOLITICAL CRISIS

II

TOWARDS ALTERNATIVE POLICIES FOR THE REGION

Xabier Gorostiaga

I. THE NEED FOR A REGIONAL ALTERNATIVE

If one can speak of a 'common regional project'[1] for the Caribbean Basin, it is that the relatively small countries of Central America and the island Caribbean — despite differences in language, ethnic composition and colonial history — display a basic similarity of economic structures and levels of development. The search for a regional alternative is in essence a response to the present economic and social crisis in Central America and the island Caribbean, one which both coincides with, and is aggravated by, the current international crisis. The international crisis is not simply about economics but about hegemony. At present, the United States finds itself unable to present a coherent project for the region, a situation which contrasts with that of the 1960s, marked by US sponsorship of the Alliance for Progress. Equally important, the older European colonial powers have shown themselves reluctant to play a more active role in what traditionally has been a US sphere of influence. Initiatives emanating from Latin America itself, such as that of the Contadora group, have been limited to counteracting the immediate danger of US intervention and have lacked any structural long-term dimension. This in part explains why the peoples of the region are, for the first time, attempting to construct their own alternative.[2]

Two factors are fundamental in understanding the nature of the region's problems and in seeking to define alternative policies. One has to do with the region's strategic location within the US sphere of influence; the second is internal and has to do with the model of politics imposed by traditional oligarchies. Our main argument is that the crisis of the region must be understood in terms of North-South relations rather than as part of the East-West confrontation (INIES/CRIES 1983). Indeed, the present US administration, by locating the regional crisis within a Cold War context, merely seeks to legitimate its traditional imperial role. While it is true that 'new international actors' have

appeared on the scene in recent years, it is also true that the influence of
the socialist camp, of Western European countries and of Latin America
does not begin to explain the underlying nature of the crisis (Gonzales
1982). But, the contribution of these new actors is fundamental in the
search for a regional alternative, particularly the contribution of the
regional sub-powers: Mexico, Venezuela, Colombia and Brazil.

II. DETERMINANTS OF THE REGIONAL CRISIS

In order to understand why a region composed of small, poor and
underdeveloped countries continues to be viewed as vital to US interests,
the various components of those interests — economic, political, military
and geopolitical — must be examined. Such an analysis is essential to
determining whether sufficient political space exists for launching an
alternative project.[3] In what follows, particular attention will be paid to
Central America (where the contradictions are most evident), though the
rest of the Caribbean will serve both as a frame of reference for, and an
essential component of, a regional alternative.

A first and striking feature is that North American economic interests
in the region are relatively small. The Central American countries taken
together represent only two percent of Latin America's GDP while the
region's importance as a market for the US, measured in terms of *per
capita* GDP, is equally small: US$472 per head versus an average figure
of US$1964 for Latin America as a whole. US trade with Central
America is only two percent of its total trade with Latin America, while
direct investment in the region represents only about 2.5 percent of US
direct investment in Latin America. In 1980, US direct investment in
Central America amounted to approximately US$1.1 billion and the
average rate of profit on such investment was considerably lower than in
the rest of Latin America. Equally important, US capital is withdrawing
from the region as a result of the region's severe economic crisis, the
magnitude of which is reflected by an absolute fall in regional GDP and
a regional current account deficit of US$2355 million for 1982. Accord-
ing to the UN Economic Commission for Latin America (ECLA),
regional per capita real income has fallen to levels of the early 1960s; in
a number of countries, nearly half the economically active population is
unemployed, and the region's terms of trade have deteriorated by nearly
25 percent compared to 1977–78. Moreover, in the past two years, the
outflow of private capital is estimated to have reached US$3000 million
while the inflow of foreign capital has fallen off dramatically. In
1981–82, US official aid to the region totalled US$828.6 million, or 70
percent of total US aid to Latin America. In addition, much of this was
military aid; in the case of El Salvador, military aid presently acounts for
nearly 80 percent of total US financial assistance (Gorostiaga 1983). This

suggests a fundamental paradox. On the one hand, the North American economic stake in the region is not high while, on the other, bailing out the region will prove extremely expensive. ECLA has estimated that more than US$20 billion would be required over the next five years to avoid regional economic and financial collapse. In short, Central America must be viewed as a net economic burden to the United States.

A second characteristic of US involvement in the region is that US economic interests are located in the sphere of circulation rather than production. In addition to its strategic value as an international financial centre, the Greater Caribbean Basin is a vital artery through which flows the bulk of US sea-trade. The obvious example is the Panama Canal, 70 percent of whose traffic originates in or is destined for the United States. Access to the Canal, moreover, greatly increases US naval mobility and allows one US fleet to be deployed in the region instead of two. As President Reagan put it in his speech of 27 April 1983, virtually two-thirds of US trade and oil imports, as well as imports of strategic metals, flow through the sea-lanes of the Caribbean off the coastal waters of the five Central American countries. Equally important are the international financial centres located in Panama, the Bahamas and the Grand Cayman Islands. Total deposits in offshore financial centres amount to some US$200 billion. The region also contains a number of vital Free Trade Zones (FTZ); the FTZ in Colón, Panama, accounts for a greater volume of trade than the rest of Central America put together. These free trade zones, together with offshore financial centres, serve largely as transnational platforms providing financial and trading services to the world market.

Still within the sphere of circulation, tourism is another activity that is of significant importance to the region and in the main controlled by the United States. In 1981 alone, regional tourism was worth US$1.1 billion. The tourist industry is particularly sensitive to political instability and it is obviously of some importance to the United States that the region should continue to provide an outlet for US capital as well as offering attractive and convenient tourist destinations.

A number of recent studies (cf. Gorostiaga 1978) have documented the rise of pressure groups in the United States with interests in the region, notably the *Council of the Americas* and the *Caribbean and Central American Action Group*, both closely associated with David Rockefeller. Also important is the influence of a group of smaller multinational corporations based in the southern United States which have used the region to establish special production and export zones in environmentally sensitive branches of production, particularly petro-chemicals. In short, while total US direct investment in the region is relatively small, it tends to be concentrated in vital areas of trade and finance, and this must be taken into account in the design of an alternative strategy.

The above argument implies that US military and strategic interests in the region are considerably more important in shaping policy than economic interests. The Caribbean Basin is perceived as part of the defensive perimeter of the United States, a perimeter which has expanded well beyond US borders to form the so-called 'fourth strategic frontier'. US military presence along this frontier is formidable. The Panama Canal Zone contains no less than fourteen military bases and is the headquarters of US Southern Command as well as the home of the *Escuela de las Americas*, the main US military training centre for Latin American army officers. In addition, one must include the military complex in Puerto Rico, the Guantanamo base in Cuba, the anti-submarine facility in the Bahamas, and the strategic air defence system in Florida and Key West. In the past two years, moreover, major new facilities have been built in Honduras, the geographical heart of Central America. It is estimated that for 1982 expenditure on maintaining these facilities amounted to about 15 percent of the US defence budget, or approximately US$20 billion. Moreover, such expenditure has been rising, in part to counter the region's political crisis, but also as part of the latest phase in the Cold War and because of its role in counteracting domestic recession.

The primacy of military-strategic over economic interests in the formulation of US policy is borne out by the author's personal experience as participant in the negotiations over the Panama Treaty. US economic interests in the Canal Zone are worth more than those in the rest of Central America combined; they include the financial centre, the Free Trade Zone, the new inter-oceanic pipeline, the 'flag of convenience' facility offered to US maritime shipping, as well as an estimated saving to the US in trans-shipment costs of approximately US$1 billion per annum (Herold 1983; Burbach 1983). A striking feature of the Treaty negotiations was that, although these interests were clearly in play, the main debate focused on military and strategic issues. Indeed, it was US intransigence over these issues which eventually forced the Panamanian government to drop the principal demands it had been making since the Canal Zone riots of 1964.

More generally, US security interests have been at the heart of all discussions of foreign policy with its Latin American neighbours. The Inter-American Dialogue, which took place in Washington over a four-month period spanning 1982–83, brought together some 50 participants from the US and Latin America (including the present writer) to define ways of improving relations in the aftermath of the Malvinas conflict. Of the various themes under discussion, including economic, social, political and institutional questions, military-strategic issues produced the most heated debate and provided the least ground for consensus, even with US liberals. One might add that most North American participants adopted a position considerably to the 'left' of the Reagan Administration. Of particular interest was the degree to which the US definition of security virtually excluded the possibility of Latin America taking up a more independent foreign policy stance, still less an independent line on Central America and the Caribbean. The Monroe Doctrine, far from being a relic of the past, appears stronger today than it has ever been (Gorostiaga 1975, 1979).

Whatever may be the economic logic of US policies towards Central America and the Caribbean, it is clear that geopolitical considerations predominate. Historically, the region has always been considered 'America's backyard'. So long as the area was thought to be secure, the US could afford to ignore it; but any threat to the status quo has always triggered an immediate response. US military intervention in the region has been more frequent than in any other part of the world. In the post-war period alone, one can cite the examples of Guatemala in 1984, Cuba in 1961, Panama in 1964, the Dominican Republic in 1965, Nicaragua in 1979, and at present, of US involvement in El Salvador and Honduras. The underlying assumption of US policy towards the region appears to be that its own geopolitical interests are incompatible with the emergence of genuinely independent nation states. In turn, viewed from the Caribbean Basin itself, it is hardly surprising that nationalism should go hand-in-hand with anti-imperialism. Today, as the nationalist struggle acquires wider economic and social dimensions, any process of transformation must necessarily call this 'informal empire' into question, implying a decisive break with a neo-colonial model of domination first challenged in the 19th century by the rise of Central American liberalism and later, in the inter-war period, by nationalist leaders such as Augusto Sandino and Farabundo Marti.

It is precisely because of the incompatibility between Caribbean Basin aspirations for genuine independence and the US perception of its own security interests that the Reagan Administration must depict the Central American conflict as an extension of the Cold War. The real question is what scope for defining new foreign policy alternatives exists in the United States itself. Clearly, the Reagan Administration's 'true believers' have no doubts about the ideological nature of their own project to which economic interests are subordinate. The Administration is not prepared to consider any form of 'delinking'; not only is the Caribbean Basin a 'preserve area' but any change would damage the self-image of US global power (Allman 1983; Feinberg 1982; Lafeber 1983). Liberal critics may disagree with the Reagan Administration over tactics and rhetoric but appear unwilling to challenge the underlying geopolitical concept of 'informal empire' (Smith 1982; Lafeber 1983). Few politicians in the US appear willing to support the view that the goal of regional political stability will best be served in the long term by recognising the sovereignty of the region, a sovereignty which must include the region's right to determine its own foreign policy.

What really matters, of course, is that regional instability is not the result of US 'weakness'; if anything, it is the extension of US power in the region which gives rise to instability. The National Security Doctrine is, today, a recipe for national insecurity, and it is increasingly clear that the majority of the region's population is unwilling to accept politically authoritarian and economically exploitative regimes in the name of perceived North American geopolitical interests. In this sense, economic and social change in the Caribbean Basin must entail a revolution in the geopolitics of the area.

Within these societies, ruling goups have traditionally accepted the US geopolitical vision as the price of retaining an exceptionally privileged standard of living, even by developed country standards. Moreover, in accepting a pro-consular role, the region's oligarchy has impeded the growth of a strong national bourgeoisie capable of building a wide socio-political alliance and establishing a new and more stable model of capitalism. What in an earlier article[4] we have referred to as the 'imperialism of ambassadors, generals and landlords' graphically illustrates the symbiotic relationship between the external geopolitical model and the internal socio-political model. It is paradoxical that where the US has occasionally supported reform, particularly 'democratis-ation' designed to broaden the narrow social base supporting oligarchic regimes, such reform has itself fallen victim to the overriding prerogatives of geopolitical strategy. As a recent study of elections in Central America concludes, it is the vested interests of the local armed forces which has constituted the chief obstacle to democracy (Bowtler & Cotter 1982). The study analyses elections in El Salvador, Guatemala, Nicaragua and Honduras between 1954 and 1981 showing how, in most cases, they have been manipulated by the military or, in the case of Nicaragua, by the *Guardia Nacional* (Somoza's personal army and that which received the most US tutelage). As the regional crisis deepens, even Costa Rican democracy is threatened by US policies aimed at undermin-ing its traditionally neutral and un-armed role. In Honduras, US presence amounts to a virtual military occupation and is serving to polarise the country both politically and socially. The US geopolitical vi-sion is thus profoundly contradictory and sacrifices long-term stability for short-term gain. Changing this doctrine is a prerequisite for peaceful political and social change, in the absence of which escalating social con-flict and growing armed struggle must lead to massive US military in-volvement. Clearly, bringing about change in US geopolitical doctrine through the traumatic experience of 'another Vietnam' constitutes the most extreme, and least desirable, outcome.

III. THE CENTRAL AMERICAN SYNDROME

Just as geopolitical logic drew the United States into the Vietnam conflict and produced the 'Vietnam Syndrome', today one can speak of a 'Central American Syndrome' in which a complex of converging interests is developing its own momentum. Indeed, it can be argued that the Vietnam experience has contributed to the emergence of a Central American Syndrome in the sense that the Right in the US sees the region as a test case for restoring American credibility in the eyes of the world. Obviously, the small countries of the region cannot themselves constitute a serious military threat to the United States. If the 'loss' of these countries is perceived as a threat, it is because US policy interests are currently defined in simplistic and intransigent terms. Just as in the case of Vietnam, economic interests are of secondary importance to the US perception of the rules and principles governing its role as a superpower. Within this geopolitical vision, any threat to US interests in the Third World is perceived as a more general political and military threat and, ultimately, as a threat to the capacity of the United States to maintain its world leadership role.

Why this should be so is not immediately apparent given that the Third World as a whole accounts for only about a third of US trade and a smaller share of US direct foreign investment. The answer, broadly speaking, is that a key function of the Cold War is to counteract the centrifugal forces of economic competition which threaten the Western Alliance. Moreover, since armed confrontation between the superpowers in Western Europe is ruled out as too dangerous, the Third World serves as a convenient theatre for acting out the Cold War, a theatre which has acquired an ideological importance quite disproportionate to its economic role. Nowhere is this more true than in the Caribbean Basin. Through no fault of its own, the region has become a test case in East-West confrontation, a confrontation the principal function of which is to reaffirm American 'leadership'. US politicians may disagree about the heavy-handedness of Mr Reagan's tactics but they agree on fundamental principles. So too does a section of political opinion in Western Europe, though social-democrats and some christian-democrats take a different view, arguing that genuine social change in the region is, in the long run, more likely to serve the interests of Western and US security.

The position of Western European critics (and of the main countries of the Greater Caribbean Basin) is that the Central American Syndrome is dangerous precisely because it coincides with a period of renewed Cold War tension between the US and the Soviet Union. It is because of the 'New Cold War' that the risk of regional conflict entails a risk of global conflict, or what is referred to in the US as the 'deadly connection'; the possibility that North-South conflict might trigger an East-West thermonuclear exchange.

Herein lies the true significance of the 'domino theory'. In its crude form, the domino theory states that revolution is transmitted from one country to another by 'subversion'. In its more sophisticated form, the theory recognises that the essential transmission mechanism of revolution is the perceived legitimacy of revolutionary governments. In this view, ideology is as important to counter-revolution as to revolution itself, and the most important task of counter-revolutionary activity is to undermine the legitimacy of existing revolutionary governments. This explains the importance accorded to Nicaragua within the US strategy for Central America, an importance which is entirely disproportionate to the country's economic and military power. Nicaragua constitutes the most important recent historical example of a social revolution whose legitimacy is widely accepted in the world community. Nicaragua enjoys the support of a significant group of countries in Latin America (including Contadora), of many Western European countries including the social democracies, and of important sections of the church and western intellectual currents. The problem for the United States, then, is that the greater the legitimacy of a revolution, the more important is its potential demonstration effects and the more likely it will act as a 'domino'. This in turn increases the perceived threat to US interests and reinforces the Central American Syndrome, leading to a proliferation of counter-domino reflexes, each more extreme than the other. Numerous spokesmen of the Reagan Administration have addressed themselves in detail to this theme. President Reagan himself, speaking to a Joint Session of Congress on 27 April 1983, declared:

There is no area in the world which is more closely integrated into the political and economic system of the United States and none which is more vital to American security than Central America. If we cannot defend ourselves there, we cannot expect to prevail elsewhere. Our credibility would collapse, our alliances would crumble and the security of our homeland would be put in jeopardy.[5]

In the same vein, the ex-Secretary of State, Alexander Haig, speaking on 31 August 1983, to the Bipartisan Commission on Central America chaired by Henry Kissinger, said:

Our problem in Central America is first and foremost global; second regional, with focus on Cuba, and third is local. If we fail to deal with these problems today in El Salvador, we may find them developing in other areas which are less ambiguous and far more dangerous.[6]

In conclusion, within the complex pattern of interests which condition United States policy towards the Caribbean Basin, it is perceived US geopolitical interests which are key. This is the fundamental problem that will need to be resolved if an alternative policy is to be defined for the region, one which is pragmatic, viable and capable of being implemented at minimal social cost. US geopolitical logic is not a conjunctural phenomenon to be confused with the 'cowboy' foreign policy of the present administration. It is an essential component of the ideological structure of Empire. The aggressively militaristic nature of the 'Reagan Doctrine' is not the result of any special Presidential psychological attribute; it is a natural response to the decline of American imperial power. Given the gravity of the situation and the danger that further militarisation of the area might entail direct East-West conflict, it is of vital importance that the search for a new alternative not be limited to the Caribbean Basin but constitute part of a new political dialogue within the world community and within the United States. Such new thinking is already emerging in certain sectors of US public opinion, particularly within the church, the peace movement, minority ethnic groups and some academic circles. One of the keys to peace in the Caribbean Basin, just as earlier in Vietnam, lies in the United States itself.[7]

IV. A REGIONAL IDENTITY

To return to our initial quesion, to what extent can one speak of a common regional identity in the Caribbean Basin? The thirty smaller countries of the Caribbean Basin share certain critical features, namely, the small, open nature of their economies, their low levels of development and per capita income and the similarity of their production structures. For most of these countries, about three-quarters of material production is directly or indirectly related to the export of a narrow range of primary products. In Central America, for example, 70 percent of gross material production is accounted for by cotton, coffee, sugar, bananas, livestock, fish and basic grains. Although the range of products produced by the island economies of the Caribbean is more diverse, their basic economic structure is not dissimilar to that of Central America. One implication is that trade patterns within the region are more competitive than complementary and that economic growth is highly vulnerable to commodity price fluctuations. Moreover, sustaining capital accumulation is difficult since, in general, these economies are poorly articulated internally. Given the limited size of each country's internal market, it is only possible to achieve long-term growth through a coordinated policy of regional trade and investment. In short, one needs to think of a different model of trade and growth if the countries of the region are to reduce their vulnerability to world market forces and, in particular, their dependency on the United States.

For historical and linguistic reasons, Central America has a stronger sense of regional identity than does the Caribbean. The Caribbean islands are linguistically and ethnically diverse and have quite different colonial histories which explain, at least in part, observed differences in political institutions. Moreover, with the exception of Cuba, Haiti and the Dominican Republic, national independence is a post-war phenomenon. For present purposes, it will be useful to distinguish between the English-speaking, French-speaking and Spanish-speaking Caribbean, each constituting different sub-regions though possessing broad underlying similarities in economic and social structure.

Geopolitics is another important factor which makes for a common regional identity. Above all, it is the United States which views the region as a geopolitical unit, a view which nowadays excludes the region's larger countries: Mexico, Colombia and Venezuela. In the long run, however, the growth of a regional identity depends on political decisions taken within the countries themselves. The formation of regional trading blocks (CARICOM and CACM) has been an important first step in this direction. The establishment of Central American and Caribbean regional trade institutions, though not resolving the problems of economic dependency, has served to widen local markets, to increase rates of accumulation, and to modernise economic and commercial infrastructure. But although impressive growth rates in the 1960s and 1970s for a time successfully masked the region's underlying problems, the present world recession has dramatically changed regional fortunes, bringing social and economic contradictions to the fore. Whatever the successes of early attempts at integration, the traditional model of growth has served to reproduce and extend external dependency and internal economic and social polarisation. Future economic integration, if it is to be stable and cumulative, must be based on an alternative model, one which serves the interests of the region's poor and not merely those of local elites. Equally, an alternative regional project must incorporate a new economic vision of geopolitics, one which emphasises the region's right to more equitable and diverse trade and aid relations, and greater economic independence from the superpowers.

The present crisis has given rise to a wide variety of initiatives in the search for a regional alternative. Major proposals have come from the United States, from Western Europe and from Latin America. All differ in their fundamental approach, though all share the common characteristic of originating outside the region. Quite clearly, what is needed is an initiative originating from within the region itself, a principle acknowledged by many of the most influential contributors to the North-South debate including the authors of the Pearson Report, the Brandt Report, and recent ECLA reports. In what follows, we examine the three most important proposals for the region, contrasting these with our own proposal in order to derive guidelines for a regional alternative.

V. THE CARIBBEAN BASIN INITIATIVE

In the past two years, a great deal has been published on the Caribbean Basin Initiative (CBI) which cannot be reviewed in detail here. (The present paper is accompanied by an extensive bibliography which includes relevant references.) Broadly speaking, most independent commentators in the US agree that the CBI is fundamentally flawed. For one thing, the volume of economic assistance proposed in the CBI is insignificant in relation to what is required. The greater part of CBI aid is, in any event, earmarked for defence, suggesting that implementation of the programme is more likely to divide the region than to promote its unity. What is also clear is that the CBI, far from resolving the problem of dependency, is likely to exacerbate it. The proposal has little to say about the social problems of the region, nor does it spell out any mechanisms for redressing inequalities of income distribution both between and within countries. One must conclude that, as a regional alternative, the CBI is largely 'cosmetic' and serves to divert world attention from the Reagan Administration's fundamental aim of strengthening US client states in the area. To make useful proposals for the region one must look at what the CBI does not say.

In our view, a genuine alternative policy would stress the following principles. First, a regional alternative should be multilateral, seeking to extend and diversify economic and political ties and to establish better relations with Western Europe, Eastern Europe, the non-aligned countries, and the rest of Latin America, particularly Mexico, Venezuela, Colombia and Brazil. Second, in contrast to the highly selective nature of the CBI, a genuine regional alternative would cover the whole of Central America and the Caribbean and would seek to strengthen existing regional institutions, while at the same time respecting the particularities of the different sub-regions. Third, a fundamental aspect of any regional alternative should be to identify areas of trade complementarity as a basis for expanding intra-regional trade. This means, *inter alia*, looking at existing patterns of production, trade and finance and presenting concrete recommendations for promoting co-ordinated policies in each of these areas. Most important, though, is the need to conceptualise an alternative model of accumulation and growth. This implies examining the way in which agriculture and industry are internally articulated and, particularly, the potential for capturing increased value-added through the processing of traditional exports; i.e. gradually moving from commodity exports to semi-manufactures and, in some cases, to finished industrial goods. This is a necessary complement to simple first-stage import substitution, a phase already accomplished in much of the region. A limited capital-goods sector could then be developed in the longer term, each country choosing a particular specialisation. Such a strategy would maximise forward and backward linkages between the primary export sector (the region's main 'engine of growth') and the rest of the economy. A process of external diversification and internal and regional integration would also require major structural reform, including, most importantly, that of the agrarian sector. This view contrasts strongly with that proposed in the CBI, one which essentially reinforces dependence on primary products while introducing further enclaves in the form of multinational export and service platforms.

More generally, the CBI treats economic growth as an end in itself and assumes that the benefits of growth must ultimately 'trickle down' to the majority. A more plausible strategy would be to reorient and strengthen domestic production capacity aimed at satisfying basic needs, the dynamic for growth being derived from increased (non-inflationary) domestic purchasing power. At the political level, an alternative strategy would stress incorporation of the majority of the population into political life as part of the process of extending genuine 'citizenship'. Moreover, emphasis should be placed in allowing for a plurality of political forms in the region within a broadly defined context of non-alignment.

Much existing criticism of the CBI, particularly in the United States, has concentrated on its implications for trade, investment and aid, the general consensus being that the CBI provides 'too little too late'.[8] The debate in the US Congress has produced a number of amendments, including one which would require 12.5 percent of the proposed US$350 million to be channelled towards satisfying basic needs. Equally, concern has been voiced over other aspects of the CBI; the reduction in the sugar quota, for example, suggests that the 'losses' for the region might well outweigh the 'gains'. With few exceptions, however, the debate in the United States, which has also had an important resonance in Western Europe, has not addressed itself to fundamental issues of social and economic development strategy.

VI. THE PROPOSAL OF THE EUROPEAN ECONOMIC COMMUNITY

In recent years, the Western European countries have begun to develop a common policy towards the Caribbean Basin region. In mid-1982, the EEC initiated a discussion on an aid package for the region and, since then, a new view of the region has gradually been taking shape, albeit one which has received rather less publicity than the CBI. The European view coincides in a number of important respects with proposals emanating from the region itself. In the first place, the EEC broadly accepts that the problems of the Caribbean Basin are fundamentally structural in nature and that any proposal which does not envisage fundamental change, particularly in agrarian structures, is of little value since it is these same structures which determine the distribution of income, employment and the standard of living of the majority of the region's population. The EEC proposal recognises that structural change is a *sine qua non* for long-term political stability. Moreover, recent European aid policy towards the region contrasts sharply with that proposed in the CBI. The Europeans have tended to include countries like Nicaragua and Grenada (under Bishop) while excluding the military regimes in El Salvador and Guatemala.

Nevertheless, the main difficulty with the European proposal is the relatively small volume of economic aid proposed, roughly US$40 million in addition to the US$150 million which the EEC already contributes to the region. But the substantive content of the proposal is political rather than economic in that it locates the Caribbean Basin problem within a North-South context rather than treating it as a dimension of the Cold War. Obviously, this opens a political door to a broad spectrum of progressive forces in the region and reflects the growing weight of particular European countries, notably those of Scandinavia though equally Spain, Greece, Portugal and Italy. At the same time, the tone of the proposal reflects growing European concern about the political capacity of the United States to respond to the problems of the Third World, including that part of the Third World within the US sphere of influence.

Doubtlessly, an important factor behind the development of an independent European position towards the Caribbean Basin is a growing concern that armed confrontation in Central America could spill over into East-West relations making present negotiations on nuclear arms control even more difficult. In this sense, Europeans have a particular stake in improving the climate of relations between the United States and the Soviet Union and avoiding a further escalation in the arms race, of which they themselves would be the first victims.

VII. THE LATIN AMERICAN PROPOSALS

Fundamental changes have also taken place in the way in which the problem of the Caribbean Basin is seen in Latin America. The role of Mexico, Venezuela, Panama and Costa Rica in helping to topple the Somoza regime in 1979 was viewed with distress by the Carter Administration which, until the final days of the war, sought accommodation with Somoza's Guardia Nacional. When, in June 1979, the US Administration attempted to pressure the Organisation of American States into sending a peace-keeping force to Nicaragua, the majority of

Latin American countries voted against the proposal. After 1979, Mexico and Venezuela launched an aid programme for Central America, formalised in the San José Agreement, which has involved more money than total US non-military assistance to the region over the same period. For the first time in recent history, the United States has ceased to be the principal aid donor to the region.

In recent years, both Colombia (under Belisario Betancurt) and Brazil have taken a more independent stance, particularly with respect to Nicaragua. (An important if generally unrecognised factor in Brazilian politics is that the three richest Brazilian States — São Paulo, Rio de Janeiro, and Minas Gerais — are controlled by the opposition.) More generally, the 'big four' (Mexico, Venezuela, Colombia, Brazil) of the Greater Caribbean area have a strategic role to play in any regional project, particularly as part of an alternative economic strategy. In the case of Nicaragua, for example, the 'big four' have been able to supply sufficient equipment, technology and raw materials to offset the effects of the unofficial US economic blockade. Equally, considerable potential exists for developing complementary trade relationships in agriculture and industry as well as complementary financial relationships. For Latin America, an important attribute of the Caribbean Basin is its potential economic size. Taken together, the small countries of the region represent a total population of 60 million and a Gross Regional Product of US$60 billion. But it is chiefly the potential of the Caribbean Basin as a 'political market'which has led to the development of an independent position. In the absence of meaningful initiatives from the United States, Latin America is now filling the political vacuum and recognises the importance both of an independent regional development strategy and of cultivating a variety of economic and political models.

This is particularly true of the Contadora Group whose peace initiatives have received international attention.[9] The proposals of Mexico, Venezuela, Colombia and Panama have been supported by the General Assembly of the United Nations and by the OAS, and in late 1983, even the United States itself was obliged to formally support the proposals. But the Contadora initiative has been strongly resisted, particularly by the Right in the United States and those Central American regimes opposed to a negotiated solution. Whatever these difficulties, Contadora does reflect a new current of thought in Latin America, a current which has gained strength particularly since the Malvinas crisis and against a background of growing trade and financial instability. Increasingly, Latin American countries are recognising the need to resolve their own problems without interference from outside powers. Although the immediate aim of Contadora is to avoid generalised conflict in Central America, this role could in future be extended to seeking a permanent negotiated political settlement in the region. What many Latin American countries now recognise is that political stability in the Caribbean Basin ultimately depends on overcoming the underlying problems of inequitable income distribution and unequal trade relations.

VIII. PRINCIPLES OF AN AUTONOMOUS STRATEGY FOR THE REGION

In the second half of this paper, we set out the 'guiding principles' of an alternative strategy as viewed from within the region itself (i.e. an 'autonomous' strategy) and ask whether such a strategy is feasible. These principles are part of more detailed research work being carried out by academics throughout the region who, over the past two years, have met under the auspices of the Coordinating Body for Regional Economic and Social Research (*Coordinadora Regional de Investigaciónes Económicas y Sociales* or CRIES). (References to detailed work are found in the bibliography.)

A first element that any proposal for the region must take into account is the distinctive national characteristics of each of the countries in question. Such a principle may appear self-evident, but it is largely overlooked in proposals emanating from outside the region. Not only are Central America and the Caribbean distinct but, within each region, one can identify separate sub-regions. Moreover, the region includes countries which, though forming part of a regional project, are not easily subsumed under a standard 'reference model'. Cuba, as part of the COMECON system, is one example; so too is Puerto Rico, a territory of the United States, and Panama with its strategic canal link. Only by respecting such particularities can a practical and viable project be defined.

Equally important to a distinctive regional vision is recognising the need for a new economic and political model. Here, one must address oneself directly to the widespread nature of class exploitation. Some may feel that the phrase is too strong, but such phrasing is necessary if the fundamental objective of the project is to remain clear. The logic of development and of political organisation is, after all, a class logic. It is what we have referred to as the 'logic of the majority', that is to say, of ordinary peasants and workers, of the unemployed, of small traders and proprietors in the productive and services sectors, of those who make up as much as three-quarters of the economically active population. Above all, the logic of the majority is about those who bear the burden of under-development. It is only within such a political framework that the notion of 'basic needs' acquires substantive meaning. Otherwise, it is only too easy for everyone — from ECLA to the World Bank, the IMF, and even the most reactionary government — to agree that meeting basic needs is a principal aim of development policy. Obviously, the main

question is which class or social group determines priorities and policies
for basic needs satisfaction. The point has not been missed by ECLA
whose regional reports reflect an increasingly detailed grasp of the
political-economy dimension. So too, albeit with some differences, do
the reports of the European Common Market Commission.

This leads us to the next principle which is that economic and political
transformation cannot be carried out *for* the majority unless it is part of
a project implemented *by* the majority. To use a more academic turn of
phrase, the majority must be the subject, and not the object, of their own
history. After all, the underlying political upheavals of the region are
themselves the expression of a growing demand by the majority to determine their own future, and it is this new historical subject which is
gradually transforming society. Nor is this subject exclusively an 'army
of the poor' since it has shown itself capable of building broad alliances
across sectors and, in some countries, includes a significant part of the
middle class as well as of the bourgeoisie. This complex alliance of social
and political forces, which differs significantly between sub-regions, is
arguably converging in a manner which makes it possible to speak of a
new social alliance at the level of the region. In some countries, such as
Nicaragua, the alliance is of a multi-class nature, though popular sectors
are ascendant. In Cuba, the alliance is clearly under proletarian
hegemony. In other countries, hegemony is being shared between
different sectors and classes. This pluralism of internal alliances is the
basis for establishing a genuine regional pluralism. The only group which
would be excluded from such an alliance would be the traditional
oligarchy. The interests of this group are fundamentally opposed to
those of the majority. In future, political stability can only be ensured
through the formation of different alliances whose internal legitimacy
will depend on the extent to which reforms necessary to ensuring basic
needs provision are implemented. The experience of Nicaragua shows
that levels of literacy, health, housing and food production can be raised
reasonably quickly and efficiently, even where resources are extremely
limited, by mobilising and organising ordinary people.[10] The eradication
of the endemic problems of under-development is not chiefly a problem
of resources; it is first and foremost a problem of political organisation.

While it is true that the incorporation of the majority into the political
process can release enormous energies and greatly simplify the task of
economic development, it is equally true that countries of the region
cannot afford a model of development which sets its sights on achieving
consumption norms comparable to those of the advanced countries.
Economic and social transformation requires accepting, *inter alia*, that
consumption levels of the well-to-do, typically modelled on those of the
North American upper-middle class, will need to be cut back, and present conventions about the proper balance between public and private

provision will need to be changed. This idea is captured in the phrase 'a civilisation of simplicity' (*civilización de la simplicidad*), a phrase which despite its Weberian associations, has a very real bearing on today's problems. The structural characteristics of these countries are such that they will be unable to compete in the international market and even against other Latin American countries unless workers become much more productive. This can only happen once basic needs have been met. The satisfaction of basic needs in turn means that non-essential consumption, including that of the upper and middle classes and of the State, must be reduced to a minimum. While such a principle appeals to humanitarian notions of social justice, it is equally rooted in a materialistic view of the necessary pre-conditions for development. The transformation of social relations and productive forces within a political culture of participation and simplicity must be part of any project aiming to create a new historical subject and a new style of development. Nor is simplicity in this sense to be confused with an egalitarian distribution of poverty. A culture of simplicity implies exploring new alternatives in the fields of health, education, participation, and the growth of both individual and collective self-reliance. It opens new alternatives not only to the poorest, but to the middle classes, to professionals and entrepreneurs who can discover new areas of creative activity, areas unavailable under the old order.

It will be useful here to consider in somewhat greater detail what we mean by a 'new model' of development. The main features of such a model can be summarised as follows. The first priority is transformation of agrarian structures. This means not only implementing a programme of land reform but significantly raising the standard of living of the peasantry, thus broadening the internal market. Land reform cannot be based exclusively on a single model of property relations, be it private or collective, but should give rise to a variety of property forms ranging from traditional small- and medium-sized private holdings to co-operatives (credit, services and production) to State property (chiefly in capital-intensive branches). Secondly, a regional project will aim to reduce net food imports, currently running at US$3 billion per annum, making use of resulting foreign exchange savings for productive and infrastructural investment in the rural sector. Equally, an important aim will be to create new forward and backward linkages between agriculture and other sectors, particularly industry and construction. Quite clearly, the region possesses an enormous potential for adding further processing stages to the production of primary commodities and while the role of the State will undoubtedly need to expand, this does not imply greater centralisation. Indeed, a strategy which attaches primary importance to agriculture should imply considerable decentralisation and regionalisation of State functions for which contemporary reforms in Nicaragua serve as a useful example. Moreover, rural transformation will imply major changes in urban policy, particularly in the reform of petty services. At present, a striking characteristic of the region is the disproportionate amount of manpower absorbed in the tertiary sector. This is because, traditionally, services have acted as a residual source of employment and income for marginal producers displaced by the spread of modern capitalist agriculture. There is a good deal of evidence to suggest that, where land reform is comprehensive and accompanied by a net transfer of resources to the rural sector, urban migration can be halted and even reversed.

How far does such a strategy require central planning and state ownership? The type of economic model proposed above is clearly not 'socialist' in the Eastern European sense, nor is it a 'mixed economy' in the Western European sense. The distinctive feature of the proposed 'mixed economy' is that the logic of private capital accumulation no longer predominates, though private capital continues to have an important role. Hence, while there must be more planning than is currently practised in capitalist economies, such planning must aim at ensuring macro-efficiency leaving the market to handle micro-efficiency. This means above all a planned pattern of investment, carried out in part directly by the State and in part by means of planning agreements with the private sector. The financial cohesion of such a State-led investment model will be chiefly ensured by fiscal reform, though also by State control of the modern banking sector and of key areas of marketing, particularly external commerce. While the balance between public and private property will vary from country to country, it seems reasonable to assume that the State will have a majority interest in modern services and an important presence in modern production, both agricultural and industrial. Taken together, this might amount to as much as one-third of GDP (comparable in magnitude if not in composition to many Western European countries) while, at the other extreme, the continued presence of a large petty-production sector (mainly in food agriculture) and of medium and large-scale capitalist production in parts of the modern sector suggests that a further one-third of GDP might originate from purely private sources. This leaves the remaining third to be shared between different forms of cooperative production largely run by autonomous producers' associations.

Although one cannot do much more than sketch the outlines of a reference model, one important implication of such a model is that it opens the way towards an extensive restructuring of productive relations, particularly in the area of workers' participation. The democratisation of economic life is an essential component of democratisation in general, and the emphasis placed on the principle of collective participation must certainly find practical expression not only in the organisation of political life but in that of economic life.

The restructuring of domestic economies around a regional project will also entail building new international economic relations. While the United States will clearly continue to be an important trading partner for the region, more diversified relations must be sought, particularly at a time when new trading powers are emerging within the world economy. In addition to the US, four broad trading blocks can be distinguished — the EEC and Japan, the socialist camp, the rest of Latin America (particularly the 'big four') and the rest of the Third World. New institutional arrangements and trading prospects will not be discussed in any detail here since they are the subject of a separate paper in the present volume. Suffice it to say that a central question will be that of improving trade relations with the EEC which largely comes down to Central America joining its Caribbean neighbours as members of the Lomé Convention. The EEC, in developing its proposal for the region, will need to pay considerably more attention to this issue than has been the case in the past.

IX.   IS A NEW REGIONAL PROJECT FEASIBLE?

Above, we have attempted to sketch the main political and economic features of the model bearing in mind that the aim of this paper is to provide guidelines rather than a blueprint and that, in practice, any realistic view of the region must accept pluralism and diversity as an end in itself. In the concluding section, we concentrate on the geopolitics of the region and set out a timeframe against which a new regional project might be measured. As before, it would be misleading to suggest that these can be treated as anything more than a set of guidelines which, as the reader will appreciate, are meant to promote and widen the regional debate, not to foreclose it.

We have already suggested that the region's foreign policy should be based on the principle of non-alignment. Now 'non-alignment' is a term notoriously open to misinterpretation. The simplest, and perhaps the most widespread view, is that non-alignment means steering a knife-edge course midway between the two superpowers. Even were this possible for one country, it would not be possible, or even desirable, for as diverse a group of countries as make up the region. In our opinion, it will be more useful to think of non-alignment in terms of regional pluralism in international relations. What matters in the present context is not whether all countries of the region pursue the same foreign policy but whether any country is allowed to diverge from the present norm which requires swearing a permanent oath of allegiance to the United States. It is this state of affairs which we find objectionable as a basis for regional foreign policy. If this objection is granted, it follows that, while individual countries of the region might wish to pursue different courses, all countries would respect one another's right to do so, and the region as a whole would maintain more pluralistic relations than is presently the case. One might then at least discuss the further question of whether each individual country should aim to steer a 'perfect middle-course' once new geopolitical terms of reference had been established.

Within this same context, certain further principles can be set out. Firstly, it is clear that given the strategic location of the region within the US sphere of influence, the region cannot align itself with the socialist camp. To propose that it should do so is merely to wave a red flag at a particularly large and dangerous bull. At the same time, to argue for strict alignment with the United States is merely to adhere to present Cold War logic. Regional non-alignment would increase the margin for manoeuvre which the region requires to be able to enter into new trade and aid relationships. Moreover, non-alignment accompanied by certain guarantees (demilitarisation, free movement of shipping, etc.) would reduce tensions, allowing the region to be removed once-and-for-all from the arena of East-West conflict. This position not only has considerable support within the region but is increasingly supported by liberal currents within the United States itself. As some North Americans have come to realise, the forced insertion of the region into Cold War politics merely serves to destabilise the region. These new currents within the United States can reasonably be expected to grow stronger.

A vexing question that invariably rises is that of Cuba. Our regional proposal starts from the premise that Cuba must be incorporated into any regional project. The exclusion of Cuba would not only reduce the perspective for realising the region's full economic potential, but it would further isolate Cuba, thus maintaining a nexus of East-West tension within the region incompatible with the purpose of the project itself. Clearly, if the United States continues to refuse granting diplomatic recognition, it is not because Cuba poses a serious military threat to the United States. After all, the US enjoys normal diplomatic relations with most socialist countries. The true reason for isolating Cuba lies elsewhere, notably in the fact that the 'Cuban threat' is a necessary ingredient to the maintenance of a US-dominated military establishment in the region as guarantor of US hegemony. To remove the region from the Cold War would therefore remove the need to isolate Cuba. And it is this isolation which, more than any other factor, explains Cuba's close alignment with the socialist camp. Any serious analysis of regional relations suggests that Cuba's re-integration into the area would increase the prospects for long-term stability, and allow Cuba to be more fully 'non-aligned'.

This brings us to the final set of arguments about the phasing of a regional alternative. In the first (or present) phase, the most important task is to set out a series of principles serving to mobilise political and public opinion both within and outside the region.[11] If such a debate is to gain momentum, it goes without saying that a peaceful solution to the Central American problem must be found. Within the region, a range of prominent political figures, academics, church leaders, etc. are presently engaged in a growing debate within the framework of shared principles set out in the present paper. Such debate must obviously be complemented by detailed empirical research. Readers who have travelled to Central America recently will appreciate the practical difficulties of engaging in serious research and genuine public debate under conditions of escalating military conflict.

A second phase of this work will require working out more detailed proposals at the level of the various sub-regions, within both Central America and the Caribbean. Such proposals must be highly pragmatic in allowing for the diversity of special features and political traditions which characterise the region as a whole. Indeed, one of the reasons why this project has been launched by independent social scientists is precisely to accommodate such diversity and to maintain a certain distance from conventional party-political debate. At the same time, one must recognise that there is a growing movement, particularly in Central America, towards building political alliances with popular movements which transcend traditional party divisions. Many of the above principles have already been incorporated into ongoing debates within regional institutions such as ECLA and SELA (*Sistema Económico Latino-americano*). Much of this same line of reasoning is also explicit in local political party discourse, engaging some Liberals and Christian Democrats but mainly Social Democrats and the 'popular front' parties of the left. Equally, many of these principles are reflected by (and indeed drawn from) debates within the Church, a most influential force in the politics of the region. The participation of the Church is not only fundamental for legitimising a new political and social project, but is significantly affecting the language of political discourse, thus enabling debate to be carried to a far wider public, particularly in North America, Western Europe and the rest of Latin America. A number of the regional and multilateral UN institutions such as ECLA, UNDP and UNESCO have also played a role in this debate, and have a more important role to play in future.

In conclusion, it is worth stressing again that our project is not a neutral one. It is a project which takes as its fundamental premise the participation and mobilisation of the region's poor as the historical subject of a new alternative. Only on this basis can a genuinely pluralistic, democratic, non-aligned and stable project be built. Nor is our regional alternative merely an academic project. It is an attempt to give structured form to part of a wider political process involving the everyday lives and struggles of ordinary people.

NOTES

1. A number of seminars have been organised by CRIES during the past few years. These include meetings in San Juan del Sur in February 1982, Managua in June 1982, Berkeley in July 1982, Managua in February 1983, Guanajuato (Mexico) in May 1983, in The Hague organised by the Institute of Social Studies in June 1983, and a meeting in Washington in October 1983 organised by PACCA (Policy Alternatives for Central America and the Caribbean). For details of these seminars see the *Bulletin* of the Nicaraguan Institute of Economic and Social Research (*Pensamiento Propio*) as well as the Working Paper Series of that Institute.

2. See Gorostiaga (1983) for a more detailed and empirical treatment of the problems covered in the present paper. In the USA the Caribbean Basin has traditionally been taken to include not only Central America and the islands of the Caribbean, but also Mexico, Colombia, Venezuela and the Guyanas. Interestingly enough, the Reagan Administration now adopts a different definition which excludes the larger countries and this makes it easier to analyse US interests in the region. In 1980 Mexico, Colombia and Venezuela alone accounted for 63 percent of the region's total exports and for 75 percent of its imports. Equally, the 1980 figure for the total population of the Greater Caribbean Basin was 160 million, the three larger countries accounting for two-thirds of this total. Again, nearly 50 per cent of North American direct investment in the Greater Caribbean Basin is in the four largest countries.

3. See Black (1982), Burbach (1983), CEPAL (1981 & 1983), Charles (1981), Fagen & Pellicer (1983), Feinberg(1982), Gorostiaga (1983), INIES-CRIES (1983), Pearce (1982), Torres Rivas (1981, 1982 & 1983), Lafeber (1983).

4. Despite the common characteristics of the Central American bourgeoisie there are a number of important differences between countries. The bourgeoisies of El Salvador and Costa Rica are both relatively strong, though very different with respect to the alliances that they have formed with other classes. The Nicaraguan bourgeoisie, by contrast, remained relatively weak as a result of forty years of Somoza rule. In general, however, the common trait of the Central American bourgeoisie is that it has remained largely subordinate to transnational capital, acting so to speak as the 'local administrator' of foreign capital. This is particularly true since the early 1960s which saw the formation of the Central American Common Market and a large influx of transitional capital into the industrial and financial centres.

5. See *Boletin de Noticias* (Embassy of the United States of America, September 1983, Managua).

6. In the course of 1983 an important group of social scientists in the United States worked on an alternative for Central America and the Caribbean which is to be publicised in the course of the 1984 Presidential campaign. See in particular the PACCA Report.

7. See in particular Feinberg et al. (1983), Zorn (1983), The Development Group for Alternative Policies (1983), Gorostiaga (1983).

8. Ibidem.

9. See the statement of the Contadora Group to the 38th meeting of the General Assembly of the United Nations in October 1983.

10. See *Pensamiento Propio*, Nos. 5 and 8 (1983).

11. The programme of work developed by CRIES aims at developing alternative proposals for major policy areas. The work consists of several regional studies on the nature of the present crisis, specific studies on the 'transitional' experiences of Nicaragua, Grenada and Jamaica, and a study on the social impact of growing militarisation in the region. The regional studies are oriented particularly towards detailed analysis of production sub-sistence; i.e. in coffee, cotton, sugar and livestock. Equally, an important study is envisaged in the area of nutritional standards and food self-sufficiency.

BIBLIOGRAPHY

Allman, T. D. (1983): 'Reagan's Manifest Destiny; The President is Playing Dominoes in Latin America and Losing', in *Harper's* (September).

Arnson, C. & F. Montealegre (1982): 'Background Information on US Military Personnel and US Assistance to Central America' (Washington: Institute for Policy Studies).

Atlantic Council of the US, The (n.d.): *Policy Papers*: 'Western Interest and US Policy Options in the Caribbean Basin'.

Atlas of the Caribbean Basin (1982) (Washington: United States Department of State, Bureau of Public Affairs; September).

Bialer, S. & J. Afferica (1982–83): 'Reagan and Russia', in *Foreign Affairs* (Winter).

Black, G. (1982): 'Central America: Crisis in the Backyard', in *New Left Review* (August).

Bouzas, R. (1981): *La Política económica de la Administración Reagan (Bases para un desorden futuro)* (Mexico: Institute de Estudios de Estado Unidos, Centro de Investigación y Docencia Económia; November).

Bowtler, G. A. & P. Cotter (1982): *Voter Participation in Central America 1954–81; An Exploration* (Washington: University Press of America).

Burbach, R. (1983): 'The Crisis of Interventionary Politics and Internal Divisions over US Foreign Policy' (Berkeley: Center for the Studies of the Americas).

Cable Centroamericano (1982): 'Centroamerica: Perspectivas económicas de mediano plazo' (February).

—— (1982): 'Centroamerica 1982: Situación de endeudamiento externo' (July).

—— (1982): 'Que esperar del Minimarshall?' (February 16).

Caribbean Review (1982): 'The New Geopolitics. Caribbean Strategies, Critiques of Left and Right, Christian and Social Democrats', Vol. XI, No. 2.

Castillo, D. (1983): *Centroamerica: Mas alla de la crisis* (Mexico: Nueva Imagen).

Centro de Estudios Internacionales(1980): *Centroamerica en Crisis* (Mexico: Colección Centro de Estudios Internacionales XXI).

CEPAL (1980): *Istmo Centroamericano: El caracter de la crisis* (Mexico: Colección Centro de Estudios Internacionales XXI).

—— (1981): *Istmo Centroamericano: El caracter de las crisis económica actual, los desafíos que plantea y la cooperación internacional que demanda* (Mexico; June).

—— (1983): *La crisis en Centroamerica: Origenes, alcances y consecuencias* (Mexico; March).

Charles, G. P. (1981): *El Caribe Contemporáneo* (Mexico: Editorial Siglo XXI).

Commission des Communautés Européennes (1982): *Action speciale en faveur du développement économique et social en Amerique Centrale* (Brussels: EEC).

Data Center (1981): 'Reagan's Foreign Policy' (Press Profile No. 6).

Development Group for Alternative Policies, Inc. (1983): 'Supporting Central American and Caribbean Development. A Critique of the Caribbean Basin Initiative and an Alternative Regional Assistance Plan' (Washington; August).

Documents of the Reagan Administration: Background on the Caribbean Basin Initiative (Washington: US Department of State, Bureau of Public Affairs; March 1982).

Dollars and Dictators (1982) (Albuquerque, The Resource Center).

Enders, T. O. (1981): *Caribbean Basin Cooperation* (New York City: Center for Inter-American Relations; September).

—— (1982): 'Commitment to Democracy in Central America' (Washington: Statement before the Subcommittee on Inter-American Affairs of the House Foreign Affairs Committee; 21 April).

—— (1982): 'U.S. Approach to Problems in the Caribbean Basin' (Washington: US Department of State, Bureau of Public Affairs; August; Current Policy No. 412).

—— (1982): 'To Promote Economic Revitalization in the Caribbean Basin Region' (Washington: 97th Congress 2nd Session; HR 5900; March).

Fagen, R. & O. Pellicer (1983): *The Future of Central America. Policy Choices for the US and Mexico* (Mexico: Fondo de Cultura).

Feinberg, R. (1982): *Intemperate Zone: The Third World Challenge to US Foreign Policy* (Washington: Norton & Company).

—— (ed.) (1982): *Central America: International Dimensions of the Crisis* (London: Holmes & Meier).

—— et al. (1983): 'The Battle over the CBI. The Debate in Washington', in *Caribbean Review*, XII, 2 (Spring).

Gonzalez, E. (1982): *Strategy for Dealing with Cuba in 1980* (California: The Rand Corporation).

—— (1983): *US Strategic Interest in the Caribbean* (California: UCLA and the Rand Corporation; April).

Gorostiago, X. (1975): *Panama y la Zona del Canal* (Buenos Aires: Tierra Nueva).

—— (1978): 'Los centros financieros internacionales en los paises subdesarrolados' (Mexico: Instituto Latinoamericano de Estudios Internacionales).

—— (1979): 'Diez tesis sobre los Tratados del Canal', in *Comercio Exterior* (Mexico; January).

—— (1982): 'Los dilemas de la Revolución Popular Sandinista a Tres Años del Triunfo', in *Cuadernos de Pensamiento Propio* (Managua: INIES/CRIES).

—— (1983): 'La crisis Regional y la Busqueda de una alternativa Propia' (Managua: INIES; February).

Grabendorff, W., et al. (1983): *Change in Central America: International and External Dimensions* (Boulder, Col., Westview Press).

Hansen, M. E. (1983): 'US Banks in the Caribbean Basin; Towards a Strategy for Facilitating Lending to Nations Pursuing Alternative Models of Development' (Paper prepared for PACCA Conference: Washington DC; October).

Henriquez Girling, R. (1982): 'The Economic Value of Central American Trade and Investments to the US Economy' (Sonoma: California State University, Department of Management Studies; February).

Herold, M. (1983): 'Worldwide Investment and Disinvestment by US Multinationals: Implications for the Caribbean and Central America' (Paper presented at the Seminar on 'En busca de una alternativa propia'; Managua: INIES/CRIES; February).

Holland, S. & D. Anderson (1984): *Kissinger's Kingdom? A Counter Report on Central America* (Nottingham: Russell Press).

Inforpress Centroamericana (1983): 'Centroamerica 1982; Análisis Económicos y Politicos sobre la region' (Guatemala; June).

INIES/CRIES (1983): 'Una politica alternativa para Centroamerica y El Caribe' (Summary and Conclusions of a Workshop held at the Institute of Social Studies, The Hague, on 6–25 June; Managua; October; in Spanish and English).

Instituto de Geografía de la Academia de Ciencias de Cuba (1979): *Premisas Geograficas de la Integración Socioeconómica del Caribe* (Havana).

Interamerican Dialogue (1983): 'Las Americas en la encrucijada' (Washington: Woodrow Wilson Center; April).

Interreligious Taskforce on US Food Policy (1982): 'Toward a Strengthened Caribbean Basin Initiative' (A statement prepared for the Committee on Appropriations, Subcommittee on Foreign Operations, US House of Representatives; May).

Irvin, G. (1983): 'Nicaragua; Establishing the State as Centre of Accumulation', in *Cambridge Journal of Economics*, 7.

Jonas, S. (1980): 'The New Cold War and the Nicaraguan Revolution; The Case for U.S. "AID" to Nicaragua' (San Francisco: Institute for the Study of Labour and Economic Crisis).

Klare, M. T. (1982): 'Beyond the Vietnam Syndrome. US Interventionism in the 1980s' (Washington: IPS).

Labastida, J., et al. (1982): *Centroamerica: Crisis y Politica Internacional* (Mexico: Editorial Siglo XXI).

Lafeber, W. (1983): *Inevitable Revolutions. The United States in Central America* (New York and London: Norton & Company).

Long, F. (1982): 'The Food Crisis in the Caribbean', in *Third World Quarterly*, 4, 4 (October).

Lowenthal, A. F. & S. F. Wells (1982): 'The Central American Crisis: Policy Perspectives' (Washington: The Wilson Center; Working Papers).

—— (1982): 'Ronald Reagan and Latin America', in: Lieber, Duye & Rothchild (eds): *A Symposium on U.S. Foreign Policy under Reagan*.

Maira, L. (1983): 'La politica norteamericana de la administración Reagan despues de La Malvinas' (Paper presented at the Seminar on 'En busca de una Alternativa Regional'; Managua; February).

Mariscal, N. (1983): *Integración Económica y Poder Politico en Centroamerica* (San Salvador: Universidad Centroamericana).

Middlebrook, K. J. & C. Rico (1984): 'United States Latin American Relations in 1980s' (Washington: The Wilson Center).
National Security Council (1983): 'US Policy in Central America and Cuba Through F.Y. 1984'; Summary paper, *New York Times* (April).
Newfarmer, R. (ed.) (1982): 'Policy Alternatives Outlined to Progressive Wing of Democratic Party' (Papers prepared for the Democratic Policy Committee, United States Senate; June).
Newsweek (1982): 'A Secret War for Nicaragua' (November).
Nuñez Soto, O. (1982): 'La Revolución Social y la Transicion en America Central. El caso de Nicaragua' (Fifth Central American Sociological Congress; 22–26 November).
Olinger, J. P. (1982): 'The Caribbean Basin Initiative' (Background Paper No. 61; July).
Ortega, D. (1983): 'Discurso pronunciado ante la 38 Asamblea de las Naciónes Unidas; 27 September 1983', *Nuevo Diario* (Managua; 28 September).
PACCA (1984): *Changing Course: Blueprint for Peace in Central America and the Caribbean* (Washington: Institute for Policy Studies).
Pastor, R. (1982): 'Sinking in the Caribbean Basin', in *Foreign Affairs*.
Pearce, J. (1982): *Under the Eagle; U.S. Intervention in Central America and the Caribbean* (London: Latin America Bureau).
Pensamiento Propia: Boletin Mensual de INIES/CRIES (Managua).
Schoultz, L. (1982): *United States Policy Toward Nicaragua* (University of North Carolina).
Smith, W. S. (1982): 'Dateline Havana: Myopic Diplomacy', in *Foreign Policy*, 48.
Stanley Foundation (1983): 'Strategy for Peace. Twenty-fourth U.S. Foreign Policy Conference Report' (6–8 October).
Tams, A. & F. Aker (1982): 'Resquebrajando el Sindrome de Vietnam, un escenario de Triunfo en El Salvador' (University of Tampa, Arizona: Faculty of History).
Torres-Rivas, E. (1981): *Crisis del Poder en Centroamerica* (EDUCA).
—— (1982): 'La crisis Centroamericana: Una Propuesta de análisis historico politico' (Managua: 1st Regional Seminar INIES; June).
—— (1983): 'La crisis económica Centroamericana: Cual crisis?' in *Cuadernos INIES/CRIES* (Managua).
TransAfrica Forum (1982): 'The United States and the Caribbean', in *Quarterly Journal of Opinion on Africa and the Caribbean*, I, 2.
United States Department of State (1982): 'Fact Sheet: Caribbean Basin Policy' (Washington, mimeographed; March).
United States Army War College (1981): 'The Role of the US Military: Caribbean Basin' (Pennsylvania: Strategic Studies Institute, final report).
Villagran Kramer, F. (1981): 'Central America in Transition: From the 1960s to the 1980s' (Washington: The Wilson Center; April).
Watson, H. (1982): 'United States Foreign Policy Towards the Caribbean' (Washington: Howard University; mimeographed).
Williams, R. C. (1982): 'The Central American Common Market: A Case Study of the State and Peripheral Capitalism' (Marietta, Georgia: Kennesow College, Department of History; March).
Wilson Center, The (1981): 'The National Interest of the United States in Foreign Policy; Seven Discussions' (Washington).
World Development (1981): 'Socialist Models of Development' (special issue), Vol. 9, Nos. 9–10.
Zorn, J. G. & H. Mayerson (n.d.): 'The Caribbean Basin Initiative: A Windfall for the Private Sector' (mimeographed).

III

THE NATURE OF THE CENTRAL AMERICAN CRISIS

Edelberto Torres Rivas

I. THE POLITICAL ECONOMY OF THE CRISIS

The present Central American crisis is characterised both by long term structural factors of an economic and political nature as well as by a number of new phenomena, of which the *Sandinista* victory in Nicaragua is obviously the most important. Structural factors explaining the crisis are related to the nature of economic development in Central America, particularly following the Second World War. Central America has experienced a particularly 'perverse' form of development which, though modifying inherited agrarian structures and introducing new forms of economic activity, has given rise to a process of growth which is profoundly contradictory, entailing heavy social costs that are at the root of the present crisis.

Nevertheless, it would be misleading to interpret such structural factors as mechanically determined by post-war capitalist expansion and the production system to which it has given rise; politics is at once a reflection of, and a conditioning factor in, this process. Economic contradictions alone cannot explain the present crisis, just as it is insufficient to suggest that the by-products of capitalist development — widespread poverty, maldistribution of income, unemployment, etc. — constitute in themselves the major threat to the bourgeois order in Latin America. The notion of economic structure as constituting the 'basic explanatory variable' obscures the fact that the laws of movement of the economy operate within the confines of a social structure which is historically conditioned by diverse forms of class struggle.

To stress the importance of an historical analysis of class struggle as part of any account of the Central American dilemma is not to suggest that such an account must be confined to political history. If economistic analysis is overly reductionist, by the same token, superstructural analysis can be tautological. Rather, what needs to be emphasised is that economic processes develop in the context of socio-political conflicts and are conditioned by them. In this sense, economic growth is only one dimension of the relations of class power. For example, it is misleading to speak of the State as 'intervening' to regulate the 'natural' laws of the market since behind the State is a particular configuration of social classes and power relations; where the invisible hand of the market is allowed to regulate economic processes, it is always the State which sanctions it.

The above remarks help to clarify the nature of the propositions set out below which, we believe, are fundamental to understanding the peculiarities of the Central American crisis. First, if all crises are necessarily about class confrontation, the characteristics of a given crisis reside in the relative strength of the opposing forces. What is taking place in Central America cannot be described as a struggle for State power between evenly matched classes, nor even between alliances of different factions within or, cutting across, classes. The class struggle is asymmetric by its very nature, and what is at stake is not merely control of the State, but the very survival of the protagonists. Second, it is not capitalism *per se* which has failed in Central America; rather it is a distinctive form of capitalist development, closely linked to the world market and foreign capital, and which has been conditioned by the need of the local oligarchy and its foreign allies to maintain exclusive control over the fruits of economic expansion. If capitalist development in Central America now appears to be a failure, it would seem preferable to speak of this failure not as one of the economics of capitalism but rather as one of the politics of a particular bourgeoisie. Finally, the development of the political conflict sometimes involves forms of confrontation between social forces which transcend conventional notions of class. In Central America in the second half of the 1970s, new social movements appeared on the scene whose multi-class character is reflected in the range of issues and interests which fuelled the growing confrontation. Instead of speaking of a single exploited class, nowadays it is more appropriate to speak of a subordinated group of classes. In short, the emergence of new historical actors suggests the need to go beyond the notion of class exploitation (an economic category) and to consider the political relations of subordination and domination conditioning the rise of mass (multi-class) movements.

II. THE CRISIS OF THE TRADITIONAL SOCIAL ORDER

In our view, the fundamental aim of analysis must be to illuminate the subjective conditions under which autonomous forms of mass action can develop, including its organisational, leadership and ideological aspects. In the present phase, the evolution of subjective conditions marks an important historical break with the past, one in which a long and drawn-out crisis of the traditional order has produced new forms of popular organisation, new historical actors, new areas of politicisation and, above all, new methods of political struggle, notably, the rise of an armed resistance. However, this 'break' does not constitute a negation of history; Central America has a long tradition of authoritarian rule and coercion has been a permanent feature of bourgeois domination. In the decade of the 1970s, this tradition was reinforced by the rise of the US-sponsored 'national security doctrine' and its accompanying military and technical apparatus. The rise of armed popular resistance was an objectively necessary response. The increased brutality required to maintain class domination led to new forms of resistance on the part of the subjugated classes.

The declining effectiveness of traditional methods of domination can only be explained, we believe, by analysing the developing crisis within the oligarchic order itself. Historically speaking, this crisis of 'oligarchic rule', by which we mean the rule of the agrarian and commercial bourgeoisies, is rooted in the fact that in Central America (unlike much of the rest of Latin America) no process of bourgeois political renovation took place which could have permitted both dismantling the monopoly of ideology and power exercised by large landowners and reforming semi-feudal forms of peasant subordination. One should add that there are significant historical differences within Central America with respect to both the particular conditions under which the oligarchic order emerged in the second half of the nineteenth century and the reversals it experienced in the period after the Second World War.

The post-war period is characterised by a process of capitalist penetration and modernisation of backward agrarian societies, a process whose main impulse is to be found in economic and political changes external to the region. This process was used, and in part directed, by a narrow fraction of the bourgeoisie within each country. However, the limited nature of such change is reflected in the fact that a proper 'settlement of accounts' between the bourgeoisie and the oligarchy never took place. There was neither a 'Jacobin' style settlement, as might have happened in Guatemala had the Arbenz reforms succeeded, nor a 'Prussian' style settlement as appeared, for a time, might be the outcome in El Salvador when a minority within the 'fourteen families' attempted to implement reforms. Indeed, an awareness of the flux and reflux of change within the ruling classes after 1945 is decisive to a proper understanding of the emergence of the present Central American crisis. At the level of economic institutions, this period is characterised by agricultural diversification accompanied by the modernisation and growth of large agricultural firms. By the end of the 1950s a significant manufacturing base existed whose further expansion required some form of Central

American economic integration. Equally, there was significant capitalist advance in the services sector; banking and finance grew and the State apparatus expanded and became functionally more diversified. Taken together, these developments not only accelerated the process of social differentiation, but also led to significant change in the economic basis of class domination. It is in this contradictory context that one must situate the crisis of the oligarchy — 'contradictory' because although the oligarchy's economic base was changing, traditional forms of political control remained intact and a 'bourgeois democratic phase' failed to materialise. The hesitant and incomplete process of bourgeoisification which affected the oligarchy was not accompanied by any significant modification in social relations of production, particularly in the countryside where traditional forms of exploitation and surplus extraction remained, and indeed were extended, though without fully transforming the peasantry into a rural proletariat. Moreover, the peasantry's access to land gradually decreased as the limits of the agricultural frontier were reached and much of the best land was transferred to new crops, creating a growing 'sub-proletariat'. In this period, El Salvador (and to a lesser extent the whole of Central America) is characterised by economic modernisation without corresponding changes in the political system. Over the period 1945–1970, total population in the region increased threefold, and increased social differentiation was reflected in the emergence of a small urban working class and a larger urban semi-proletariat. Traditional forms of peasant organisation were eroded as landless labourers increased on the one hand and, on the other, a small but important middle peasantry emerged. While the landowning oligarchy did not disappear as a class, it underwent a significant transformation which, so to speak, turned 'landowner capitalists' into 'capitalist landowners'. Equally important during this period is the rise of what might be termed 'rural monopoly capital' closely allied to fractions of the industrial, commercial and financial bourgeoisie.

It is important to recall, briefly, that since the 1930s the political power base of the Central American oligarchy has been under increasing threat. With the exception of Costa Rica, the decade of the 1930s was marked by the rise of a series of military dictatorships whose function was to uphold the existing social order by force of arms. The price paid for such a solution was, in general, economic stagnation and the maintenance of the traditional peasant economy. The end of the Second World War brought new democratic currents to the fore, helped by higher prices for coffee. Although this process took different forms in particular countries, there was in general a growing demand for participation and political integration of those social forces which had been excluded from power in the pre-war period. This was a struggle not merely for recognition but for the political right to exist and, in consequence, posed an increasingly open threat to the oligarchy. The struggle for political democracy, for the right to organise, for a nation-state oriented towards new social and economic objectives (as indeed, the struggle to build a new national culture, to extend education to all, to ensure the automony of the universities, to make suffrage universal) fundamentally threatened the nature of oligarchic culture.

This struggle took on increasing momentum throughout Central America in the 1950s and involved, as in any process of superstructural change, new political actors of which the urban middle-class was perhaps the most important. Such new actors were more easily identified by the causes that they championed than by their economic and social positions. Above all, they were conscious of the historical possibilities of the moment and of the need to define a new historical reality for Central America capable of transcending the formalism of late nineteenth century liberalism. The peasantry was not at this stage a central protagonist in the anti-oligarchic offensive; indeed sections of the peasantry often actively lent their support to the ruling class. In this period, a lasting political presence was established by professionals, by university students, and by elements of the urban artisan class, of the political bureaucracy, of small and medium commercial and industrial sectors and, of course, of intellectual groups. As these organisations grew, their ranks were swelled by rural and urban workers as well as by sections of the urban semi-proletariat, forming what came to be known as the 'popular classes'. But el pueblo, using the terminology of the day, were led and represented almost exclusively by the middle class.

The particular form which the crisis of the oligarchy took in the 1950s helps to explain the subsequent historical course of each country. With the exception of Guatemala, growing radicalism failed to identify or to question the economic basis of the oligarchic power structure. Typically, criticism was limited to abuses of power by the State or, in some cases, the nature and style of the institutions of political domination. If one can speak of an offensive against the oligarchy, it was largely doctrinal in nature. The 'coffee economy' and its supporting agrarian structure continued to function relatively successfully, which partly explains why during this period there was no fundamental ideological attack on the inherently exploitive nature of the primary export model.

Without fully exploring the history of this period, some reflections on the experience of particular countries will be useful, particularly in the cases of Guatemala, El Salvador and (to a lesser extent) Honduras, where successful struggles were waged against military caudillos representing the interests of the oligarchy. The process was most radical in Guatemala where, once the traditional Liberal Army had been discredited and partially dismantled after 1947, it was replaced by a more technical and professionally competent army enjoying United States backing. With the disappearance of the Liberal Party, new space opened up for popular political organisations. The agrarian reform of 1952, and the expropriation of the United Fruit Company in 1953, mark the culmination of the democratic, anti-oligarchic and anti-imperialist movement. The defeat which followed in 1954 did not result in the full restoration of the system that had existed under the Liberal dictator, Ubico, but did re-establish the power of the coffee growers and, in general, of the most reactionary sectors of the agrarian ruling class.

In El Salvador, the fall of General Hernandez Martinez (who was responsible for the murder of 30,000 peasants in 1932) was also the work of a multi-class coalition, national in scope and headed by professionals and younger sections of the military. But in April and May of 1944, the popular movement suffered a severe setback when its leaders were executed by the dictatorship.[1] A crisis took place within the armed forces and, although the most reactionary elements ultimately prevailed, in the period 1944–1948 (after Colonels Osorio, Polanos, Villalta and others had staged a successful coup), a number of modest reforms were implemented which helped to democratise Salvadorian political life and, above all, to facilitate economic growth. In short, the modernising fraction of the military was able to turn back a mass offensive against the oligarchy and for some years thereafter to implement piecemeal reform.

In Honduras, the anti-oligarchic struggle took place on a more limited scale and was directed against the personal dictatorship of General Tiburcio Carias. Traditionally, large landowners and the armed forces had played only a limited role in politics. The alliance between the State and the foreign-owned plantation sector was sufficient to guarantee the stability of traditional *caudillismo* which was not threatened by the rise of popular coalitions, unlike the cases of Guatemala and El Salvador. It was not until 1964 that the country began to experiment with democratic institutions under the civilian and constitutional government of Villeda Morales, and only in 1970, under General Lopez Arellano, was a first attempt made seriously to modify the agrarian structure. This in part explains why, in the course of the 1970s, Honduras did not experience the acute forms of political crisis which affected its three neighbours.

The Nicaraguan experience is of particular importance. It will be recalled that Somoza Garcia was re-elected for the first time in 1943, just as the Second World War was entering its final phase. One year before, the country had experienced its first protest movement led by the youth wing of the Conservative Party. In Nicaragua, the oligarchy was closely associated with the 'Somoza solution' imposed by American intervention; for the oligarchy, the *Partido Conservador* had always represented the main opposition to the Somoza dictatorship even though successive splits in this party had provided Somoza with numerous accomplices to help manipulate the electoral process. Despite this 'opposition', anti-oligarchic forces within the Conservatives were insignificant. While the Conservatives were anti-Somoza, they could not be said to be supporters of democracy, modernisation, and the full social and political integration of the nation. Rather, it was within the State itself (under the leadership of Somoza) that attempts were made to resolve the political crisis that was spreading throughout Central America. Because of this crisis, and despite his enormous personal power, Somoza failed to have himself reelected in 1947 although he retained control of the National Guard. Nevertheless, after a brief interregnum, he once again took direct control of Government.[2] The other decisive element in understanding why the political crisis was postponed is of an economic nature: since the mid-1940s, the country had been experiencing a boom in cotton production accompanied by rates of growth in productivity and exports unparalleled in the history of the region. With the creation of this new primary export sector, which benefited both Somoza's Liberals and the Conservatives, intra-oligarchic feuds acquired less importance and economic growth held the crisis at bay.

Finally, the case of Costa Rica is quite distinctive in that the oligarchy had much stronger links with commercial capital (control of profits arising from export activities) and was less dependent on extensive land use. The relative importance of medium and small coffee growers gave political life a more democratic and participatory dimension. Social control depended less on the use of force than on ideological mechanisms as reflected in the educational system, religious institutions and an ideology of peasant egalitarianism. The civil war of 1948 laid the institutional basis for gradually closing the gap between economic and political modernisation. During the 1950s, the oligarchic crisis was mitigated by the democratic traditions of Costa Rica and, above all, by fundamental changes that took place in the relationship between the coffee growing bourgeoisie and the State. Costa Rica constitutes an exceptional case in which a rural society, steeped in conservative values, was able to undergo a process of political modernisation, fractured briefly by the short civil war of 1948.

In the main, it was not until the 1970s that particular conditions developed under which the diverse experiences of democratic struggle, which had so long been frustrated, began to generate currents of armed insurrection. In Guatemala, where democratic reform had been brutally halted at an early stage, armed movements first appeared in 1964–66. In Nicaragua, the insurrectional opposition of the FSLN began to gain force after 1974. In El Salvador, the guerilla organisations were formed between 1972 and 1975. The prevalence of fraudulent elections, the systematic destruction of the trade union movement, the barring of revolutionary parties, the growth of violence against the peasantry, and the collapse of reformist programmes — all products of a bourgeoisie lacking the most elemental appreciation of the conditions for its own historical survival — provided the ingredients for a situation in which popular forces could no longer remain incorporated within the institutions serving to reproduce the system. The lack of a bourgeois strategy to establish normal mechanisms for consensual integration of the dominated classes gave rise in the end to 'subjective conditions' capable of becoming an objective reality. It is in the 1970s that the movement of the people at last took the form of mass political organisations with their own military structure. All of this could not have arisen *ex nihilo*; rather, these developments marked the culmination of a long history of defeats and repression whenever common people had attempted to organise. The political-military resistance organisations that arose in Nicaragua, El Salvador and Guatemala were distinguished, above all, by their methods of struggle and forms of organisation. But for the first time, their political analysis went beyond attacking the traditional oligarchic order and attacked the bourgeois order itself which, in the changing economic climate of the 1970s, was beginning to show serious signs of strain.

III.   THE TWO STAGES OF THE CENTRAL AMERICAN CRISIS

The 19th of July 1979, and above all the conjuncture of events immediately preceding and following the fall of Somoza, are of extraordinary significance not only for Nicaragua but for the whole of Central America. The Right initially underestimated the political significance of the Sandinistas, focusing instead on the anti-dictatorial dimension of the struggle. With the triumph, the whole Central American perspective has changed and new questions are emerging about the nature of the region's economic problems, the power position of different classes, the role of North American imperialism, the relations between neighbouring countries, etc. Changes have affected both the old and the new. The oligarchic crisis, deeply rooted in the history of the region, is now seen as a problem for which no bourgeois solution is available; on the other hand, the forced militarisation of Honduran society, the threat of North American intervention in El Salvador, and the increased probability of internationalisation of the conflict are all new factors. Below, we concentrate on how these new elements have changed the nature of the crisis, and particularly on its economic aspect, an increasingly important 'unknown' for the guardians of the present social order.

It is now generally agreed that the Sandinista victory coincided with a particularly favourable historical conjuncture. Insurrections in the rest of Central America are unlikely to follow the Nicaraguan path, either in replicating its internal features (the breadth and multi-class nature of the opposition; the conjunctural combination of urban insurrection, guerilla war, general strike; the praetorian nature of the army; Somoza's narrow dependence on a particular fraction of the bourgeoisie) or its international dimension (a solid anti-Somoza front in several neighbouring countries; the active sympathy of eleven members of the OAS; the support of a number of European social democratic govenments and, most importantly, the conjunctural failure of the United States to articulate a new internal alliance). In short, what is unrepeatable is the socio-political and historical context in which the triumph took place. Moreover, creating a Latin American and international coalition capable of blocking US intervention seems particularly difficult under existing circumstances in Central America and the Caribbean.

A key feature of the Nicaragua experience was the breadth of the multi-class front mobilised against the dictatorship and first articulated by the FSLN. The broad national character of the FSLN was strengthened by the creation of the *Movimiento del Pueblo Unido*, effectively gouping the whole of the Nicaraguan left. Later, the scope for developing successful tactical alliances resulted in the creation of the *Frente Patriótico Nacional* in which the forces of the small and medium bourgeoisie, and even individuals representing the most powerful fractions of national capital, joined together in the offensive against the dictatorship. This aspect has been analysed by various authors and is well known.[3] The conflict between dictatorship and democracy (the struggle for bourgeois democracy) need not be the expression of class contradiction since it normally takes place within the existing structure of domination. In Nicaragua, a corrupt and repressive apparatus of class domination associated with foreign interests constituted a particularly vulnerable feature of *Somocismo*. In such cases, the scope for confrontation is broader at the political level than at the economic level. Nevertheless, deterioration of the Nicaraguan economy after 1975 contributed to drawing in the mass of the population, and national democratic demands were radicalised as the conflict turned into an armed struggle.

It is precisely this characteristic which distinguishes popular revolutionary movements — class struggle is subordinated to the struggle between the ruling fraction and the people as a whole. Within the Central American crisis where, prior to 1979, change was perceived as the slow transformation of the conditions of reproduction of class domination, the revolutionary element has a number of aspects. As the crisis deepens, it is transformed into a crisis of the State which leads to a revolutionary or pre-revolutionary situation. Nevertheless, the scope and character of progressive class alliances in El Salvador or Guatemala has been distinct from, and generally weaker than, its impressive homologue in Nicaragua. These differences reflect not only the unequal development of capitalism in the region, but also the precise form of crisis taking place within the ruling class itself. The Guatemalan ruling class, already under threat in the 1950s, has had to resort to nearly twenty years of counter-revolutionary violence to maintain bourgeois domination. In El Salvador, on the other hand, the myth of the 'democratic bourgeoisie' has taken a long time to dispel. However, in both cases, social movements are increasingly engaged in armed *class* struggle as opposed to armed *popular* struggle. Widening the social base of the revolutionary movement is not so much a problem of time as of tactics. The national democratic project and the popular mobilisation required to effect it, in these cases, do not coincide as neatly as in the Nicaraguan case. This is not to deny the breadth of popular backing for such a project; rather, it is to point out that the alliance of classes which must be mobilised to confront the State effectively is narrower in the case of El Salvador and Guatemala than in that of Nicaragua.

If the above is true, the revolutionary process in these two countries is entering a distinct phase of class struggle which, while not necessarily impeding military advance, does imply the need for new definitions at the level of political and social confrontation. A major problem since the triumph of the Sandinistas has been, on the one hand, to appreciate that the political contradiction between the bourgeois state and subordinated sectors of the population arises from the economic contradiction between capital and exploited classes and, on the other hand, to distinguish the qualitative differences between national and revolutionary forms of struggle.

Revolutions in the twentieth century, notwithstanding the predictions of theory, have largely been national revolutions that are not easily exported. The subjective conditions of revolution arise strictly at a national level, even if many of the objective conditions are present at a regional level (even in countries like Costa Rica). The emergence of the main social actors and the degree to which these actors are swayed in one direction or another is a product of national history and of the particular forms and relations of conflict between the protagonists. While the different forms of crisis in Central America share the same time frame, each has its national particularities. The 'domino' theory, whether in its right-wing or left-wing version, is without foundation. Indeed, the tragic irony is that counter-revolution is much more readily exportable than revolution itself, confirming what might be termed the 'anti-domino' theory. A successful revolution which undermines the bourgeois order and its system of values in one country is 'contagious' only in the sense that it provokes a strong reaction in the ruling class of neighbouring countries. That is precisely what we are observing today in the case of Nicaragua, and the general lesson to be learned is that revolutionary victory in one country will strengthen rather than weaken the forces of reaction in other countries. Popular struggle today must take place in a generalised and increasingly brutal environment of counter-revolution, a condition which did not apply in Nicaragua.

Nevertheless, the fall of the *Somocista* State and of that fraction of the industrial and financial bourgeoisie to which it was allied is, without doubt, a culminating moment in the Central American crisis with important implications for the process of change in the region. Firstly with the fall of Somoza the crisis of the Nicaraguan oligarchy was finally resolved, opening the way for a new and successful offensive against large landowners and in favour of the peasantry. Equally, the crisis within the bourgeoisie, which had deepened in the period of revolutionary struggle, was finally resolved in favour of a new national leadership within which the bourgeoisie was unable to exercise dominance. Finally the crisis of the system of domination was resolved quickly, its extreme weakness demonstrated in the overnight collapse of Somoza's apparatus of repression. Overall, Nicaragua illustrates the case of a bourgeoisie which lacked the experience of a long period of hegemony, and of a military apparatus whose cohesion was guaranteed personally rather than institutionally. Again, at another level, one must not forget that the second Somoza (Somoza Debayle) was not only the leader of Nicaragua but was a leading member of the Central American bourgeoisie, exercising decisive influence in the highest military levels of the region as well as being North America's most trusted ally. These factors are key to understanding the force of the counter-revolutionary offensive being experienced today, a counter-offensive which is crucial to the new period of Central American history now unfolding.

Such a characterisation does not mean that the political crisis will necessarily be resolved by a victory of the Right and the accompanying dismemberment of the popular forces. The counter-revolutionary climate in which revolutionary forces now operate has several dimensions: ideological, military and political. The bourgeoisie has renewed its defences, and though history provides numerous examples of successful counter-revolution (the Paris Commune, the insurrections in Canton and Shanghai in 1927, the fall of Arbenz in Guatemala in 1954, etc), counter-revolution is always defensive in its orientation since it must hold back the rising consciousness of the oppressed classes. In Central America, revolution is not being pushed back but is, rather, encountering new forms of opposition. The key to this opposition is the decision by the United States to prevent the fall of its allies at any price. This decision has local and international support on a scale never experienced by the Sandinistas.[4]

A further aspect to be examined is the role of the United States. North American presence in the region has grown, in part reflecting a new interpretation of the doctrine of national security according to which all conflict is the result of the East-West confrontation and therefore constitutes a direct threat to the national security of the United States. Even before the emergence of the new hard line in Washington, the United States was establishing a new presence in Central America. Below we consider certain key features of this new presence.

United States presence in the region is not merely military in character, even if its military aspect is the most visible feature. Central American armed forces have long been recipients of North American aid, and US influence can be broken down into three phases. First, there is the period after the Second World War which saw the professionalisation of local armies and their technical modernisation; second, after 1960 when the doctrine of national security was used to integrate local armed forces into a common defensive front; and finally the current period which is marked by new forms of training and tactics in counter-revolutionary warfare. However, it is only in the current period that Central American armed forces have been confronted with generalised armed insurrection and have therefore been converted into direct instruments of counter-revolution.

Since it was founded in 1946, the *Escuela de las Americas* (Fort Gullick, Panama) which is run by the United States army, has trained some 13,200 Central American officers which is equivalent to 31 percent of the region's total.[5] Recently, military cooperation has taken the form of North American officers being integrated into the command structure of the national armed forces. In El Salvador, there are (at the time of writing) 53 military 'advisers' and an unknown number of intelligence officers. Honduras is the most tragic example: the United States, in using the country as the main military base for counter-revolution, has effectively laid the basis for its destabilisation by promoting the militarisation of civilian life, strengthening the apparatus of repression and reducing a legitimate civilian government to a mere administrative pawn.

Total direct military aid to El Salvador and Honduras has risen from US$9.9 million in 1980 to US$232.2 million in 1982. The quantum of resources transferred in the form of 'economic' aid is even greater, to which must be added American resources appearing under the somewhat misleading heading of multilateral aid and financial contributions. For 1982, economic aid amounted to US$583.5 million for El Salvador and US$202.4 million for Honduras. In both cases, United States assistance has created growing dependence on external resources, resources given less for economic than for political reasons in keeping with American strategic designs. In effect, El Salvador and Honduras are being converted into protectorates, and the United States has assumed responsibility for domestic affairs and even for the administrative budget of central government.[6] The counter-revolutionary role which the United States is playing in the region often entails taking on responsibilities that

complement, or in some cases substitute for, traditional public sector activities.

If Honduras has been assigned the role of playing host to counter-revolutionary military personnel and becoming a base for a new Bay of Pigs operation, Costa Rica has been given the function of organising those anti-Sandinista forces which are not Somocista. Moreover, Costa Rica has been charged with leading the diplomatic and ideological offensive against Nicaragua, the principle theme of which is to contrast growing 'totalitarianism' in Nicaragua with 'pluralistic democracy' in Costa Rica. But Costa Rica's exemplary image rests on an increasingly precarious base. In order to maintain the country's democratic tradition, the United States has quietly undertaken a large and successful food-aid programme which is estimated to benefit nearly 300,000 people. The North Americans are intuitively aware of the 'laws' which academics labour so diligently to discover, notably, that bourgeois democracy is important for the control and integration of subordinated classes. Equally, they understand that when social conflict rises above traditional historical levels, this reflects a form of political malaise which cannot be attributed to the rhetoric of left wing cadres. Thus, the successful application of PL 480 (better known as the Food-for-Peace Programme) which, since 1981 has enabled 15 percent of the Costa Rican population to receive free food, is an important element in convincing the masses that the country's economic difficulties are only temporary.

To complete this picture, one would need to refer to other forms of ideological control, including the rise of millenarian religious movements financed from the United States. What is significant in all of this is that the offensive against democratic and revolutionary social forces has increasingly been directed by, and from, the United States. Since July 1979 this offensive has taken on a variety of expressions ranging from military actions on the northern frontier of Nicaragua to the construction of offensive bases in Honduras, direct command of the counter-revolutionary war in El Salvador, the food programme in Costa Rica, the 'change' without reforms in Guatemala, etc. All of this has decisive consequences for the second phase of the Central American crisis. When one argues that internal confrontation is increasingly turning into confrontation with the United States, it is because the interests of the regional superpower find material expression at the geographical centre of the crisis. To the extent which the United States now determines the global strategy of counter-revolution, many of the localised aspects of the crisis take on a secondary role. In effect, the 'backyard' of the United States is quietly being transformed into its 'front garden' in which the horizons of American imperial power are defined. Regionalisation of the crisis, one must repeat, is not a result of the political and military policies of the Sandinista Government; it is a result of the way in which US response to the crisis has drawn in and affected every country in the region.

The main features of the political scenario being built in Central America are now clear. A military solution is, in itself, not sufficient. The counter-revolution must recruit new actors: not only right-wing politicians and the highest ranks of military and ecclesiastical authority, but also leaders of certain socio-political groups ostensibly untainted by the counter-revolutionary tradition or the apparatus of State terror. These new protagonists are recruited from the so-called 'apolitical right' and constitute, in terms of counter-revolutionary strategy, a 'third option'.

This aspect points to a dimension of the crisis which has to do with the ultimate nature of power and domination confronting popular forces. Popular forces have not emerged from within traditional 'democratic' politics, nor are they content to act within the limited space assigned to the 'legal' opposition. The popular mass movement, as an historical actor, has come of age in an environment characterised by fierce repression and it struggles to resist a class which is itself increasingly divided, as reflected in the growing intra-bourgeois struggle for State power. But the break-up of bourgeois hegemony and weakening of State political power, though facilitating revolution, does not necessarily lead to revolution. What this gradual disintegration does reflect is the increased difficulty of controlling the oppressed classes. It reveals the fundamentally anti-democratic nature of oligarchic domination and exposes the ideological poverty of official anti-communism. Faced with this crisis of bourgeois power, we are observing today what, in ancient Greece, was used to maintain and perpetuate the social order — the organised solidarity of *Amos*, or rulers against slaves, which requires not only superior military might but superior organisation as well.[7] The empty instrumentality of violence is insufficient to ensure continuity, but the warning implicit in the victory of Nicaragua's subjugated classes (recalling the slogan 'superior solidarity of the ruling class') has not been heeded and can perhaps no longer be heeded in Guatemala and El Salvador. It is this collapse of ruling class solidarity and cohesion which lies at the centre of the crisis of bourgeois power. What the North Americans have understood is that power must be shored up or rebuilt, according to local circumstances, on the basis of new political resources, and this means finding new leaders. Prior to 1979, the term 'third force' (in the language of Jimmy Carter) was mistakenly used to designate that political space occupied by individuals or groups associated neither with the subversion of the left nor the repression of the right. It is the search for allies in a context increasingly polarised and paralysed by violence which has led to the disappearance of the 'third force' option. While the actors of the political centre live on, their space on the political stage has almost vanished.

The Salvadorian experience is exemplary in the sense that the room for manoeuvre available to a Duarte or a Majano ultimately depends not on the Left but on the Right. If new centrist political forces are to appear today, their success will depend on two conditions being met. Unfortunately, these conditions are mutually exclusive. The first is that 'extremists of both camps' should be disarmed, which would mean asking the guerilla movement to lay down their arms and the military to return to their barracks. The second is that substantial reforms should be implemented, be it only to deal with the effects of the economic crisis. However difficult or impossible meeting these conditions may appear, the search for new allies is still being attempted by the United States as part of its strategy of containment. But the United States cannot abandon its old allies any more than it can bring back to life the many democrats who have died. Nevertheless, there do exist social forces capable of filling the political centre, though its members are often obscure figures of the Right or have temporarily retreated from politics. In the immediate future it appears unlikely that such a new coalition can be built, a coalition which the magazine *Polemica* has aptly characterised as representing 'the authoritarian road to democracy'.[8]

However, if there is a chance of building a 'third force', its success depends on new elements emerging from the crisis. On the one hand, it is undoubtedly true that significant sections of the population, caught between armed struggle and State repression, have grown tired and demoralised. This is particularly true of the middle class which is most threatened by the constant insecurity that, in countries like El Salvador and Guatemala, has become a way of life. Broadly speaking, one can argue that the roots of centrist politics today lie in the urban middle classes who, though a minority of the population, form the majority of 'public opinion'. The second factor is the rise of a new 'extreme right' that enjoys a certain degree of popular support (something which should surprise no-one), in part because of its extreme nationalism, and in part because in an atmosphere so permeated by violence, the slogan 'death to the enemy' appears to some the only means of resolving the crisis. Hence the emerging struggle within the ruling class has given rise, in El Salvador, to 'new faces' such as Major d'Aubuisson, or in the case of Guatemala to a process of coup and counter-coup.

In brief, under the direction of the United States, new initiatives are being taken to create fresh political parties, new 'apolitical' trade unions (drawing on the resources of CLAT), to hold elections and generally to try to shore up the view that time has not yet run out. Within the region, Christian Democratic and other similar forces may still have some role to play in such an initiative. While one may doubt their chances of success, such initiatives should not be ignored.

NOTES

1. In January 1944 Hernandez Martinez ordered the execution of a group of civilian leaders and eight of his own young officers. The general strike in April and May 1944 forced him to resign, handing over power to another General (Menendez) who in turn was later forced out of government by Osmin Aguirre, a Colonel belonging to the most reactionary section of the army.

2. Under internal pressure and pressure from the USA, Somoza aproved the candidacy of Dr Leonardo Arguello who won the elections of February 1947. Two months later Arguello was pushed to one side and Somoza named Benjamin Lacayo Sacasa to form an interim government under which elections were called three weeks later and won by Victor Roman y Reyes. Both these men were uncles of Somoza.

3. See, for example, Bayardo Arce: 'Nicaragua: Revolución', in *Cuba Socialista* (December 1981; Havana), p. 101.

4. The prediction of Franz Borkenau has proved correct. Writing about the Spanish Revolution 45 years ago, he said: 'A dreadful contrast exists with previous revolutions. In the past, counter-revolutionaries needed to depend on reactionary governments because they were often technically and intellectually inferior to the revolutionary forces. This has totally changed with the advent of fascism. Today, any revolution will be confronted by the use of the most modern, most efficient, and the most inhuman weapons in existence. In effect, we are experiencing the end of that epic in which revolutions were free to evolve according to their own laws,' (Quoted in H. Arendt: *On Violence*; Mexico 1970; p. 44.)

5. The figures are: Nicaragua 4693; Honduras 2628; El Salvador 2327; Costa Rica 1987, and Guatemala 1571. See: 'U.S. Prizes its School for Latin Military', *The Washington Post*, 23 May 1983, p. 15.

6. Although the deficit in public spending is a generalised phenomenon, Honduras has the highest relative figures. It has become the Central American country most vulnerable to economic crisis and therefore most keen to accommodate itself to the type of aid that it now receives.

7. The ultimate aim of the Greek *Polis*, as Xenophon reminds us, was to permit citizens to protect themselves against slaves and criminals such that no citizen would die violently. Even the most repressive of governments must, in addition to its capacity to exercise violence, maintain a command and leadership structure superior to that of the oppressed classes. It is this capacity that is being eroded in the present Central American crisis. The degree of decomposition reflected in the 'fall' of General Romero in El Salvador in September 1979, or the successful military coup against General Lucas Garcia in Guatemala in March 1982, served to accentuate how important it is for the United States to rebuild its strategic alliance in Central America. Violence is only instrumental in character and cannot be divorced from the question of its ultimate end.

8. See *Polemica*, No. 7.8 (San José, Costa Rica), p. 6.

IV

BETWEEN NEGOTIATIONS AND CONFLICT: US POLICY IN CENTRAL AMERICA

Edgar Jimenez

I. INTRODUCTION

In recent years, three new factors have contributed to substantially modifying the relationship between the United States and Latin America, a relationship which today has become a focus of world concern. The first of these factors is the Malvinas war which significantly changed United States' perceptions of the region. The importance to world opinion of the conflict between Britain and Argentina had to do not so much with the local military aspect but rather with the global significance of Latin America in international security. The second factor is the growing political crisis in El Salvador and Guatemala, and related developments in Nicaragua and Honduras. The question of 'human rights' is only one aspect of the political consequences (and dangers) that the regionalisation of the conflict would entail. A third factor is the enormous growth of Latin America's external debt, which has made the region particularly vulnerable given that the United States is the region's principal creditor.

The Central American situation, by reason of its extreme volatility, is critically important to the current climate of international relations. Various parties have sought to promote a viable political solution to the conflict. The Franco-Mexican Declaration is one example though other international actors have figured as well. The Socialist International, which has broadly supported national liberation struggles including that of the Sandinistas in Nicaragua, has voiced its concern over present US policy at successive annual congresses (Madrid, Panama, Caracas, etc). International Christian Democracy has been divided over whether to lend full support to the strategy of the Reagan Administration. For its part, the United States has launched a wide range of initiatives aimed at influencing regional and world opinion ranging from the Caribbean Basin Initiative to the Kissinger Commission proposals and the recent missions of the Secretary of Defence, Casper Weinberger (timed to coincide with naval and land force exercises in Honduras). A further actor in the Central American conflict is the Contadora group (Panama, Colombia, Venezuela and Mexico) which, with limited success, has sought to play a mediating role in defusing the danger of generalised conflict. The object of the present paper is to analyse the various political alternatives which exist in Central America and to assess the chances of successfully negotiating a peaceful solution to a situation characterised by increasing local militarisation and a growing threat of direct US military intervention legitimised through the re-activation of the Central American regional defence pact, CONDECA.

II. BACKGROUND TO US FOREIGN POLICY IN THE REGION

US foreign policy towards the Central American region in the post-war period can be divided into a number of distinct phases. In the first phase, marked by the signing of the Inter-American Reciprocal Assistance Treaty in 1947, both the military and ideological dimensions of the Cold War were institutionalised in the region. The next phase, triggered by the Cuban revolution in 1959, saw the creation of the Alliance for Progress to lend support to limited reformist currents in the region; what President Kennedy called the 'new frontier'. At the same time, the concept of continental security was redefined, local military forces were modernised, and the new 'counter-insurgency' doctrine took concrete form with national armies being encouraged to take part in 'civic action' programmes. In effect, Kennedy extended the definition of US military response beyond that of a simple nuclear exchange between the superpowers to cover the area of sub-nuclear or conventional response where US interests were perceived as threatened, in turn enabling President Johnson to intervene in the Dominican Republic in 1965. In this phase, peaceful (nuclear) coexistence between the superpowers was complemented by the principle of the legitimate use of conventional force within a superpower's sphere of influence.

The third phase is more complex. It is marked by the appearance of the Johnson Doctrine under which a 'discrete' US military presence in the region was seen as necessary in order to prevent further Cuban-style revolutions. Successes were registered in the Dominican Republic as well as in defeating guerilla movements in Bolivia and Venezuela. This phase extends into the Nixon-Kissinger period though, with the electoral victory of Allende in Chile, US strategy underwent a number of important modifications. Underlying this change were the twin assumptions that, first, direct confrontation between the superpowers was increasingly less likely and that, second, conflict between the superpowers would increasingly take the form of internal subversion. Hence the United States increased its role in training client armies and new weapons were added to the cold war arsenal (including that of economic destabilisation). At the same time, Dr Kissinger proposed his 'new dialogue' which was initiated at the meeting of foreign ministers held in Tlatelolco (Mexico) in February 1974. Here, reciprocal military assistance was discussed as an important mechanism for dealing with potential internal conflict.

The fourth phase coincides with the years of the Carter Administration. The ideological dimension of global confrontation was rejuvenated via the 'human rights' doctrine and traditional East-West polarisation was modified to accommodate the emergence of a plurality of actors in the western camp: i.e. trilateralism. At the same time, the need for a more flexible response to growing unrest in Latin America and other parts of the Third World was codified into a doctrine of 'crisis management'.

The most recent phase, which involves a fundamental redefinition of American strategy, starts with the election of Ronald Reagan. In this phase, the reassertion of traditional American prerogatives, including undisputed military and ideological leadership of the 'free world', is the central component of a project designed by the 'New Right' to reestablish US political credibility (damaged by Vietnam and Watergate) and to restore US economic competitiveness threatened by a deepening world recession, a weak dollar, and a growing US trade deficit. A central aspect of Reagan's project is the relaunching of the global arms race which, domestically, has both political and economic advantages. Perceived Soviet successes in the Horn of Africa and US failures in Iran and Nicaragua are used as justifications for reviving the Cold War. Social tensions in the Third World, acutely sharpened by the crisis in international trade and finance, are once again ascribed to communist subversion. Guerilla movements are termed 'international terrorism' and US geographical frontiers are superseded by a US 'strategic frontier'.

It is within this framework that one must try to understand the unconditional support extended by the Reagan Administration to the forces of repression in Central America. Initially, several responses were developed by the United States to deal with an increasingly serious military situation in El Salvador and the growing instability of the region. The main political response was the launching of what was initially referred to as the 'Mini-Marshall Plan' in collaboration with a number of other countries, including Canada and Venezuela; if the original plan was scrapped, it is largely because of the amendments proposed by Mexico. Similarly, missions headed by Lawrence Eagleburger and Vernon Walters were despatched to Latin America and Europe with the objective of mobilising support for United States policy in El Salvador. At the same time, the American Secretary of State, Alexander Haig, declared in Washington (21 February 1981) that the crisis in El Salvador was a typical case of communist aggression in the western hemisphere with the Soviet Union acting through its Cuban 'proxy'.

Subsequently, in October 1982, the State Department made it known that negotiations might take place with the Salvadorean *Frente Democrático Revolucionario* (FDR) and that a political solution was considered desirable. The objective here was to encourage the Salvadorean Government, following the Venezuelan, Mexican and French initiatives, to negotiate with the FDR while isolating the FMLN (*Frente Farabundo Marti de Liberación Nacional*). This attempt to split the political and military wings of the Salvadorean opposition failed and the Salvadorean Government quickly returned to its initial position of pursuing outright military victory.

The initial US position, adopted in 1981, was that military victory would only be possible if the Salvadorean Government increased its political credibility in the world at large and modernised its armed forces both technically and politically. It was for this reason that the United States linked the holding of elections in March 1982 with its commitment to the training of Salvadorean army units, in particular the training of a Salvadorean 'rapid deployment force', on US territory. In the event, neither of these measures proved particularly successful. The rapid deployment force proved incapable of defeating the guerilla army while the March elections gave rise to 'unexpected' results (the victory of the extreme right over the centre right) which created new internal political contradictions and further reduced the international credibility of the regime.

III. THE MODIFICATION OF US FOREIGN POLICY

With the approval in March 1982 of a new set of directives proposed by the US Secretary of Defence, Casper Weinberger, aimed at strengthening the capacity of US forces to fight a non-conventional war, US foreign policy changed direction once more. This new military emphasis implied a closer working relationship between the military forces of the US and its respective allies. In October 1982 the policy was put into operation with the creation of a Special Operations Command at Fort Bragg, North Carolina under US Army supervision. Military strategy was based on two postulates: first, that US forces should be capable of confronting aggression and not merely responding to it[1] and, second, that the twin pillars of counter-insurgency doctrine, military force and political reform, should be applied more aggressively. In effect, this meant establishing a significant US military presence in the region and, in the case of El Salvador, shifting from a conventional war footing to one of institutionalised counter-insurgency; i.e. the use of 'search and destroy' tactics, the setting up of strategic hamlets, and the replacement of conventional army units by smaller and more mobile special forces such as the *Atonal, Atlacatl* and the *Belloso* brigades.

As US foreign policy towards Central America changed and as the political and military problems of the region grew, the Reagan Administration drew up five broad options:

1. to give unrestricted support to its allies at national level;
2. to regionalise the war with the support of the southern cone countries;
3. to regionalise the war through the reactivation of the CONDECA Pact;
4. to negotiate; and
5. to intervene directly using US combat troops.

These options reflected a fundamental change in underlying strategic philosophy towards Central America and the Caribbean. Two aspects are particularly crucial. First, Central America was now officially considered to be a 'zone of vital strategic interest' for the United States or what has come to be known as the 'fourth strategic frontier'. As President Reagan said in his 1982 'Star Wars' speech, more than half of US foreign trade passes through the Caribbean, including all oil imports from the Middle East. Equally, consensus was now emerging around the proposition that in order to defend the new strategic frontier, a permanent US military presence must be created in the area. The Central American base was, logically enough, Honduras. The above options were not considered to be mutually exclusive. Rather, they constituted a set of parallel 'tracks', the relative importance of which in overall policy could be modified according to circumstances. How far each of these has been explored, and with what degree of success, is a question to which we turn below.

IV. FIRST OPTION: SUPPORT TO ALLIES IN THE REGION

The attempt to 'resolve' the Central American crisis by relying exclusively on internal mechanisms within each of the countries concerned has failed. Increased aid, whether to a Christian Democratic Government in El Salvador or to the army in Guatemala, cannot itself provide a solution though, quite naturally, aid continues to be given as part of a broader strategy. Hence, in September 1983 Casper Weinberger went before the US Congress to request US$84 million in additional funding, arguing that the President was moving along the 'right lines' in Central America and that increased support to the Salvadorean army would make 'military victory feasible in the short term'.[2] The President had previously requested US$110 million in military assistance to El Salvador of which only US$26 million had been approved by Congress. To broaden his basis of support, the new package presented in September 1983 asked for a further US$41 million for Honduras and US$5.5 million for Panama.

More generally, between 1980 and 1983, total economic and military aid to El Salvador came to US$793.5 million (excluding the September 1983 request). Moreover, over the same period, the proportion of aid required for security purposes rose dramatically in relation to economic development aid. In 1980, the security component of aid represented 26.3 percent of the total, the remaining 73.7 percent going to the various non-defence components of the programme. In 1981, security-linked aid jumped to 61.5 percent of the total; the figures for 1982 and 1983 are 77.4 percent and 79.1 percent respectively. Thus, US assistance to El Salvador, initially directed towards aiding the economy, has now become almost exclusively military.

Moreover, not only has the proportion of 'economic aid' shrunk, but an increasingly larger share of this aid has been of direct strategic and military importance. In one sense, of course, such a distinction is purely formal since an important aspect of counter-insurgency must be to ensure the continued functioning of productive plant and infrastructure. In effect, what has happened is that the burden of shoring up the economy against total collapse has been borne increasingly by multilateral institutions. A simple example of how the costs of the war are indirectly financed is reported in the US State Department's congressional presentation.[3] Of the US$232.4 million which the Salvadorean Government received from the International Monetary Fund, the World Bank and the Inter-American Development Bank in 1982, less than 20 percent was directed towards meeting the basic needs of the population. The balance was used for infrastructure development and servicing foreign debt.

Another important illustration of the Reagan Administration's determination to maintain US political and military hegemony in the Central American region is the growing discrepancy between aid to the region and aid to Latin America as a whole. For 1981 and 1982 taken together, US aid to Central America amounted to US$828.6 million or almost 70 percent of the total aid package to Latin America. Military aid to Central America over the same period was equivalent to approximately 60 percent of total military aid to Latin America.

Within Central America, Honduras has come to play an increasingly important role in US geopolitical strategy. The rise of Colonel Gustavo Alvarez is instructive. Having first been named to head the Honduran armed forces, Col. Alvarez was subsequently elevated by the Honduran Congress to the title of Commander-in-Chief (November 1982), a title previously reserved for the President of the Republic. If Honduran politics has become increasingly militarised, US military and economic assistance has played an increasingly important role in this process. From (fiscal) year 1980 to 1983, US military aid to Honduras jumped from US$3.5 million to US$41.8 million, an increase of 1091 percent! Between 1979 and 1982, the Honduran Air Force was neally doubled and six new naval bases have been constructed. A further US$21 million has been invested in modernising landing strips, notably at Mesa, Goloson and Palmerola, in order to provide the necessary infrastructure to transport US or regional rapid deployment forces. A new military training base has been established on the Atlantic coast at Puerto Castilla which services not only Honduras but Salvadorean troops. Under the supervision of North American military and intelligence personnel, Honduras has experienced the growth of a new 'civilian defence' organistion modelled on its Salvadorean counterpart, ORDEN, as well as, for the first time, the rise of an anti-communist terrorist group (MACHO) similar to those in El Salvador and Guatemala. In short, in the space of only three years, Honduras has been converted into a major regional military power and its forces are now involved in fighting on the Nicaraguan and Salvadorean frontiers.

If the role assigned to Honduras is that of acting as military henchman to the USA, that assigned to Costa Rica is of acting as political handmaiden. Growing US ties with Costa Rica are in part the result of that country's economic crisis. Over the period January 1980 to September 1982, Costa Rica received nearly US$320 million from the International Monetary Fund; by the end of 1983, the Reagan Administration had provided a further US$276 million in addition to the US$100 million granted in the previous year.[4] For its part, Costa Rica has adopted a new and distinctly anti-Nicaraguan foreign policy. In the final quarter of 1982, the Costa Rican and American Presidents met no less than three times. Interestingly enough, during that same period two new US-sponsored organisations set up headquarters in Costa Rica, the *Comunidad Democrática Centroamericana* (CDC) and the *Foro Pro Paz y Democracia*.[5] In December 1982 the Costa Rican Government also announced the formation of a number of military units as parts of its new security plan: the *Organización para la Emergencia Nacional* (OPEN) has approximately 10,000 men and receives technical assistance from Israel, Taiwan and South Korea.[6]

V.   SECOND OPTION: REGIONALISATION OF THE WAR WITH HELP FROM
THE SOUTHERN CONE

The second option is based on obtaining the support of specific Latin American countries for the Reagan Administration's Central American policy. Specifically, the strategy requires that Venezuela act as political proxy and that Argentina act as military proxy. (The Venezuelan Christian Democratic party and, particularly, the figure of Aristides Calvani, are key in the case of El Salvador.) In this connecion, the visit to San Salvador in late 1979 of the Latin-American Christian-Democratic Organisation (ODCA), headed by Sr Calvani and including Sr Rene de Leon Schlotter, General Secretary of the Christian-Democratic 'International', and the ex-Chilean Senator, Sr Tomas Reyes, was particularly important. Co-operation between the Christian Democratic parties of El Salvador and Venezuela was further aided by a meeting in Washington on 21–23 May 1980 to discuss the theme 'The State of Centrist and Christian Democratic parties in Latin America and the Caribbean'. Broad agreement was reached at these meetings that Christian-Democratic parties would have a key role to play vis-à-vis military regimes since Christian Democracy constitutes a centrist civilian alternative equidistant from the extremes of Marxist socialism and right wing nationalism.[7]

The posture of the Reagan Administration towards strengthening Christian Democracy in the region and, in particular, increasing Venezuelan influence, was defined in a document produced by the National Security Group created in 1981. In this document, an outline plan was presented for enabling the United States to make up lost ground in Central America; the US objective being:

To undertake a more active diplomatic campaign to influence opinion in Mexico and amongst Social Democrats in Europe. In the immediate future, to try to isolate the impact of the above parties on Central American policy while seeking more active support amongst Christian Democratic parties and free trade unions.

In order to realise this objective a conference was called in Western Europe[8] chaired by the Belgian Prime Minister, Leo Tindermans. The conference agreed to create a foundation based in Western Europe to finance projects in Central America. Agreement was also reached on holding a congress in San José, Costa Rica, on 'peace and democracy in Central America' in keeping with the decisions taken by the Washington conference in 1980. Moreover, the European meeting included the following phrase in its final declaration: 'Anti-democratic forces seeking international destabilisation are those responsible for attempting to replace traditional American hegemony in the region by a new Soviet-Cuban hegemony.' However, with the advent of the Malvinas war, US strategy suffered a serious setback. Argentinian military support for the Central American operation diminished, while Venezuela joined the Contadora group. Elections in both these countries have since brought to power new governments concerned to distance themselves from American policy towards Central America.

VI.   THIRD OPTION: CENTRAL AMERICANISATION OF THE CONFLICT

The Central Americanisation of the conflict depends, on the one hand, on the reactivation of the CONDECA Pact, originally created in 1963 to ensure the region's mutual defence and, on the other hand, on fomenting a conflict in Nicaragua 'similar' to that in El Salvador. Underlying this option is the American strategic view of the region as a whole rather than simply as a collection of nation states. Hence, for the United States, the war in El Salvador and that in Nicaragua must be increasingly linked to each other, in effect bringing about a regionalisation of the conflict at Central American level. To analyse whether such a strategy can succeed, three aspects must be considered in turn.

The first aspect concerns the degree to which the United States can effectively equate the Somocista and counter-revolutionary forces in Nicaragua with those of the FMLN in El Salvador or the opposition groups in Guatemala. To this end it is necessary to argue that Nicaragua constitutes the heart of the problem. By supporting and controlling the 'contras' in the Nicaraguan conflict, Washington has introduced a new actor; hence negotiations in El Salvador take on a quite different meaning from that originally intended by the Contadora group. This new scenario makes negotiations multi-dimensional: between contending social and political forces, between national governments and between the US Government and particular national government and social forces. By complicating the nature of the regional scenario, the use of negotiations as a political instrument becomes more difficult, an east-west dimension is inserted into the conflict, and political space is created for direct US military intervention.

A second aspect concerns the land and sea manoeuvres which the United States has undertaken in the region. In January 1983 'Operation Big Pine' took place involving the use of 1600 US troops and 4000 Honduran troops in the *Misquitia* area close to the Nicaraguan frontier. This was intended to act as a warning and deterrent to Nicaragua. Subsequently, between the 5th and the 12th of February, a combined 'national security' operation was mounted in Costa Rica using US army forces and special contingents from the Costa Rican Public Defence Force along the Atlantic Coast stretch of the Nicaraguan border. Between the 11th and 17th of February 1983 operation 'Kindle Liberty 1983' saw 4500 US troops involved in joint manoeuvres with 500 troops of the Panamanian National Guard in a simulated defence of the canal zone. On the 10th of March, the annual 'Redex' naval exercise took place involving 41 US vessels and 36 vessels of US naval allies. Subsequently, on 15 July, a North American naval task force consisting of eight warships was despatched towards Central America and the Caribbean. The purpose of the training exercise, according to the Pentagon, was 'to demonstrate US support for friendly countries in the region'.[9] A few days later, the US Secretary of Defence confirmed that a second task force, led by the carrier *New Jersey* and accompanied by four destroyers and one frigate, was on its way to the Caribbean. Together, these two naval task forces constituted the most powerful naval presence in Caribbean waters since the Second World War. In the words of Richard Stone, speaking in Bogotá, 'the extended naval manoeuvres which the two US task forces are to undertake in the Atlantic and Pacific coastal regions of Nicaragua are an important stabilising factor in the Central American region.'

The above, it would seem, is part of a wider objective of constituting a rapid deployment force capable of operating anywhere in the world numbering up to 120,000 men with land, air and sea capability.[10] According to Senator Edward Kennedy, only 31 percent of total US military forces are presently deployed inside the USA.[11]

Increasing direct US military presence in the Central American and Caribbean regions shows that the US administration considers the situation to have reached a critical point. This has led a number of analysts to question whether, in the light of the 1984 elections, the Reagan Administration has not decided to abandon its long term plan for Central America and opt for direct intervention in the short term. Such a strategy is of course extremely risky, and these risks have not gone unnoticed by the Administration's critics, or even by some members of the Administration itself. One of the main concerns of the US Administration is how to deal with US public opinion. Apparently, there is lack of consensus between the State Department, the Pentagon and Reagan's advisors in the White House about how far the 'fight against subversion' in the region can be taken without provoking a reaction in Congress and in the public at large. In any event, what is clear is that in the past three years, US military presence in the region has been quantitatively and qualitatively transformed.

The third fundamental aspect is that of the reorganisation of the CONDECA Pact. On 30 September 1983 a meeting of Central American military chiefs was convened by Guatemala to discuss the reactivation of this regional body. Those present included the Ministers of Defence of El Salvador, Honduras, Guatemala and Panama and the US Chief of the Southern Command based in Panama. In effect, a new military triangle was set up, consisting of the armed forces of El Salvador, Honduras and Guatemala and aimed at 'containing' Nicaragua. At the same time, the US Secretary of Defence, Casper Weinberger, toured the Central American region in order to discuss new arrangements and inspect military installations.[12] During this trip, he suggested that direct military intervention could not be ruled out and reaffirmed the principle of the need to 'work together in combating communism, the enemy of the West.' Mr Weinberger's visit, just as that of Mr Mottley, Under-

Secretary of State for Latin American Affairs, together with the multiplication of US military manoeuvres in the region, suggests that the Central Americanisation of the conflict is becoming an increasingly important option in the Administration's thinking. It is already clear that exercising such an option involves meeting a number of conditions.

Militarily, a strategic and tactical intelligence network must be consolidated to cover the region as a whole. Permanent bases must be established for counter-insurgency training for both Honduran and Salvadorean forces and CONDECA must be successfully reconstituted as an effective body. Politically, it is important to prevent the Sandinista Government from consolidating its position further in Nicaragua. Reagan himself has approved the CIA backed counter-revolutionary operations based in Nicaragua as part of the package of 'covert operations' approved on 16 September 1983. Moreover, it would seem that the political meaning of the US Secretary of State's Central America trip is that the position of the Pentagon and the National Security Council in defining and implementing foreign policy towards the region has been strengthened vis-à-vis that of the State Department. This is why Weinberger was sent rather than Schultz, the Secretary of State. Finally, US public opinion is being reminded daily of the growing Soviet threat in order to counteract the effects of the 'Vietnam Syndrome'. The South Korean airline disaster was particularly helpful in this respect as were events in Grenada.

VII.   FOURTH OPTION: NEGOTIATIONS

To understand the 'negotiations' option, one must consider three separate but inter-related sets of events. The first is the setting up of the Bipartisan Commission on Central America under the chairmanship of Dr Kissinger. The second is the role played by Richard Stone and, in particular, his three meetings with representatives of the FDR while, finally, there is the role of the Contadora group.

In June 1983 President Reagan named Henry Kissinger to head the Bipartisan Commission. The Commission has spoken to a wide range of people including ex-Presidents of the United States, Sandinista leaders, representatives of the Nicaraguan counter-revolutionary groups, leaders of the FDR, and the President of the Salvadorean Legislative Assembly, Major d'Aubuisson. The objective of the Commission was to present a series of recommendations on Central America to the Reagan Administration in early 1984. In effect, the role of the Commission was to create a new national consensus on Central America in order to counteract growing hostility in the US Congress and to bring the Republican and Democratic parties closer together.

In similar vein, the naming of Richard Stone as special emissary to 'sound out' the Salvadorean opposition is largely due to the pressure of US public opinion and, in particular, opinion within the liberal wing of the Democratic party. Mr Stone's assignment has been to demonstrate President Reagan's 'good faith' in seeking a negotiated solution. Mr Stone's brief, however, has been too narrow to allow for any meaningful negotiations. The aim of his mission was to ascertain whether elements of the FDR could be persuaded to participate unconditionally in the elections scheduled for March 1984. The possibility of negotiating FMLN–FDR participation in Government prior to elections was not included. The mission itself included a series of trips to the region and to Mexico as well as a series of conversations which took place in August and September 1983 between Mr Stone and diplomatic representatives of the FMLN–FDR in Bogotá and San José.

The various offers and counter-offers made in the course of these discussions involve a set of issues which can be reviewed under five headings: (1) the suspension of US arms shipments to El Salvador; (2) the participation of the FMLN–FDR in the 1984 Salvadorean elections; (3) the formation of a broadly based Government; (4) the negotiation of a cease fire; (5) the search for a peace formula acceptable to all sides.

In the course of his mission, Mr Stone reiterated his optimism about a settlement on a number of occasions. At the beginning of September 1983 he said that the United States was seeking to 'substitute democratic struggle for armed struggle' and looking for a 'peaceful process of participation'; at the same time he affirmed his support for the initiatives of the Contadora group.

Various other proposals for a negotiated settlement have been advanced, notably by Cuba, by Nicaragua and by Central American foreign ministers. Cuba has offered to withdraw its advisors from Nicaragua on condition that the United States does the same in El Salvador. The Sandinista Government has supported this idea and has spoken of a possible regional settlement which would involve ending all shipments of arms to El Salvador. Nevertheless, the positions of Mr Stone and of the FDR appear to be irreconcilable. For Mr Stone, the Soviet Union bears the fundamental responsibility for what is happening in the region and this amounts to no less than an 'offensive against the security of the hemisphere'. For Dr Guillermo Ungo of the FDR, the fundamental problem resides in the nature of the policies pursued by the Reagan Administration, in particular its support of a dictatorship of the extreme Right, and it is these policies which endanger hemispheric security and the security of Central America.

As to the Contadora group, their main objective has been to prevent the conflict from escalating into a regional war. A number of factors, however, have weakened the Contadora position. One is the heterogeneity of views it represents; Panama, for example, has been somewhat less conciliatory than other members of the group. In considering how the Contadora position has evolved, two events are of decisive importance. The first was the Cancun meeting, attended by Presidents Miguel de la Madrid of Mexico, Luis Herrera Campins of Venezuela, Belizario Betancurt of Colombia and Ricardo de la Espriella of Panama (16 and 17 July 1983), at which a document entitled 'Peace in Central America' was drafted expressing the basic political philosophy of the Contadora group. Given that neither the OAS nor the United Nations has been able to mount a regional initiative, Contadora has attempted to develop sufficient solidarity and credibility to become an effective regional negotiating body. But at the recent General Assembly meeting of the United Nations, differences were clearly apparent in the Venezuelan and Mexican postures. Despite nearly total support for a negotiated settlement within the international community, the limits of the Contadora process are clear and internal divisions have not entirely healed, particularly differences in views about the comparability of the conflicts in El Salvador and Guatemala. Nevertheless, Contadora has succeeded in establishing an effective mechanism for discussing the principles of a peaceful solution to Central American conflicts, thus forcing the international community to choose between intervention and negotiation. President Reagan, conscious of this situation, has worked behind the scenes to undermine the Contadora process, arguing that the weakness of Contadora is in itself a justification for continued US military involvement. An example is his speech in Seattle (23 August 1983) where he reaffirmed that 'peace must be built through strength'.

VIII. CONCLUSIONS

In the present paper, we have attempted to show how successive US Administrations have pursued policies towards Central America which have resulted in increased US involvement at a military level. It has been argued that under the Kennedy Presidency, traditional US policy, based on a doctrine of massive retaliation, was extended to include new forms of political and military response in the Caribbean Basin and Latin America. After the Bay of Pigs fiasco, however, President Johnson extended the notion of counter-insurgency to include 'discrete US military involvement', one of the factors contributing to the defeat of guerilla movements in the late 1960s. During the Nixon and Kissinger period, economic destabilisation was added to the arsenal of counter-insurgency while, under Carter, 'tri-lateralism' served to widen the international basis of support for crisis management. However, in the latest phase, President Reagan has adopted a decidedly more aggressive foreign policy stance and has launched a new ideological and military cold war with Central America now defined as the 'fourth strategic frontier' of the United States.

We have attempted to set out the broad 'options' faced by the Reagan Administration and the changing emphasis which has been placed on each. The distinctive logic of the Reagan strategy has been to divide the political opposition in order to gain time for erecting a military infrastructure capable of containing, and ultimately reversing, revolutionary gains in the region. US military aid to the region has expanded enormously and, more recently, US military presence has grown ominously. At the same time, successive diplomatic initiatives have been launched, more with the aim of neutralising foreign critics and appeasing domestic critics than of seeking a genuine negotiated solution.

In the final months of 1983, direct US military intervention for a time seemed imminent, particularly in the weeks following the US invasion of Grenada which boosted President Reagan's rating in US opinion polls. However, a rapid and massive military mobilisation by Nicaragua and new Nicaraguan and Contadora peace initiatives appear to have forestalled direct intervention by the United States. At the beginning of 1984, with the US election campaign underway, it appears unlikely that the Reagan Administration will attempt a full scale invasion of Nicaragua for the time being, though intervention in El Salvador cannot be ruled out. Thus, in the short term (up until the November 1984 presidential elections in the USA), a certain degree of stability can be expected, military conflict probably remaining at its present level. In the medium and long term, any serious examination of the options open to the US Administration suggests that space for a political solution is narrowing and, *per contra*, military intervention leading to a generalised regional conflict is becoming the only option. Whether the drift towards war can be reversed and how the outcome of the US elections will affect this process is now the fundamental question for the Central American region.

NOTES

1. See *New York Times*, 21 August 1982.
2. See *Uno mas Uno*, 20 September 1983.
3. See US Department of State: *Congressional Presentation: Security Assistance Programmes*, Fiscal Year 1983 (Washington DC) p. 457.
4. See *Aid Memo* (Centre for International Policy, 1 October 1982).
5. See *Uno mas Uno*, 5 October 1982.
6. See *Uno mas Uno*, 19 December 1982.
7. Those present at the conference were Aristides Calvani and Rafael Caldera of Venezuela; Antonio Morales Erlich and Adolfo Rey Prendes of El Salvador; Vinicio Cerezo of Guatemala; Edward Seaga of Jamaica, Adan Fletes of Nicaragua; José Miguel Alfaro of Costa Rica; Leo Tindermans, Prime Minister of Belgium; Helmut Kohl, Prime Minister of the Federal Republic of Germany. Also present for the United States were

Richard Allen, Roger Fontaine and Pedro Sanjuan, all of whom are members of the North American 'new right'.

8.   The event was organised by the European Popular Party which brings together European Christian Democratic fractions; also present were: the Chilean, Andres Saldivar, new President of the Social Democratic 'International'; Aristides Calvani, General Secretary of ODCA; and Napoleon Duarte of El Salvador.

9.   The task force was made up of the aircraft carrier *Ranger*, the cruiser *Harn*, the destroyers *Lynde* and *McCarmick*, the frigate *Marvin Silheds*; the tanker *Wichita* and the support ship *Camden*. All were under the orders of the Atlantic Command which controls the Caribbean.

10.   We are referring here to the possible installation of 572 missiles in Europe; the sending of 550 air force advisors to the Sudan; the presence of 800 marines in Lebanon; the amphibious operation in Somalia; operation 'Bright Star' in Egypt; the manoeuvres in Lebanon and US military participation in the French force in Chad.

11.   See *Time*, 22 August 1983.

12.   During his visit to the region he went to Howard Air Force base, the inter-American military school at Fort Gullick in Colon; he also spoke with the Salvadorean Minister of Defence, Eugenio Vides Casanova, and with President Alvero Magana. In addition he met the head of the Honduran armed forces, General Gustavo Alvarez, and the Honduran President, Roberto Suazo Cadova; in Panama, he met President Ricardo de la Espriella and the Chief of the Panamanian National Guard, General Manuel Antonia Noriega.

V

WESTERN EUROPEAN RESPONSES TO REVOLUTIONARY DEVELOPMENTS IN THE CARIBBEAN BASIN REGION

Erik Jan Hertogs

I. INTRODUCTION

This paper deals with the question of whether it is feasible that Western Europe might play a similar role in the dissolution of the *Pax Americana* in the Caribbean Basin Region (the term Carribbean Region is used to refer to Central America and the Caribbean) during the 1980s as that which the United States played in helping to break-up the European colonial empire in the first half of this century. First, we present a brief overview of European reactions to US interventions in the region in the 1950s and 1960s. This is contrasted with European responses towards revolutionary developments in Nicaragua, El Salvador and Grenada in the late 1970s and the early 1980s. A number of possible explanations for this change in policy are set out and we refer to the cases of West Germany, France, the European Community and the Socialist International respectively. Finally, suggestions are advanced as to how Europe might act as a counterbalancing force to US hegemony in the region in the future.

European influence on recent developments in Nicaragua, El Salvador and Grenada differs both quantitatively and qualitatively from European reactions to earlier instances of US intervention in revolutionary or reformist experiments. When a US trained and supported group of mercenaries invaded Guatemala in 1954, the Western European response was lukewarm. A request by Guatemala to have this invasion placed on the agenda of the United Nations General Assembly was opposed by the French and English delegations (under pressure from the United States) and the question was referred to the OAS, a forum in which, at the time, the United States enjoyed unanimous support (Blasier 1976: 171).

At the time of the Bay of Pigs invasion in 1961, American involvement again went largely unchallenged. Although West-European Social Democratic parties initially reacted positively to the Cuban Revolution, when it came down to defending its results, all members of the Socialist International, with the exception of the Japanese Social Democratic Party, chose to support their ally, the United States (Papadopoulos n.d.: 6–7).

In 1965, United States Marines were used to intervene in the Dominican Republic as a preventive measure to ensure that Juan Bosch would not take power. Here again, the UN Security Council had to decide whether the issue fell under the jurisdiction of the UN or of the OAS. It is illustrative of the slow drift in international realities that this time France voted against moving the discussion of the conflict to the OAS and that, within the OAS, the United States was barely able to put together the two-thirds majority needed to authorise the formation of an inter-American peace-keeping force[1]

In all three cases, the leaders of the countries under siege called on Western Europe to stand by them. Arbenz attempted, unsuccessfully, to get weapons from Western Europe. When he finally succeeded in buying weapons from Eastern Europe, the US used this as proof that Guatemala had become a 'Communist beachhead' and the invasion was authorised. Castro had also sought weapons from Europe; he got no response from England, but was able to obtain a shipment from France (though the ship exploded, presumably with CIA complicity, in the port of Havana). Juan Bosch, during his seven-month presidency, tried to develop economic relations with Western Europe and when, two years later, a pro-Bosch junta headed by Colonel Caamano came to power, it made overtures toward the governments of France, England and a number of Latin American countries hoping that, contrary to US wishes, the new regime would be recognised (Bell 1981: 80–81, 89).

Today by contrast, hardly any book on the Central American crisis fails to mention Western Europe or the Socialist International. In some cases reference is made to the complicity of European governments in present American policy but more frequently emphasis is placed on European initiatives to counter it (Andino, Mies & Schmidt 1982: 254–59). The most recent example of opposition to US policy is that of the Grenada invasion on which European condemnation was unanimous. An explanation for this independent European policy is usually sought in Europe's increasing economic ties with, and especially investments in, Latin America. In the words of James Petras: 'the pink flag of social democracy will give way to the green light for West German capital' (1980: 15). As George Black writes in his book on the Nicaraguan revolution:

More than any other Western government, German foreign policy is shaped by a pragmatic need for foreign markets, and stability coupled with increased local purchasing power could make Central America an attractive target for West-German exports. (Black 1981: 303)

However, such a direct link between politics and economics presupposes extreme foresight on the part of capitalists and, furthermore, assumes that foreign enterprises will find a more favourable climate for business in a 'revolutionary' developing country than in a country with a Western–oriented dictatorial regime. Evers (1982) has examined several explanations for the German social democratic 'offensive' in Latin America and concludes that there is no direct economic rationale which links the penetration of Latin American markets by West German capital: explanations should focus more on the political and ideological level (Evers 1982).

For the Caribbean Basin Region as a whole, no predominant European capital or commercial interests exist. Investments by the countries of the European Community in Central America are insignificant: in 1978 only 0.3 percent of total overseas investments were placed in Central America and in 1979 only 0.5 percent of the Community's total trade was with Central America (Commission of the EEC 1981: 3). On the other hand, the European Community *is* important for Central America since in 1979 24.0 percent of Central America's exports were to the Common Market (versus 34.9 percent to the USA) (Ibid: 2) and, in 1975, 26.7 percent of foreign investments in Central America were of Western European or Japanese origin (Castillo Rivas 1980: 186).

On the other hand, tax havens in the Caribbean seem to be of significant importance to European capital. Table 1 gives the breakdown of West German investments in the Caribbean Basin Region showing that investment in the tax havens makes up nearly 90 percent of total investment in the Region. It is thus difficult to argue that the independent policies derive from Europe's need to protect its investment since these are limited almost entirely to tax havens. Nevertheless, economic interests cannot be completely dismissed in an account of European policies vis-à-vis the Region. France, for example, has very close economic ties with Mexico. Among West European countries, France is after Spain the main importer of Mexican oil, and Mexico is after Brazil the most important purchaser of French products in Latin America. Moreover, in 1979, France was the fourth largest supplier of products to Mexico (Schwarzbeck 1982: 19). In political terms, Mexico is considered a key country in the region. Thus, the French–Mexican initiative recognising the FDR/FMLN as a representative political force reflects not merely a shared view of developments in El Salvador: French support of this essentially Mexican initiative must also be seen as a gesture to consolidate its special relationship with Mexico.

Of greater importance than economic interests in the region are considerations of a global political nature. The crisis in Central America could be the catalyst for a larger international crisis, especially since the Reagan Administration appears deliberately to be fostering confrontation. It is thus not only in the Caribbean Region or in Latin America that

Table 1. *Accumulated West German Private Direct Investments in the Caribbean Region (in millions of DM at the end of each year)*

Country	1963	1973	1975	1977	1979	1981
Latin America (incl. Caribbean Region)	1477	4080	5284	7355	8609	10887
Caribbean Region (excl. tax havens)	18*	122*	189*	177	201	n.a.
of which:						
Central America (without Panama)				40	54	64
Costa Rica				10	17	23
El Salvador				11	15	15
Guatemala				13	15	15
Honduras				1	2	2
Nicaragua				5	5	9
of which:						
Caribbean Islands (excl. tax havens)				137	149	n.a.
Jamaica				2	2	2
Dominican Republic				3	3	3
Trinidad & Tobago				97	104	n.a.
West Indies				2	2	n.a.
Tax havens				1311	1321	1777
Bahamas				25	29	58
Bermudas				58	65	66
Cayman Islands				27	23	494
Neth. Antilles	92	522	672	996	1009	850
Panama**	37	135	165	205	106	309
Latin American share (in %)						
(a) in all West German foreign investments	24.3	13.6	13.0			
(b) in West German investments in developing countries	67.8	42.3	n.a.			

*Only the Neth. Antilles and Panama excluded.
**Excluding the Panama canal zone.

Compiled on basis of information in von Gleich (1978) and Deutsch-Sudamerikanische Bank (1978-1983).

European interests are being affected, but throughout the world. European policies must therefore be placed in a global context.

At the international level, the most important consequence of US Central American policy is the deterioration in East–West relations.[2] It is in the interest of Western Europe to prevent such a deterioration since *detente* has enabled profitable economic relations to be established with the Eastern European countries and the Soviet Union. Furthermore, the renewal of the Cold War impairs the manoeuvrability of European countries in many areas and resurrects the threat of a nuclear holocaust which most likely would take place on European soil. But varying conceptions exist in Europe of the East–West relationship, and distinct views of the price to be paid for opposition to US policy in Central America. It is within this framework that the 'anti-intervention' policies of West Germany, France, the European Community and the Socialist International, in turn, are analysed below.

II. WEST GERMANY

The German reaction to the American-supported invasions of Caribbean Basin countries in the 1950s and 1960s differs markedly from that to American interventionist policy of the late 1970s and early 1980s. In the former case, the US had no reason to fear criticism from West Germany, whereas in the latter, under the Schmidt Administration, disagreements on an appropriate policy vis-à-vis revolutionary developments in the Caribbean Region became an important source of tension in German–American relations. The policy of West German social democracy, however, was characterised by a certain ambivalence: on the one hand serious attempts were made to influence the course of events in a direction explicitly rejected by the United States (i.e. by pushing for negotiations between the government and guerilla movement in El Salvador and by supporting the Sandinista government in Nicaragua), while on the other hand, German politicians strove to minimise their role in the region and were very reluctant to defend German initiatives in the face of US objections. This ambivalence caused German policy to be executed primarily on a sub-state level, i.e. via social democratic institutions such as the SPD, the Friedrich Ebert-Stiftung and the Socialist International, but also via Germany's lobbying within the European Commission for an active European policy. On the more visible and official level German policy was characterised by extreme reserve: the Federal Republic did not endorse the Franco–Mexican initiative; in the United Nations, the introduction of resolutions denouncing human rights violations in El Salvador was left to other countries; and German participation in President Reagan's 'Mini-Marshall Plan' for the Caribbean was, in Schmidt's own words, 'neither advisable, nor necessary'.[3]

Since the 1960s, Germany's growing economic and political weight suggests that it now has the potential to play an important role in the Caribbean Basin Region. In addition, Latin America happens to be that part of the Third World with which West Germany has the closest economic and political ties; Latin America comes closest to being a German 'sphere of influence' as expressed, among other things, by the network of political affiliations which the large German parties have established in Latin America. German Social Democrats have increasingly been opposed to the US attempt to force the problems of the Caribbean into an East–West mold, arguing that this raises the danger that a regional crisis might aggravate relations between East and West, a point of special concern among German Social Democrats who place high priority on the normalisation of relations with the countries of COMECON. Germany's trade with Eastern European countries is indispensable for many German firms and, by importing raw materials and energy from these countries, the Federal Republic hopes to decrease its dependence on the United States and on certain politically unstable areas of the Third World, primarily the Middle East (Zieburg 1982). But West Germany has not only come into conflict with the United States in the field of East–West relations. Since its 'over-industrialised' economy is very dependent on the continuous export of technology-intensive capital goods, competition between West Germany and the US in this branch has increased throughout the 1970s (Schlupp 1980: 60). This has resulted not only in economic but in political rivalry, since the 'politicisation of the economy' has permeated most deeply in the high technology, investment goods sector of the economy. A striking illustration of this political-economic rivalry is offered by the German–Brazilian nuclear treaty, which has caused much friction between the two countries (Carriere 1980). At the same time, no country in Western Europe is so strongly intertwined with the United States as West Germany. Therefore every conflict with the US rapidly takes on dramatic proportions, and debates about alleged German 'anti-Americanism' and 'neutralism' flare up in Bonn and Washington.

This relationship enables us to understand what is at stake if Germany opposes Reagan's policy in the Caribbean Region. An independent German policy, aimed at 'containment' of the international tensions caused by revolutionary developments, is in the interests of a Bonn-sanctioned climate of detente, but can only be implemented at the expense of German–American relations. (The North–South dimension of German social-democratic policy in the Caribbean Region will be dealt with in the section on the Socialist International.) Under the Schmidt Administration this dilemma led to the ambivalent policy mentioned above. The present CDU/CSU/FDP Government seems to be willing to give up this balancing act in favour of improving German–American relations at the risk of a deterioration in relations with its Eastern neighbours and with developing countries. For German policy towards the Region, this implies that aid to Nicaragua will probably be reduced, and that the German Ambassador in El Salvador, who had been recalled 'on security grounds', will most likely be reinstated. Development aid projects, which had been stopped 'due to technical reasons', can be expected to resume.[4]

III. FRANCE

French social-democratic policy contrasts with that of Germany in the sense that France has openly attacked American policy in the Caribbean Region. Examples of this are the Franco–Mexican initiative, arms sales to Nicaragua, diplomatic activities in the United Nations and public condemnations of America's policy by President Mitterrand and the Minister of Foreign Affairs, Monsieur Cheysson. One of the reasons for the difference in approach between France and Germany is that Germany, because of its political presence in Latin America and its dominant role in the Socialist International, has recourse to political channels not available to France. Therefore France has little choice other than to make use of the standard public and diplomatic channels. Another reason is that France has a foreign policy tradition underscoring its independence vis-à-vis the major power blocs. From the French viewpoint, both the Soviet Union and the United States impinge on the sovereignty of developing countries, coercing them into involvement with one camp or the other. In this context, French aid to Nicaragua, Grenada and the Salvadorian guerillas is presented as offering a 'third road'. Having profited much less than Germany from the normalisation of East–West relations, France is relatively less concerned about possible effects on detente. It also has less to fear from a cooling in Franco–American relations since its economy is less intertwined with America's and its own nuclear 'force de frappe' makes it less dependent on American military protection (Wells 1981). Revolutionary developments in the Caribbean Region have also offered Mitterrand a welcome chance to enhance the 'socialist' dimension of French Third World policy. Such modifications are especially necessary since under the French Social Democratic government, very little had changed in France's semi-colonial relations with French-speaking Africa and French possessions in the Caribbean (French Guyana, Guadeloupe and Martinique). Although France, with its greater manoeuvering room vis-à-vis the United States, could potentially play a leading political role in the Caribbean Region, not too much should be expected. French relations with the Third World are primarily with its former (mainly African) colonies, and France has neither the economic nor the political weight to enable it to be concerned with several continents at once; hence, the largely verbal and symbolic character of French policy in the Caribbean Basin Region. In concert with such regional powers as Mexico and Venezuela, however, the French role may nevertheless be an important one.

IV. THE EUROPEAN COMMUNITY

In March 1981 a long interview appeared in *Le Monde* with Claude
Cheysson (then member of the Commission of the European Community
and responsible for development aid) under the title of 'Les divergences
s'accentuent entre les Etats-Unis et la C.E.E. au sujet de l'Amerique
Centrale et des Caraibes' (Clerc 1981). What led to the interview was
American criticism of European humanitarian aid to Salvadoran
refugees in Honduras ('the aid could fall into the hands of the *guerrilla*')
and of European aid to Grenada designed to help modernise its international airport ('the airport could be used to transport Cuban troops to
Africa') (Pearce 1981: 189). In his interview, Cheysson sharply denounced American involvement in European matters and stated that it
was Europe's duty to help countries to develop without being forced to
lean towards either the United States or the Soviet Union. He pointed out
that the European Community is linked via the Lomé Treaty to nineteen
political entities in the Region (of which Grenada is one), and that the
responsibilities entailed herein extend to neighbouring countries such as
those of Central America. The European Commission, therefore,
refused to bow to US pressure and went ahead with granting aid to the
Salvadorean refugees (after the International Commission of the Red
Cross had made assurances that the aid would not fall into the wrong
hands). Aid was also granted to Grenada.

In addition, the European Commission set up a plan for 'Special
Action in Favour of the Economic and Social Development of Central
America', the central component of which is aid for agrarian reform in
the countries of the Isthmus, Haiti and the Dominican Republic.
Although West Germany provided the main impetus for the plan, it was
nevertheless difficult to reach consensus among member states of the
Community. The Netherlands protested against the plan's inclusion of
El Salvador, Haiti and Guatemala, because of the violations of human
rights in these countries. Great Britain opposed the inclusion of Nicaragua,
arguing that Nicaragua was 'spending its resources on military build-up
rather than development' and that the 'Nicaraguan regime is becoming
increasingly repressive and Soviet and Cuban influence there is growing'.[5]
The final version of the plan includes only Honduras, Nicaragua, Costa
Rica and the Dominican Republic, and the amount to be donated in
1982 has been set as US$30 million, bringing the total European Com-
munity aid to these countries to US$80 million in 1982.[6]

It is difficult to judge whether this European initiative should be interpreted as a form of rivalry with the US, but it is clear that the premises
underlying the plan for Special Action differ quite substantially from
those of the US Caribbean Basin Initiative (CBI). In its introduction, the
latter analyses the economic problems of the region as caused by a

negative balance of trade which 'threatens political and social stability throughout the region and creates conditions which Cuba and others seek to exploit through terrorism and subversion'.[7] The analysis of the region's economic problems given in the European plan, however, considers the balance of payments problem secondary to the problems caused by the rural sector's rigid integration into the world market and the unequal distribution of land (Commission of the EEC 1982: 3). As a result of these differing analyses, the solutions proposed differ as well: the CBI essentially propounds stronger integration into the world market, whereas the Special Action Plan stresses agrarian reform.

In the European Parliament a resolution rejecting the legitimacy of the Salvadorean elections of 28 March 1982 was accepted with 84 votes in favour, 4 abstentions and 54 votes against (Leijte 1982a, 1982b). The resolution stated that the elections cannot be considered free since no political freedom was guaranteed, and politicians of the opposition could participate only at the risk of death. In addition, American policy was denounced for hindering a dialogue between government and opposition in El Salvador, and Lopez Portillo's offer to mediate was supported. Finally, the European Community gave a substantial amount of aid to Nicaragua: in the period 1979–1981 US$16 million, making the EEC Nicaragua's third largest donor after Cuba (US$42.5 million) and Mexico (US$39.5 million) (UNGA 1981: Table 3). (For European aid to Nicaragua see Tables 2 and 3,)

These surprisingly enterprising policies of the European Community can partially be accounted for by Germany's preference for multilateral rather than bilateral initiatives. But one should also take into account the

Table 2. *Donations in Cash and Kind from Western European Countries to Nicaragua in the period 1979–1981 (in million US dollars)*

Source	1979	1980	1981	Total
EEC	5.277	10.634	0.078	15.989
Sweden	5.296	6.229	0.985	12.510
Netherlands	6.281	5.852	0.206	12.339
Spain	12.224	—	—	12.224
West Germany	2.222	1.585	—	3.807
Switzerland	2.763	—	—	2.763
France	1.000	0.052	—	1.052
Italy	0.669	0.284	—	0.918
West Europe total	35.732	24.636	1.269	61.637
World total	62.695	89.411	42.465	194.571
Share West Europe in world total	57.0%	27.5%	3.0%	32.5%

Calculated from: United Nations General Assembly (1981), 4–5, Table 3.

Table 3. *Bilateral Loans by West European Countries to Nicaragua
over the period 1979–1981 (in million US dollars)*

Source	1979	1980	1981	Total
West Germany	17.6	11.2	—	28.8
Netherlands	—	17.5	10.0	27.5
Italy	—	24.5	—	24.5
France	—	12.2	—	12.2
West Europe total	17.6	65.4	10.0	93.0
World total	17.6	184.6	315.8	518.0
Share West Europe in world total	100%	35.4%	3.2%	18.0%

Calculated from: United Nations General Assembly (1981), 5, Table 3.

fact that the European Commission and the European Parliament must distance themselves from American policy if they are to generate recognisable policies of their own. However, the Foreign Affairs Ministers of the European Community member countries are first responsible to the governments of their own countries. Since the political diversity within the Community is so great, it is nearly impossible to formulate a clear political line for the group as a whole. Furthermore, individual countries are under direct pressure from the United States to conform to US policy (Tudyka & van Hobbelen 1982: 64). With the European Community subordinate to the Council of Ministers, and the European Parliament in a position of almost total impotence, the European Community cannot hope to compete with the United States in the Caribbean Basin Region. What the Community *can* do is to demonstrate a degree of independence from US policy. The European Parliament can also be expected to take certain humanitarian initiatives.

V. THE SOCIALIST INTERNATIONAL

The role of the Socialist International (SI) in formulating a European policy different from that of the United States is often exaggerated. A striking example of this is *El desafío europeo en Centroamerica* (*The European Challenge in Central America*), a book by Pierre Schori, Secretary for International Relations of the Swedish Social Democratic Party and Secretary of the International Committee for the Defence of the Revolution in Nicaragua. In his book, Schori ascribes virtually all progressive initiatives by European governments in the Caribbean Region to the influence of the SI. However, since the SI has only limited budgetary means at its disposal, no political cadres of its own, and little real power over its affiliated parties, the only weight it has can be attributed to the individual prestige of Social Democratic leaders endorsing a particular resolution. Beyond this, the SI performs tasks involving the co-ordination and dissemination of information, but these rather nebulous functions are difficult to gauge in terms of impact.[8]

The SI's involvement in the Nicaraguan Revolution began in September 1978 when it declared its solidarity with the bourgeois forces of the Nicaraguan opposition, the FAO and UDEL. In November 1978, support was extended to the FLSN as well and a promise made to donate US $50,000 per month in humanitarian aid, an amount that was actually paid only once (Rathgeber 1982: 284). Following the Sandinista victory, the SI called for aid to Nicaragua, and at the XVth Conference of the SI in Madrid, a 'Committee for the Defence of the Revolution in Nicaragua' was formed under the presidency of Felipe Gonzalez; other members included Brandt, Kreisky, Perez, Palme, Mitterrand and Manley, while Pierre Schori became its secretary.

In the case of El Salvador, SI involvement began in January 1980 when one of its member organisations, the *Movimiento Nacional Revolucionario* (MNR), withdrew from the governing junta. Three months later, when the non-military opposition groups united to form the *Frente Democrático Revolucionario* (FDR) under the leadership of MNR President Guillermo Ungo, the SI declared its solidarity with the FDR and declared it the legitimate representative of the Salvadorean people (Ibid: 296).

In November 1981, the SI split on its policy towards Nicaragua. The SI's special committee on Nicaragua failed to agree on a statement of support after its emergency meeting in Madrid, and three months later, the fourth meeting of the regional committee for Latin America and the Caribbean, scheduled to take place in Caracas, failed to meet when the host, the Venezuelan Social Democratic party, *Acción Democrática*, protested against inviting the Sandinistas, using the argument that they were neither social democrats nor members of the SI (Schori 1982: 256). There are strong indications, however, suggesting that the real reason for Venezuela's objection was pressure from the United States (van Traa 1982: 29). After the cancellation of this meeting, Brandt invited the 21 SI vice-presidents (plus two special guests, Carlos Gallardo Flores from Guatemala and Guillermo Ungo from El Salvador) to Bonn. During this informal meeting (1–2 April 1982) a resolution was passed giving qualified support to the Sandinista government:

The *Sandinista* Government of Nicaragua must receive support in its commitment to pluralism, social justice, democracy and non-alignment, and must receive support condemning every attempt, whatever its origin to destabilize and interfere against its sovereignty. (Schori 1982: 408)

With respect to El Salvador, the resolution stated that the elections of 28 March offered no solution and called for negotiations involving all political sectors willing to accept the democratic process, including the FDR/FMLN. Qualified support was expressed for Maurice Bishop's government in Grenada 'in its efforts to work out a constitution with the objective of organising elections' (Ibid: 408). At the XVIth Conference of the SI in Albuferia, Portugal (7–10 April 1983), the final resolution largely restated these passages, albeit with more generous phrasing for the support for the New Jewel Movement in Grenada and an unequivocal denunciation of American policy vis-à-vis these countries (Socialist International 1983: 145).

The activities of the SI in Latin America are undoubtedly largely inspired by the West German SDP. For the SPD, the SI is an ideal instrument for developing contacts in the Third World, the SI is essentially only useful inasmuch as it is able to work as a countervailing force offsetting America's dominant position in developing countries. Therefore it is of crucial importance that the SI continues to resist US pressures, even in cases where the revolution has become more radical than its Social Democratic supporters.

VI. CONCLUSIONS

At the start of this paper we posed the question of whether Europe's role in helping to dissolve the American neo-colonial position in the Caribbean Region might be comparable to that which the United States played in the dissolution of the European colonial empire. The thrust of America's decolonisation policy was to ensure the establishment of an 'open door': free and equal access for all capitalist metropolitan powers to raw material, trade and investment opportunities in the peripheral countries. As a result, the decolonisation of the Third World enabled the United States to gain access to markets previously closed to American interests. Economic factors were a clear motivating force behind American policy. Such economic motives, however, cannot be ascribed to European policies vis-à-vis revolutionary developments posing a possible threat to America's hegemony in the Caribbean Region. In the aftermath of the successful revolution in Nicaragua, in Grenada until October 1983, and soon perhaps in El Salvador, no important 'doors' could be expected to open for European economic interests. Development aid requirements will far outweigh any potential profits to be made in small, poverty-stricken countries devastated by civil war.

European policies can be accounted for only in the light of specific developments at the end of the 1970s and in the early 1980s. The Caribbean Basin revolutionary movements arose in a period when the United States had begun to distance itself from the process of detente and hoped to strengthen US leadership of the 'Free World'. This new tone in American foreign policy met with dismay in Europe and, when the

Reagan Administration attempted to use the crises in the Caribbean Region to alter the global political climate, this difference of opinion took on a fundamental character.

Simultaneously, the initiative for defining a Western policy acceptable to the Third World began to shift from the United States to social-democratic Europe. It became important for Europe's Social Democrats to prove to the Third World that Europe could supply reliable support to developing countries unwilling to orient themselves towards either the USA or the USSR. Revolutionary movements in the Caribbean Region were interpreted as opening such a 'third road'. Finally, the formulation of a policy distinct from that of the US offers certain advantages for the European Community. This was most true for the Socialist International and for France: both used the opportunity to project and sharpen their images in adopting a stance critical of the United States. At the same time, their relationship with the US created a strong impediment to the formulation of a policy of their own, for, when it comes down to it, even European Social Democrats accord first priority to maintaining the Atlantic Alliance.

What conclusions can be drawn from this analysis? In the first place one must recognise that Western European policy is formed by a complex set of interests. These interests differ according to country and are to a certain extent contradictory. It is likely that, on the whole, Europe will continue to oppose policies leading to generalised conflict in the Caribbean Basin Region. But, depending on the political conjuncture within each individual country and the state of its relations with the USA, the initiative for formulating an independent policy will shift over time from one country to another. Also the political rhetoric of a government may be quite different from that government's actual policy. All this means that the Region's revolutionary leaders must keep abreast of political developments within Western Europe in order to be in a position to react quickly to changes. Thus, the Sandinista government, for instance, has recently commissioned a study on international development cooperation with Nicaragua (FIR 1982).

Second, the fluctuations in European policy make it more susceptible to outside influences. In this context the importance of the solidarity movement in Europe should be noted, for these committees can help in investigating possibilities for European support to revolutionary movements and in ensuring that potential support actually materialises. Here again, Nicaragua serves as an example: initially, following their victory, the Sandinistas had little time and energy to attend meetings of the Nicaragua Support Committees in Europe, but within a year-and-a-half they rediscovered the importance of the solidarity movement in making contact with political parties, trade unions, churches and the media, and ties with the solidarity committees were promptly reinstituted. [9]

And third, given the fact that global interests of Western Europe are at stake in the conflicts in Central America and the Caribbean, European political leaders are wise to act upon these interests even though they might deepen the divisions in the Western camp. The contradictions between European and US policies are an historical inevitability which can only be resolved on the basis of a new foreign policy approach. In his book *The Intemperate Zone: The Third World Challenge to US Foreign Policy*, Richard Feinberg outlines such an alternative policy, labelling it 'neo-realism'. Hopefully, a 'neo-realist' Western consensus on the need to accommodate to revolutionary change in Central America and the Caribbean can be achieved in the not too-distant future.

NOTES

1. See *Keesings Historisch Archief*, 14 May 1965, p. 291, and 21 May 1965, p. 306.
2. The importance of the East-West relationship in this case is also noted in Wolf Grabendorff (1982: 4) and Schwarzbeck (1982: 31).
3. See 'Schmidt: Marshall-Plan für Karibik', *Frankfurter Allgemeine Zeitung*, 5 May 1981.
4. See 'Latin Letter', *Latin America Weekly Report*, 17 December 1982, p. 3 and 'West Germany: Hardening the Line', *Latin America Weekly Report*, 31 March 1983, p. 7.
5. See 'Central America ...', *LAWR*, 1 October 1982, p. 4, and 'Bonn Moves Closer to Washington', *LAWR*, 10 October 1982, p. 10.
6. See 'Ayuda a America Central', *Europa*, No. 14 (January–February 1983), p. 3, and 'Central America ...', *LAWR*, 10 December 1982.
7. See 'Feature Caribbean Basin', *Department of State Bulletin* (April 1982), p. 7.
8. For detailed information on the SI's activities in Latin America see Kopsch (1982).
9. See the interview with Hans Langenberg of the European Secretariat of Nicaragua-Committees in Steenhuis(1982).

REFERENCES

Andino, R. C., D. Mies & R. Schmidt (1982): *Revolution in Mittelamerika* (Frankfurt am Main: Verlag Marxistische Blatter).
Bell, I. (1981): *The Dominican Republic* (Boulder, Col.: Westview Press).
Black, G. (1981): *Triumph of the People: The Sandinista Revolution in Nicaragua* (London: Zed Press).
Blasier. C. (1976): *The Hovering Giant: U.S. Responses to Revolutionary Change in Latin America* (Pittsburgh: University of Pittsburgh Press).
Carriere, J. (1980)): 'Europe and Latin America: The Nuclear Connection', in *Europe and Latin America: An Annual Review of European-Latin American Relations* (London: Latin America Bureau).
Castillo Rivas, D. (1980): *Acumulacíon de Capital y Empresas Transnacionales en Centroamerica* (Mexico: Siglo XXI).
Clerc, J.-P. (1981): 'Les divergences s'accentuent entre les Etats-Unis et la C.E.E. au sujet de l'Amerique Centrale et des Caraibes' (Interview with Claude Cheysson in: *Le Monde*, 13 March).
Commission of the European Community (1981): *Europe Information: Foreign Relations* (Brussels; November), 53/81.
—— (1982): *Special Action in Favour of the Economic and Social Development of Central America* (Brussels; 21 June; COM 82 257 final).
Deutsch-Sudamerikanische Bank (1978–1983): *Kursbericht über Lateinamerika*.

Evers, T. (1982): 'European Social Democracy in Latin America: The Case of West Germany', in Jenny Pearce (ed.): *The European Challenge: Europe's New Role in Latin America* (London: Latin America Bureau), 80–129.

FDCL (1982): *Sozialdemokratie und Lateinamerika* (Berlin: FDCL).

Feinberg, R. (1983): *The Intemperate Zone: The Third World Challenge to U.S. Foreign Policy* (New York & London: W. W. Norton & Co.).

Fondo Internacional para la Reconstrucción (FIR) (1982): *Estudio de las Políticas y Mecanismos de la Cooperación Internacional* (Managua).

Gleich, A. von (1978): 'The Economic Relations Between Germany and Latin America and the Significance of the European Community', in: J. Grunwald (ed.): *Latin America and the World Economy: A Changing International Order* (Beverly Hills & London: Sage Publications).

Grabendorff, W. (1982): *The Central American Crisis and Western Europe: Perceptions and Reactions* (Bonn: Research Institute of the Friedrich-Ebert-Stiftung).

Kopsch, U. (1983): *Die Rolle und Aktivitat der Sozialistischen Internationale und ihrer Mitgliederorganisationen in Lateinamerika seit 1976* (Hamburg: Institut für Iberoamerika-Kunde, Series Arbeitsunterlagen und Diskussionsbeitrage, No. 17).

Leitjte, H. (1982a): 'Kritiek EG op Salvadorbeleid', *Het Parool*, 10 March.

—— (1982b): 'Commissie VN: politieke oplossing in El Salvador', *NRC Handelsblad*, 12 March.

'Nicaragua: Mit der Sozialistische Internationale für mehr Unternehmerfreiheit', *Lateinamerika Nachrichten*, 105 (July 1982), 33–37.

Papadopoulos, P. (n.d.): *The Socialist International and the Decolonization Process of the Cuban Case* (University: University of Amsterdam, unpublished manuscript).

Pearce, J. (ed.) (1982): *The European Challenge: Europe's New Role in Latin America* (London: Latin America Bereau).

Petras, J. (1980): 'La Social-Democratie en Amerique Latine', in *Le Monde Diplomatique* (June), 15–17.

Rathgeber, T. (1982): 'Sozialdemokratische Solidaritat mit Nicaragua und El Salvador', in: FDCL: *Sozialdemokratie und Lateinamerika* (Berlin: FDCL), 277–310.

Schlupp, F. (1980): 'Modern Germany and the International Division of Labour: The Federal Republic of Germany in the World Political Economy', in: *The Foreign Policy of West Germany: Formation and Contents* (Beverly Hills & London: Sage Publications), 33–100.

Schori, P. (1982): *El Desafio Europeo en Centroamerica* (San José: EDUCA).

Schwarzbeck, F. (1982): *Lagenotiz betr. bilaterale Beziehungen ausgewahlter westeuropaischer Staaten zu Mittelamerika und der Karibik: eine Uebersicht* (Ebenhausen: Stiftung Wissenschaft und Politik; SWP-LN 2344 Fo.Pl.IV).

Socialist International (1983): 'Resolución del 16° Congreso de la Internacional Socialista'; reprinted in *Nueva Sociedad* (March–April), 131–147.

Steenhuis, A. (1982): 'Nicaragua wil niet terugvallen op het Oostblok', in J. J. Teunissen & A. Steenhuis (eds): *Revolutie en Realisme: De Economische en Politieke Uitdaging in Nicaragua* (Amsterdam & Utrecht: Transnational Institute and Nicaragua Committee), 108–117.

Traa, M. van (1982): 'Hard werken aan politieke oplossing', in *Voorwaarts*, 15 March, 25–30.

Tudyka, K. & W. van Hobbelen (1982): 'Ueber die Voraussetzungen einer "europaischen" Politik', in *Weltpolitik, Jahrbuch für Internationale Beziehungen*, No. 2, 58–65.

United Nations General Assembly (1981): *Assistance to Nicaragua: Report of the Secretary-General* (5 November; A/36/280).

Wells, S. F. (1981): 'The Mitterand Challenge', in *Foreign Policy*, No. 44, 57–69.

Ziebura, G. (1982): 'Die Krise des transatlantischen Systems und die Zukunft der deutsch-amerikanischen Beziehungen', in *Weltpolitik, Jahrbuch für Internationale Beziehungen*, No. 2, 15–42.

VI

A NOTE ON MEXICO:
EXPECTATIONS AND REALITY

Olga Pellicer

I. INTRODUCTION

The year 1983, which saw growing involvement by Honduras and Costa Rica in the North American Strategy to bring down the *Sandinista* Government in Nicaragua and to contain the revolutionary forces in El Salvador, may with hindsight prove to have been decisive in the regionalisation of Central American conflict. Looking back over the year, instability has increased throughout the region and it is likely that there will be increasingly frequent border clashes between Nicaragua and Honduras, possibly leading to open war, further pressure to increase the isolation of the Nicaraguan Government, social disorder in Honduras (as a result of the attempt to destabilise Nicaragua), internal divisions in Costa Rica's traditional political parties, and an intensification of the guerilla struggle in Guatemala and El Salvador.

Obviously, it is difficult to predict what will emerge from this new *noche larga*. One thing seems certain, however; the forms of internal domination which had characterised the area before the fall of Somoza, the undisputed hegemony exercised by the United States, and the use of inter-American institutions to justify US intervention whenever necessary are all part of the system which can no longer be reconstructed. The time is past when Central American oligarchies could guarantee political stability and the process of capital accumulation, and when the United States could freely intervene in Guatemala or Santo Domingo with the backing of the OAS. Central America at the end of the 20th century can no longer be adminstered under the aegis of 'Pax Americana', and will either be turned into an enormous battleground (for which there is no lack of historical precedent) or will become a region in which a genuine attempt is made to build, whatever the difficulties, a new model of development based on greater social and economic equality, the participation of working people in the exercise of power, and a regional order guaranteeing pluralism and peaceful co-existence.

It is within such a perspective that one needs to locate Mexico's policy towards the region. For present purposes, one need not reflect on the desirability or otherwise of Central America becoming the exclusive focus of Mexican foreign policy. It is possible that in Mexico, for tactical reasons, Central American policy may for a time be accorded somewhat less attention. What concerns us is, on the one hand, Mexico's potential contribution towards creating international conditions conducive to the construction of more just societies in Central America and, on the other, the impact of political events in Central America on the orientation of Mexico's own political future. In effect, Mexico's view of its own national security would be somewhat different if it accepted the domino theory; i.e. that Nicaraguan and Cuban subversion must ultimately affect Mexico's own stability. Equally, the ideology sustaining the Mexican State would need to change substantially if Mexico were to cease lending its support to the notion of change and the principle of non-intervention in Central America. Moreover, to accept a regional order in which traditional North American hegemony could continue to be exercised without restraint would seriously restrict the margins of Mexico's own national sovereignty.

What is taking place in Central America cannot be divorced from Mexican national interests; on this principle, even the most sceptical observers of Mexican foreign policy are agreed. Nevertheless, there is less agreement about Mexico's precise relationship with different Central American political currents, about the particular role that Mexico should play in the crisis, and about constraints on more effective Mexican participation in the construction of a new regional order. The present paper is intended as a contribution to this debate.

II. MEXICO'S RELATIONSHIP WITH DIFFERENT CENTRAL AMERICAN POLITICAL FORCES

Mexico's influence in the region is conditioned by its sympathy towards the rise of political forces reflecting majority aspirations. It is such new currents which ultimately will determine the future of the peoples of Central America; hence, if Mexico's voice is to have legitimate resonance, it must speak for those in Central America who are becoming 'the authors of their own history'. While no detailed analysis has yet been undertaken of the relations between the Mexican government and different political groups in Central America, certain general propositions can be advanced based on the evolution of economic and political relations with the region. Traditional ruling groups in Central America have tended to view closer relations with Mexico with considerable scepticism. In the mid-1970s, when Mexico took steps to strengthen economic ties with its southern neighbours, it became clearer that, while

Central American elites were pleased to take full advantage of new opportunities for tourism, they remained sceptical about the benefits of closer economic ties which some perceived as a form of 'Mexican Imperialism'. This, in part, explains the accent placed by Mexico in its trade talks on the notion of 'equitable benefits', and the fact that Mexican joint ventures in Central America were governed by the principle of minority association with local capital.

Despite repeated assertions of this principle, the resistance to economic association with Mexico was considerable. A good example is that of the State corporation FERTICA (which produces fertilisers), one of the Mexican government's most important attempts at promoting joint ventures in Central America. While certain criticisms can be made of Mexican management of this venture, what is true is that Central American pressure groups successfully blocked the project by, for example, refusing to grant favourable tax and tariff concessions (already available to other importers of fertilisers) and preventing participation of public sector enterprise, using the argument that this field should be reserved for private initiative. The latter argument is indicative of the sorts of difficulties encountered in building better economic relations, given the very distinct philosophies governing the role of the public sector in Mexico and its Central American neighbours. The Mexican State, with its long tradition of public ownership, has always had great difficulty in dealing with Central American elites systematically opposed to State intervention in the economy. In countries like Guatemala, El Salvador and Honduras, for example, the public sector's share in GDP as late as 1980 was less than 20 percent.

These divisions between the Mexican Government on the one hand, and governments based on archaic economic and political structures on the other, have tended to deepen as the political crisis of the region has grown, and particularly so given Mexico's support of the Sandinista government in Nicaragua and of opposition forces in El Salvador. In Guatemala, anti-Mexicanism is deeply rooted in 19th century history which saw the annexation to Mexico of the regions of Chiapas and El Soconusco. It was only in the 'revolutionary' period of Guatemalan history (1944–54) that such attitudes began to change. More recently, fanning anti-Mexican sentiment has served the political ends of the Lucas, and Rios-Montt and Mejia Victores governments in the struggle against the guerilla movement. The proximity of the guerilla struggle to the Mexican border and the flow into Mexico of refugees created by the Guatemalan 'scorched earth' policy have been factors reinforcing the concern with which Guatemalan political leaders view Mexico's proximity as a threat to their own political control. As a consequence, frontier incidents have multiplied and an already fragile *modus vivendi* between the Governments has weakened.

A very different climate characterises relations between Mexico and governments such as that presently in power in Costa Rica. In the Costa Rican case, an important section of the *Partido de Liberación Nacional* has always favoured close relations with Mexico. If stronger ties have not emerged, it is because Mexican politicians have paid insufficient attention to promoting such relations. At the same time, one should not overlook the fact that in recent years, conservative sections of the Costa Rican bourgeoisie have shown growing hostility towards Mexico, a hostility echoed by sectors of the mass media. One example, in early 1982, was the accusation of overcharging made against PEMEX by the office of the Controller-General of Costa Rica which related to a joint venture between the two countries in the field of petroleum exploration. This accusation, and the widespread public outcry against PEMEX to which it gave rise, was widely aired in the Costa Rican press.

All these experiences suggest that within Central America, it is in left-of-centre circles that sympathy for Mexico is to be found. Therefore, it is interesting to speculate about what expectations exist in such circles with respect to Mexico's future role in the Central American region. To begin with, a confusing element in this debate is the idea, emanating principally from sections of the Communist Party, that Mexico's policies towards the region principally reflect the expansionist drive of the Mexican bourgeoisie. In reality, Mexican direct private investment in the region is insignificant and Mexican businessmen show little interest in the relatively small economies of Central America. However, the argument is awkward since it encourages a form of economic reductionism which obscures the more complex political factors conditioning Mexican policy and, in particular, the coincidence of Mexican interests with those of progressive forces in Central America.

Another source of suspicion is the apparent disjuncture between Mexican global initiatives and Mexican initiatives in the field of bilateral relations. Hence, for the more progressive sectors of the *Partido Liberal* in Honduras, or of the *Partido de Liberación Nacional* in Costa Rica, it is disconcerting that so much attention should be paid to the Franco-Mexican Declaration, or to the presentation of the peace plan for Central America while, on the other hand, little interest is paid to lending direct support to political groups in Central America closely identified with Mexican positions. According to this view, Mexico is more concerned with gaining international prestige than with providing tangible support to those forces which, in their different ways, are struggling for the transformation of economic and social life in the region.

A third and most significant fear concerns the way in which Mexico might seek to regulate the pace of political and social change in Central America. A particular example is that of the expectations raised by events during the final months of the Sandinista struggle. While it was clear that countries such as Mexico, Venezuala, Costa Rica and Panama directly supported the Sandinistas in the final insurrectionary phase, the circumstances of this support were exceptional given both the breadth of feeling against Somoza and the 'human rights' orientation of the Carter administration. Today, five years later, just as international conditions have changed, so too has the nature of the internal struggles taking place in countries like Guatemala and El Salvador, struggles which have assumed a dimension of direct class confrontation rather than merely being popular uprisings. Hence, not only is the revolutionary process likely to be longer, but its internal alliances will be different in nature from those which characterised the Nicaraguan situation. Equally, United States foreign policy now shows a degree of intransigence reminiscent of the worst period of the Cold War. The insistent theme of the Reagan Administration, that Central America is a focus point of communist subversion, has been repeatedly echoed by the transnational mass-media with considerable effect on the rest of Latin America.

In such circumstances, it is difficult to imagine that Mexico's commitment to aiding change in Central America will take the same form as it did in Nicaragua in 1978–79. The problem is well stated by Adolfo Aguilar: 'Mexico will continue to define its policies and initiatives in a way which corresponds to the reality of revolutionary change taking place in Central America, but Mexico will never attempt to become the author of such change ....' In short, although Mexico will remain an ally in the struggle, it will not become directly involved in revolution.

However astute this observation, the distance which Mexico has maintained from internal armed struggles has produced a degree of disillusionment, particularly amongst the Guatemalan opposition for whom Mexican help at this juncture would be decisive. It is understandably difficult for the Guatemalan guerilla movement to accept that Mexico will not allow the southern provinces of Chiapas and Tabasco to be used as sanctuaries or bases for arms traffic. Undoubtedly, it will take some time for conditions of generalised insurrection and seizure of power to reach a stage such that the Mexican Government might collaborate more directly with revolutionary forces. In addition to these preoccupations, a further factor is the growing concern on the part of the Nicaraguan revolutionary leadership as to whether Mexico will continue to provide economic aid on the same scale as in the past. The present crisis of the Mexican economy suggests that there will need to be a rationalisation of economic aid and that, while certain priority programmes will be maintained, Mexico may be less generous in some fields; i.e. the subsidisation of crude oil supplies.

For all the above reasons, there is a growing feeling in certain circles of the Central American Left that Mexico, in contrast to Cuba, is a 'vacillating ally'. In our view, such conclusions reflect the mistaken premise that Mexican foreign policy can play an active internal role in the revolutionary process. Such a premise is unsubstantiated either by the reality of Mexico's economic situation or by the nature of the Mexican State and its traditions of foreign policy. This is not to say that Mexico has not, and cannot, play a significant role in Central America; this role, however, will be limited to shaping the external conditions for revolutionary advance and, in particular, helping to create an international environment which inhibits US intervention, promotes peaceful co-existence, and thus facilitates the full development of those progressive forces acting for social change which must ultimately prevail in Central America. In short, Mexico's role is to promote an international order conducive to Central American self-determination.

A number of points are worth examining in order to ascertain how far Mexico can significantly affect international conditions in a manner that will favour progressive forces of the regions. A first question concerns the political and ideological tradition of the Mexican State and, in particular, how far Mexico's view of its national interest and security requirements entails increased autonomy relative to the United States. As already pointed out, the defence of national sovereignty is an issue closely linked to how far Mexican military circles are willing to accept US hegemony. Starting from the hypothesis that it is in Mexico's own national interest to act as a countervailing force to US power, there are a number of reasons why Mexico's influence in international circles, its relationship with the United States, and its reluctance to become directly involved in revolutionary processes in Central America all contribute to defining a special role for Mexico.

A useful context in which to judge Mexico's influence at the level of international politics is to contrast its position with that of the other main regional actor sympathetic to the forces of change, Cuba. However important and prestigious Cuban help has been to many Third World countries, such help at times reinforces the tendency towards polarisation and circumscribes the political space for resolving international conflict through consensus. Given the need to build as broad an alliance as possible against intervention in Central America, Mexico's role in cementing such an alliance is of key importance. Ample evidence for this argument is to be found in examining the record of resolutions passed on Central America in the different United Nations Organisations, from the Commission on Human Rights to the Security Council. Equally, Mexico's capacity to act as interlocutor vis-à-vis the United States Government has been significant, so much so that certain strategists in the Reagan Administration have attempted to mount 'a diplomatic campaign intended to change the position of Mexico and of European Social Democracies while, in the meantime, isolating them from Central American problems.' What is certain is that the theme of Central

America is always at the top of the agenda whenever high level discussions take place between Mexico and the United States. The Mexican Government is highly experienced at dealing with the United States over Central America, not merely on general questions but regarding the roots of the region's political and social problems, or indeed, on immediate points such as the suspension of the Nicaraguan sugar quota. Nor has the Mexican Government shown any sign of changing its position as a result of its dialogue with the US. Indeed, Mexico's concern for its own dignity under adverse economic conditions has strengthened the determination of its leaders to keep to a firm line. What is at stake is no less than Mexico's pride and prestige. This was clearly demonstrated during the visit to Mexico in April 1983 of the US Secretary of State (accompanied by the Secretaries of Commerce and the Treasury). The visit had been preceded by a propaganda campaign led by President Reagan to convince US public opinion of the grave threat posed to Mexican security by 'communist subverson' in Central America. This view was decisively rejected by Mexican leaders, and Mexico's position is clearly reflected in the final joint communique which stresses the importance of seeking all possible forms of dialogue in order to avoid armed conflict in Central America. A further feature of the continuing US/Mexican dialogue is the increased access given to pressure groups in the United States (Congressmen, journalists, business leaders), the function of which has been to help promote a view of the region's problems within the US distinct from that offered by the Reagan Administration.

A final theme concerns non-alignment as a *sine qua non* for viable change in Central America. Any realistic appreciation of United States National Security leads one to conclude that, for a new regime in Central America to be acceptable to the US Government and American public opinion, it must avoid open association with the Soviet Union. One point on which most political observers agree is that, in the present century at least, the 'Cubanisation' of Central America is impossible. This is not to deny that there are those within the Reagan Administration who would like to force the Sandinistas into a closer alliance with the Socialist camp; such a move would legitimise the belief that Communist subversion has always been present in Nicaragua and would undermine European and Latin American support for the present Nicaraguan Government. Indeed, the Nicaraguan leadership is well aware of this trap and has taken considerable care to maintain internal pluralism, a mixed economy, and a non-aligned foreign policy. It is precisely in the area of lending credibility and support to the non-alignment of Central American revolutions that Mexico has an important role to play.

In summary, Mexico's major contribution in future will be to help build coalitions within the international community which oppose US intervention and favour self-determination in Central America, to act as interlocutor vis-à-vis the United States in order to defend all forces seeking change in the region, and to act as guarantor of the non-alignment of the Central American revolution. Mexico is an actor who can contribute to the creation of conditions facilitating change in the region or, at the very least, the creation of conditions inhibiting the most violent expression of North American intervention. Nor are these propositions mere speculation. The Mexican position has been firm and consistent, whether at the Consultative Meeting of the OAS in 1979, at various meetings with US leaders (including Presidential meetings) over the past several years, and most recently through the initiatives of the Contadora group. Such an argument should not be interpreted as an attempt to vaunt Mexico's prestige or negotiating strength or to suggest that the Mexican State has some unique ability to influence international politics. Rather, our argument stresses the particular factors which serve to define and circumscribe Mexican foreign policy. Such an analysis could equally be applied with different qualifications, let us say, to Venezuela. What is important in this characterisation of the international and regional political system is the fact that the interests of peripheral countries are becoming increasingly differentiated from those of the great powers. It is in the interests of a country like Mexico to support the creation of a regional sub-system in Central America and the Caribbean which will reduce East-West confrontation, facilitate self-determination, and institutionalise non-alignment and peaceful co-existence. This is not to suggest that such objectives can easily or quickly be realised; establishing such a new order may require many years, and it is even possible that, for a time, Central America may be transformed into the 'Middle East' of Latin America, Ultimately, however, we believe that a new regional sub-system will emerge and that a number of countries, Mexico amongst them, must participate in constructing a more equitable international order.

Finally, it would be naive to suppose that Mexico's foreign policy will not suffer setbacks or that expectations will not, in some cases, be frustrated. In the years to come two basic factors, we suggest, will strongly condition Mexico's foreign policy. The first has to do with the growing difficulty which may be experienced in generating a consensus within the political elite and the public at large on policy towards Central America. This will be particularly difficult in a period when certain voices turn their full energies toward discrediting the Central American Revolution, backed by sections of the Mexican media closely linked to the United States. The second factor has to do with the extreme complexity of what is happening in the region and the difficulty of dealing with a rapidly changing situation in which so little time is available to reflect properly on the political implications of policy choice. Nevertheless, clarity will be at a premium in the debate about the nature and viability of the new social and economic order to be built in Central America. Clarity over this aspect will greatly facilitate the work of those who are fighting to establish a new regional order and help to prevent Central America from being converted into a battleground.

PART TWO

PERSPECTIVES FOR A NEW
ECONOMIC ORDER

VII

PLANNED ACCUMULATION AND INCOME DISTRIBUTION IN THE SMALL PERIPHERAL ECONOMY

E. V. K. FitzGerald

I. THE PROBLEMATIC

A central historical feature of modern socialism that tends to be overlooked in economic history is that not only did mature capitalist societies (with their advanced development of the forces of production and socialisation of productive relations) not provide the first cases of transition, but also all the attempts to construct socialism since 1950 have taken place in small, open, under-developed primary-export economies on the periphery of the world market system. Thus, to the burden of poverty must be added the problem of dependency, as the current developmentalist terminology would have it.[1] This means that the form of classical and modern debates[2] about the economics of the transition — based as they are on the concept of a large and mainly self-sufficient economy with a growing capital-goods industry (i.e. its own 'Department I') where foreign trade is a marginal item — is a suitable basis for economic analyses: even though other characteristics of that 'classical' model (such as the existence of a large peasant sector) may still obtain. Although there are considerable differences between these 'new transitions', there do seem to be enough common characteristics to permit the logical relations between accumulation and distribution in such economies to be worked out.

Without attempting a proper description of these social formations, we can identify some characteristics of relevance to this paper. First, the 'incompleteness' of the economy, in the sense of not having a substantial producer goods capacity, and relying on raw material exports to lend dynamic to the economy and permit capital accumulation; thus the insertion into the international division of labour is a crucial determinant of the model of growth and distribution. Second, the existence (in the early stages of transition, at least) of a large 'peasant' (or more strictly, petty commodity production) sector which supplies food to the towns, seasonal labour to the export sector, and small scale artisan wage-goods.

In other words, the bulk of the population is not proletarian, nor all production 'modern'. Third, the state itself directly controls the 'modern' (i.e. wage-paying, capital-using) sector of the economy, but its direct planning capacity is limited to this sector; it must respond to specific exchange conditions with both the world economy and the peasant sector, through the external and internal terms of trade. Economies as diverse as Cuba, Algeria, Mozambique, Tanzania, Vietnam and most recently, Nicaragua — have reacted to this structural problematic in different ways, but there does appear to exist a certain common logic which is worth exploring. It may be possible to clarify particular problems that arise in practice; such as the choice of technique in the export sector, the supply of wage goods (or 'basic needs' as they are now called), and pricing policy; as well as more theoretical issues, such as 'primitive socialist accumulation' or the role of markets in the planned economy.

We shall not attempt in this paper to give empirical evidence for these 'stylized facts',[3] but they are generally recognizable ones. The analytical method used is broadly that set out by Kalecki (1972), whose work includes a number of useful analytical elements although he never addressed the topic of the peripheral socialist economy directly. The exposition is made up of three elements: the first is a general characterisation of the structure of such economies and the articulation of the various sectors: second, this analysis is used to produce determinate (i.e. planned) solutions to the classical problem of accumulation and distribution during the transition to socialism, where the rate of investment must be raised but popular incomes not excessively depressed; the third is a brief illustration of the application of this analysis to the experience of Nicaragua in its first three years of revolutionary government. A more formal model of such an economy, which serves to show how the domestic pricing pattern is determined by the planned distribution of income, how this distribution is derived from the balance of payments, and how this in turn depends on the rate and composition of investment is published elsewhere (FitzGerald 1985). It should be stressed that the argument in this paper is highly tentative, serving to open a discussion rather than report definite conclusions.

II. THE STRUCTURE OF THE PERIPHERAL SOCIALIST ECONOMY (PSE)

The two output sectors in the classic formulation (Kalecki 1972) are producer goods (Department I), wage-goods (Department II). It is useful to distinguish, as Kalecki does, between necessities (Department IIa) and non-necessary consumption goods (IIb), for a number of reasons, as we shall see. The main differentiating characteristics of the PSE are in

Departments I and IIa. Department I is lacking much if not all capacity to produce heavy plant and equipment, technologically advanced inputs, and in many cases oil as well, all of which must be imported at given international prices; primary exports (usually agricultural products such as coffee, cotton and sugar on the one hand, or minerals on the other) are not primarily raw material inputs to industry but rather sources of foreign exchange when exported (at given international prices) to import producer goods. In this sense, the primary export sector is the 'heavy industry'of such economies,[4] and in many cases is itself relatively capital-intensive; the other component of fixed capital formation is construction, which is a major component of Department I. As we shall see, the expansion of this sector provides much of the dynamic of the economy. Department IIa, wage-goods, has two components. The first is food supply, which is based on a small-scale 'peasant' production sector employing a labour-intensive technology; this is complemented by artisan-type production of other wage-goods such as clothing. 'Early' industry (textiles, soap, etc.) completes this list. The second component is the provision of social services such as elementary education, primary health, water, electricity, housing, local infrastructure and so on; again, this may well make up as much as half of the total 'wage-goods' supply. In modern parlance, Department IIa is the 'basic needs' sector.[5] Finally, Deparment IIb is made up of much of the manufacturing sector proper (factories, other than those in primary exports, producing 'rural inputs' such as tools and kerosene; raw materials for wage goods such as cloth, leather and fats, construction materials, and some non-basic consumer goods, with a broadly 'international' technology and imported equipment, on the one hand; and a series of non-basic services such as entertainment on the other. These elements of non-basic consumption are not only for technicians and adminstrations but also the 'upper-end' of the consumption of workers and more prosperous farmers. Thus Department IIb goods are used to exchange with the peasantry for food (i.e. increase output in Department IIa) and to stimulate worker productivity in Departments I and IIb.

The balance between these three sectors will be discussed below but it is worth observing here that the PSE generally appears to be constrained by foreign exchange and labour supply, the former creating a 'trade-off' between Departments I and IIb, while the latter leads to one between Departments I and IIa. Thus the organization of the insertion into the international division of labour and the relation with the informal sector are central to the structure of the economy and underly its social relations of production (Preobazhensky 1965).

In terms of 'operational variables', the ouput of export and manufactures is under state control, but food supply depends largely on pricing policy (i.e. exchange conditions with small farmers or cooperatives; the prices of exports are exogenous, while those of food depend on the desired food supply; so only manufacturing is subject to complete planning. In other words, the law of value still holds for a large part of the economy, and determines its dynamic.

This is not the place to embark upon a discussion of the social relations of production in the PSE, which will be historically specific to individual cases. Ownership, however, may reflect some general characteristics. Department I (primary exports and construction) is part of the state-enterprise sector, subject to central planning in output decisions, although international market conditions mean that export prices are not planned; of course, there is also the issue of the degree of decentralisation of the enterprises in this sector. The labour force, however, is necessarily a highly seasonal one in export agriculture, possibly also in construction (weather conditions preventing work or cyclical demands for labour in agriculture) and also migratory in mining in many cases. There is a 'sharing' or even competition for labour with Department IIa; therefore, in the case of agriculture, there may also be implicit competition for land between the two sectors. Department IIb is also part of the state sector, subject to central planning of production and prices, but relying on imported technology (equipment) to some extent and absorbing exogenous input prices. This sector, in fact, is the one that is most 'plannable' in the sense of responding wholly to state decisions. However, it employs only a minor part of the national workforce which, with the permanent workers — a minority — from the primary export sector, forms the 'proletariat': in the strict sense of constituting a relatively small proportion of the total workforce. The output of wage-goods and 'wage services' (e.g. small bars) is in the petty mercantile or petty commodity sector — that is, peasants and artisans organised in family units of production, without permanent wage labour or profits as such, nor more than a basic minimum of reproducible capital. This sector will probably be organised in cooperative form, however, ranging from service and credit to production cooperatives; it may well include the greater part of the workforce, and provide seasonal labour to the state sector.

This is not a dual economy in the 'Lewis' sense, because it is articulated by labour and wage-goods interchange between the 'modern' and 'traditional' sectors. Moreover, the economy is controlled by the state, which manages wholesale trade, foreign trade, banking and 'organised' services ranging from agricultural extension services to air transport. The key elements are two: first, that the proletariat is small and in the state sector, while the 'semi-proletariat' and 'sub-proletariat' are large[6] and in the non-state sector so that state control over the labour process is limited; second, that state ownership (and, more importantly, effective control) is limited to Departments I and IIb, and severely limited by the exogenous dynamic of world markets in Department I.

This means that the socialisation of the *relations of exchange* may be almost as important as the socialisation of the relations of production in the transition process, particularly since state ownership as such does not ensure such socialisation (Bettelheim 1975) and may well lead to great adminstrative inefficiency as well as undesirable bureaucratisation. These two elements are no more than a reflection of the underdevelopment of the economy itself; their objective limitations on central planning are now widely recognised, not only implicitly in government pronouncements but explicitly in encouragement of petty producers and merchants, so long as they engage in simple rather than expanded reproduction — in other words, that an essentially private process of capital accumulation and differentiation does not emerge. What has not been worked out at the level of theory or methodology is just how this sort of economy should be planned.

The standard of living of the majority of the population will depend upon the volume of wage-goods in (food, clothing, primary health, etc. — or 'basic needs' as they are now known) supplied by Department IIa, for except in emergency, imports would generally be confined to producer goods. Clearly, at the centre of the economic strategy must be the increasing supply of basic needs: this is an end in itself (and a necessary condition for continued popular support in peacetime) and a requirement if the effective contribution of the workforce to production is to be realised. The distribution of basic needs will still depend partly on the relative scale of nominal wages: this is an issue of considerable importance, often expressed as 'moral versus material incentives' or the long-run objective of eliminating wage relations as opposed to the need to maintain or increase labour productivity. This is not only a matter of relative wages (between skill levels, for example), but also one of encouragement for increased workers' effort as a whole, and if this is expressed in nominal wages, it must also be met by increased supply of wage-goods. More Department IIb goods play a crucial role which is usually ignored in planning models. But as a greater part of the workforce is not in regular wage employment, the internal price structure, summarised in the internal terms of trade, determines their incomes. The 'classical' problem is usually expressed as a conflict between real wage and food prices — between the standards of living of proletarians and peasants (Preobazhensky 1965). It is true that the market in wage-goods 'clears' at the balance between peasant supply (itself responding positively to the terms of trade) and wage expenditure, and that improved terms of trade benefit real peasant incomes but the key policy element (under planning control) is the price and supply of manufactures by the state sector, which determines the real incomes of both peasants and proletarians. A simple model of this balance is shown elsewhere (FitzGerald 1983): the implication is also that attempts to increase the surplus by reducing the supply of Department IIb output to Department IIa (by manipulating the internal terms of trade) will only depress real wages as peasants reduce food supply, without greatly increasing the investible surplus, which depends on the export sector.

The second element in the popular standard of living — the basic needs package — is the services of health, education and housing. A characteristic of PSEs is that these have involved (albeit in varying degrees) mass mobilisation of the workforce itself or their families, in their spare time, with central political direction but without central economic adminstration, in the form of literacy campaigns, construction of local schools and clinics, sanitation and inoculation, 'site and service' schemes for community house building, minor public works projects and even the stimulation of folklore. All these can be seen as a way of mobilising otherwise underutilised labour (especially of women and youth) in order to raise considerably the output of Department IIa without either central adminstration or a purely individual approach; but perhaps more importantly, it gives the people an opportunity to control their own living standards when, of necessity, accumulation and production decisions in Departments I and IIb of a small economy are highly centralised.

In sum, the rising standard of living is defined by the expansion of Department II above that of the population itself; its distribution depends on government pricing policy, particularly the internal terms of trade.

An economy that relies on the import of producer goods to maintain production (import-substitution for the small economy will rapidly reach the limits of efficiency) will also depend upon its export sector for growth; and in our case those exports are basically semi-processed primary products. Given that basic consumption is equivalent to the output of Department II, the surplus is, by definition, the output of Department I less the imported input requirements of the economy — essentially for Departments I and IIb. Thus the balance of payments (determined by endogenous import and export volumes, exogenous world trade prices, and net foreign finance) defines not only the investible surplus but also its relation to the current level of output. In other words, the balance between consumption and investment is defined by the external account, whatever the internal financial, fiscal and monetary equilibria may be; indeed, as we shall see, it is essential to adjust the internal macroeconomic equilibrium to this balance. The foreign exchange allocation is of course planned, as is the volume of exports, in line with the growth objectives. The key point here is that it is the balance of payments, rather than 'savings' relationships, which transmits the investment decisions through to the pattern of current output, pricing and income distribution; this is because it is through the world market that labour power is transmuted into capital goods.

The nature of the surplus arising from the export sector is important, not only in theoretical but also in practical terms. In its realised form, it is net foreign exchange earnings, allowing for the direct and indirect input requirements of production: indeed, it is in this sector of the planned economy that the 'modern' methods of project appraisal based on 'border' accounting prices are more appropriate[7] and allow for rational choice of crops, new investments and so on to gain greatest advantage from the international division of labour. In other words, 'economic calculations' will be necessarily based on world prices. The choice of technique, however, will depend on the overall accumulation strategy, and not on microeconomic considerations. The generation of that surplus is potentially composed of three parts: normal profits, super-normal or 'excess' profits, and rent. The normal profit arises from a reasonable charge for the equipment used, possibly expressed as interest payable by the export enterprise on funds advanced by the central accumulation fund; as Dobb points out (1970), this will depend upon the overall growth targets for the economy. Excess profit, upon which much of the pre-revolutionary project would have relied and which may still be present, derives from the payment of wages below the normal rate; this would rapidly disappear with the normalisation of wage rates to some socially desirable basic needs requirement, but may still be implicit in the use of seasonal (or 'semi-proletarian') labour which guarantees its own subsistence and reproduction through the peasant sector, and to some extent even by the communal social services mentioned above. Nonetheless, it will essentially depend upon the output of Department II.

However, a considerable part of the surplus will take the form of differential rent on an international scale (Flichman 1982): that is, income arising from the fact that natural resource availability (soils, weather, location, mineral deposits etc.) is such that the costs of production of the marginal exporter (which, with the metropolitan control over the terms of trade, determine the international price)[8] are higher than those in the economy in question. This rent (of the 'first type' in Marx's classification) which would only be a transfer payment in a closed economy, and a charge on profits at that, becomes a major source of accumulation for the PSE given that it is both effectively a charge on metropolitan profits and productively reinvested. This, and not the turning of the terms of trade against the peasantry, is the source of 'primitive socialist accumulation' for the PSE. The exploitation of the peasantry, leaving aside its undesirable political consequences in a social formation of the type we are discussing, does not in fact assist accumulation, because what is needed is more foreign exchange. To export peasant-produced food would, however, be unwise because of the low level of productivity and thus the requirement to depress peasant incomes to extract an investible surplus as well as severely restricting wage-goods supply to the towns. This concept of primitive socialist accumulation based on international differential rent, is a distinguishing characteristic of the PSE although traces of this concept can be found in earlier 'classical' writing.[9] This, of course, does not mean that such economies should not attempt to build up a capital goods sector or export manufactures. This is a descriptive model, not a normative one.

Finally, the adminstration of the export sector itself, both in production and marketing, may require a certain degree of enterprise decentralisation to improve efficiency. The correct financial procedure would seem to be to base wages on productivity relative to the norm and retained profits on approved expansion requirements but reserve the rent element for the central accumulation fund, arising as it does from the national ownership of natural resources. Similarly, costs and prices in Department IIb would be set at world prices in order to ensure foreign exchange efficiency.

III.   CAPITAL ACCUMULATION AND PLANNING

We have now identified the main components of the PSE, and suggested how income distribution, pricing, output and foreign trade are related. This model derives from the need to articulate three 'forms of production' in the peasant, state and foreign sectors. The determination of the correct balance is incomplete, however, without the rate of investment. It is planned growth rate, therefore, that defines the current equilibrium, rather than the other way around, principally of consumer goods. In this section we shall explore the determination of the growth rate and the correct sectoral balance; the implication of this for economic planning will then be discussed.

The key question is how imported capital goods are to be allocated between the two capital-using sectors (exports and manufacturing, Departments I and IIb), which determine future investment and consumption levels, respectively. This is because Department I will supply future foreign exchange to import more machines; and because Department IIb is for exchange with food producers and to stimulate worker productivity. But labour must also be allocated between the two sectors that need it most (exports and wage-goods): the combination of those two 'trade-offs' over time, in combination with the desired rate of real wage growth, sets the overall growth rate of the economy. The problem is not unlike the classical (i.e. Feldman[10]) form, but with a different linkage and logic: not only are the sectors different, but their balance is found through foreign trade. The maximum attainable rate of expansion of the export sector and thus rate of accumulation in the economy as a whole, is determined by past investments in the sector and present consumption requirements. It can be simply shown that the key determinants of the possible growth rate of Department I are three: the terms of trade and the import coefficient; the planned rate of growth of wage-goods supply; and the capital-output coefficients. The maximum rate is determined by the minimum tolerable rate of consumption growth (i.e. the population growth rate). As to labour supply, if the peasant food sector, which is the main competitor for labour (or possibly land, but the argument is much the same), is to grow at or above the population growth rate without rapid technological change (i.e. without large-scale capitalisation and collectivisation) then the export sector will have only a 'natural' growth in labour too. Thus, if techniques of production do not change, export growth and accumulation will be very limited.

In fact, it is precisely the export sector where techniques can be changed by mechanisation, unlike the petty commodity production sector on the one hand, and manufacturing (constrained to a more or less given international technology) on the other; this is done by changing the capital-output ratio. The correct choice of technique will thus arise from the balancing of the foreign exchange and labour constraints on accumulation over time: the foreign exchange equations provide the 'supply' conditions for capital goods in the sense that a higher consumption growth rate (Department IIb) reduces the amount of capital equipment available for investment; the labour equations provide the 'demand' conditions in that a higher need for labour in the wage-good sector requires more mechanisation in the exports sector. The solution of two equations in the three variables (export growth, consumption growth, and export sector technology) is determinate for a chosen consumption growth rate.

There are a number of further points that should be mentioned before passing on. First, that much of the investment will not be in material production, as we have implied, but rather in infrastructure; this may be economic (roads) or social (housing), but will not increase production directly, although it does occupy a large part of the fund; for any one rate of growth, the accumulation effort must be proportionately greater for perhaps half of fixed capital formation may be in such infrastructure. We have also suggested that investment is directed towards greater output or labour productivity; in fact it may be concerned with the reduction of import coefficients (i.e. import substitution). Although the scope for this is limited in the small economy, the main criterion for such investment would be the net foreign exchange savings generated thereby. Second, that the employment constraint we have discussed would not bind in the early stages of transition, while underemployed labour is absorbed. As Kalecki points out, this permits more rapid growth as labour productivity need not be increased, while a fixed real wage will still result in rising consumption and improved income distribution.[11]

This period of rapid growth may be deceptively short if much of the 'underdeveloped' labour is in fact of a semi-proletarian nature which cannot be simply transferred into state enterprises. Nonetheless, such a period of rapid growth may be an appropriate one for the use of foreign loans, which can be repaid from increased export earnings. Third, that the central part played by the external terms of trade in the accumulation balance means that as the terms of trade deteriorate it may be necessary to invest even more in the export sector and sacrifice consumption growth in order to maintain accumulation — which amounts in effect to a 'backward sloping supply curve' (Braun 1973). Uncertainty over future fluctuations may vitiate planning: in general this means 'investment' in foreign exchange reserves may be desirable; in particular the structure of the PSE is such that export goods can be converted into wage-goods but not the other way around, so that faced by an unanticipated deterioration in the external terms of trade, the investment programme can only be maintained by disproportionate[12] cuts in consumption or else sacrificed, while an equal improvement can simply be converted into imported consumption goods, to maintain the desired balance. Thus there are strong arguments, in the presence of uncertainty, for planning a higher rate of export growth than otherwise.

So far in common with all approaches (including those of Kalecki, Bettelheim and Dobb)[13], we have implied that in order to 'solve' the planning model, it is necessary to introduce an exogenous decision as to the choice between the rate of growth of investment and consumption; that is between consumption now or later, what Kalecki calls a 'decision curve' and Dobb calls 'time preference'. The underlying presumption is that lower rates of real wage growth are associated, via the higher rate of investment so generated, with higher rates of productivity growth; this arises not just from the increased capitalisation as such, leading to a higher output from a given labour force, but from the fact that mechanisation itself leads to a higher rate of growth of labour productivity (Kalecki 1972: 53–54). This 'accumulation model' is indeterminate having (so to speak) more variables than equations; a specific point on the downward-sloping curve of wage growth against productivity can only be chosen by stipulating a 'political' choice between investment and consumption. However, in practice planned economies have found that there is a relationship between productivity and real wages. If resistance to the increased rate of exploitation implicit in mechanisation without wage increases takes the form of nominal wage claims and strikes in capitalist economies, in the PSE it tends to take the form of reduced productivity and absenteeism (cf. Brundenius 1981). To the extent that there does exist a direct relationship between wage growth and 'realised' (as opposed to 'potential') productivity growth — albeit not a mechanical one, for labour discipline is also affected by national morale (e.g.

external threats) and forms of enterprise organisation (e.g. worker participation in management) — then this, and not the 'decision curve' is the 'missing equation' that solves the system. In other words, there is a determinate rate of productivity and wage growth which is determined by the intersection of the 'accumulation' curve (lower wages leading to more investment and potentially higher ouput per head) and the 'labour process' curve (higher wages leading to greater willingness to use new technology to the full). This implies that, although there will be a considerable degree of flexibility, the rate of growth cannot be raised beyond a certain 'natural' value. If the accumulation rate is set too high and thus wages growth too low, potential productivity will grow more rapidly than what the labour force is willing to provide, equipment will not be properly used and the true productivity (and output) growth will be much lower; by the same token, setting the accumulation rate too low will lose potential production.

In this way, therefore, the only possible 'investment structure' (i.e. allocation of capital funds between exports and wage-goods production) will be determined; and from this the growth of Departments I and II are derived. In other words, for a given set of international market conditions and relationships with domestic petty commodity producers, the equilibrium growth pattern of the Peripheral Socialist Economy is extremely constrained. Successful planning will be based more on the recognition of those constraints and working within those, than on trying to achieve radically different growth paths which lead to serious foreign indebtedness or suppression of the workforce.

Given an accumulation strategy, this much should be possible to implement. However, the PSE cannot be a completely planned economy in the sense that prices, wages, output, consumption and investment are subject to centralised control, and in some sense the law of value can be superseded. On the contrary, both the foreign trade sector and the peasant/artisan sector operate in market terms. Thus the Plan must be framed in terms of market forces, and instruments other than plan directives — ranging from banking to local democracy — must be employed to ensure the desired outcome. In particular this requires far more attention to pricing, credit and foreign trade than is normal in plans, and in general, the exercise of 'macroeconomic policy' consistent with the plan objectives.

At a national level, these arguments (which are well described by Bettelheim [1975] for the large economy in transition) for decentralisation seem to be compelling. However, at the international level the PSE is far more vulnerable than its larger cousins, in terms both of the exposure to fluctuations in world markets and the macroeconomic effects of single investment projects. In consequence, the need for central control of the economy (or at least Departments I and IIb) is very great;

a compensation may be that the information and communications problems which so hamper central economic control in large socialist economies do not obtain in the smaller ones.

IV. CONCLUSIONS AND REFLECTIONS ON THE NICARAGUAN CASE

In this paper, we have tried to set out the elements of a simple theory of Peripheral Socialist Economy, adapting the theories laid out by Kalecki, Bettelheim and Dobb to the small, open, underdeveloped economy. We have suggested how certain elements of the 'structuralist' approach to peripheral economies might be applied to some advantage[14] in order to analyse the articulation of different forms of production. The object of the exercise has been to define the particular heterogenous structure of the PSE, describe the nature of wage and surplus determination, and adapt the 'classical' models of socialist accumulation to the case in hand.

We have suggested that this logic is generalisable. This is not to imply that all PSEs are identical: Cuba for instance, has had a minority peasant sector in agriculture and state-run retail trade until recently (although both of those are being 'unwound'); while Mozambique has export cotton produced by peasants and large farms to feed the cities. The analysis presented was initially worked out in the context of discussions about the economic aspects of transition in Nicaragua,[15] so that some brief comments may be useful: not of the quantitative details, but rather on how the logic of the 1980 and 1981 Economic Programmes on the one hand, and the 1981 Agrarian Reform law on the other, relate to the analysis in this paper.

In the autumn of 1979, when the *Gobierno de Reconstrucción Nacional* started to plan the economy of Nicaragua, the first stage in the 'transition to the new economy' was seen as the balanced revival of consumption after the deprivations of civil war, within a destroyed and disorganised productive apparatus (FitzGerald 1982). The lesson of the Chilean experience, and to some extent the Cuban one too, was that increases in the nominal wages would only push up food prices at the expense of the poor, so the only way to expand with an improving income distribution was rapidly to increase wage-goods supply. Thus priority was given to credit and input support to peasant farmers and food donations. Even so, expansion in wage-goods supply would necessarily be slow, so that basic needs provision was increased by the mass mobilisation of secondary and tertiary students for literacy and public health campaigns. At the same time, imports of non-basic consumer goods were cut back as foreign exchange was directed towards production inputs.

The result, over the 1980–82 period, was to redistribute real income from the supply side, raising the lower and depressing the upper ends of distribution, independently of nominal incomes, which could not be directly controlled in an economy with a large petty commodity sector. Real wages were held in towns and raised in rural areas, redistributing wage income towards the newly-employed and farm workers, within a constrained wage-goods availability. Inflationary pressure was reduced by adjusting the fiscal-financial balances within the plan itself, and price rises sharply biased towards non-necessary consumption. The logic[16] of the 1980 and 1981 plans is explicitly based on this 'Kaleckian' approach, where stabilisation is founded on wage-goods supply. The internal terms of trade were deliberately shifted towards peasant food producers and the poorest urban dwellers protected by subsidised distribution of the 'basic needs basket' in selected neighbourhoods as well as the factories. In rural areas, the Ministry of Internal Commerce concentrated on the distribution of manufactured goods to underpin the 'real' internal terms of trade, and purchase enough basic grains to control their nominal value. Supportive control of import permits by the central bank completed the 'market' strategy of consumption planning for basic needs necessary in an economy where over half the workforce was outside the enterprise sector and only a quarter in state employment.

Nicaragua is an agrarian economy, where three-quarters of exports and over half of material product are in agriculture or agro-processing, while two-thirds of the population is rural; so the *Reforma Agraria*[17] was central to the development of the relations of production. It is of interest to note that considerations of economic structure were also central to its design. The greater part of the rural work force are 'semi-proletarians' (small family food farmers supplying seasonal labour to commercial export estates) while only one-sixth are permanent labour on such estates: thus land reform based on worker control of the estate would not benefit the rural poor. Collectivisation of the peasantry was judged inefficient and politically undesirable so that food production was organised in cooperatives where inputs are controlled by the state but labour is organised by the families. A considerable concern was expressed for the possible conflict between exports and food production over labour supply, which required an articulation of such cooperatives with export estates and a shift away from cotton and coffee (with severe seasonable peaks) towards (mechanised) sugar and cattle. The function of agriculture in both Departments I and IIa is clearly recognised. In a land-surplus economy, the previous articulation of capitalist and peasant forms of production through labour repression and profits based on super-exploitation clearly could not continue: but a new form of articulation and higher productivity would have to replace it which would guarantee wage-goods supply and allow export rents to be used on the basis for accumulation. The *Programa Alimentario Nacional* is designed to organise petty commodity producers of food through prices, marketing, storage, fertilisers, transport and so on; the *Area de Propiedad del Pueblo* will extend to cover the rest of the large export units (of which in 1981 it had over half) and already takes a quarter of the long-term national investment budget; and medium farmers are 'surrounded' by credit controls, state marketing and regionally determined production programmes. In essence, the objective is to articulate various forms of production and to guarantee the planned expansion of both accumulation (exports) and consumption (food) as part of the transition strategy.

Finally, the realistic recognition (MIPLAN 1980, 1981) that exports will continue to be the source of growth in the medium term, and the decision not to attempt extensive industrialisation — except in agroindustry and energy — does contain a certain element of risk, not only of deteriorating terms of trade but also of dependency. A first task is to invest in domestic hydroelectric and geothermal energy sources (a quarter of the investment budget) in order to reduce the present total reliance on imported oil; while oil supplies themselves are guaranteed by the regional non-aligned power, Mexico. Export markets for the main products (coffee, cotton, sugar, meat, gold) have reasonably free world markets — unlike the Cuban experience. Financial aid has also been available from non-aligned countries and Western Europe. Again, technology (i.e. equipment and skills) are available from 'newly industrialising countries' such as Mexico and Brazil. All this reflects the breakdown of US hegemony over the world capitalist economy, and thus considerable freedom of manoeuvre therein, as well as the possibility of balanced links with the COMECON. Rather than a reduction of dependency as such, the diversification of dependency is the aim; by the same token, the maintenance of a wide range of exports and negotiation of long-term supplier's contracts or barter agreements are aimed at the mitigation of the negative effect of the external terms of trade on accumulation.

Nonetheless, in the longer run, the transition strategy must involve a greater degree of industrialisation to overcome the structural heterogeneity we have identified in our model; this will have to take the form of integration with other economies in the region. In one case (Cuba) this is not too difficult, and offers valuable complementarities, of primary versus industrial products, but to build a truly regional industrial system would require profound transformations in Costa Rica, El Salvador and Guatemala. Meanwhile, therefore, the model of the Peripheral Socialist Economy we have discussed in this paper will remain the basis of the Nicaraguan *transición a la nueva economía*.

NOTES

1. See, for example, the survey in *World Development* (1981). It is unfortunate that this

collection, while containing much valuable information, does not contain serious economic or political analysis.

2. See, for example, Preobazhensky (1965), Domar (1957) on Feldman, and Dobb (1970).

3. But see, for example, Brundenius (1981) on Cuba, Wuyts (1981) on Mozambique, and the brief discussion in Section IV below on Nicaragua.

4. This leaves aside the crucial role of capital goods production in the generation of technological advance; of course, it is worth noting that this definition means that these basic services must then be defined as 'productive'.

5. This is worked out excellently by Brundenius (1981).

6. For a discussion of this concept in the Nicaraguan context, see FIDA/FAO(1981). It is worth noting that stable semi-proletarianisation, as opposed to the dualist concept of peasants or proletarians, was also the dominant form of labour organisation in pre-industrial Europe. See Lis & Soly (1979).

7. A methodology for this can be found in FitzGerald (1978) or Irvin (1978).

8. Braun (1973) works this out in a formal Sraffa-type model.

9. Preobazhensky (1965) considers this option, but discards it implicitly — presumably because it was not geopolitically relevant to the USSR at that time. The connection between 'resource-rich' colonies, over-exploitation and national liberation struggles, and the consequent viability of a 'rent-based' model, deserves more thought.

10. Domar (1957) provides an excellent exposition, despite his incomprehension of the issues involved.

11. Kalecki (1972 and 1976) for the example of Cuba.

12. To be precise, the inverse of the manufacturing import coefficient, or about five times.

13. Kalecki (1972), Bettelheim (1979) and Dobb (1970) all provide approaches to the problem of time preference for consumption, but all imply that this is in the end a 'political' choice.

14. Noyola (1978) was an ECLA (i.e. 'structuralist') economist who worked for the revolutionary Cuban government.

15. When the author was working as Senior Economic Advisor to the Ministry of Planning.

16. MIPLAN (1980, 1981), especially Chapter III: 'Dinámica y Tensiones de la Reactivación' in both documents. The two parts of this income distribution strategy are also manifested in the respective titles of these annual economic programmes — that for 1980 being 'economic revival for the benefit of the people' and that for 1981 being 'austerity and efficiency'.

17. JGRN (1981). Some background is given in FIDA/FAO (1981).

REFERENCES

Bettelheim, C. (1959): *Studies in the Theory of Planning* (London: J.K. Publishers).
—— (1975): *The Transition to Socialist Economy* (Hassocks, Sussex: The Harvester Press).
Braun, O. (1973): *Imperialismo y Comercio Internacional* (Buenos Aires: Siglo XXI).
Brundenius, C (1981): *Economic Growth, Basic Needs and Income Distribution in Revolutionary Cuba* (Lund: Univeristy of Lund Research Policy Institute).
Dobb, M. (1970): *Welfare Economics and the Economics of Socialism* (Cambridge: Cambridge University Press).
Domar, E. (1957): *Essays in the Theory of Economic Growth* (Oxford: Oxford University Press).
FIDA (1981): *Informe de la Misión Especial de Programación a Nicaragua* (Rome: FAO/International Fund for Agricultural Development).
FitzGerald, E.V.K. (1978): *Public Sector Investment Planning for Developing Countries* (London: Macmillan).
—— (1982): 'The Economics of the Revolution', in T.W. Walker (ed.): *Nicaragua in Revolution* (New York: Praeger).
—— (1983): 'Kalecki on the Financing of Development: An Elucidation and an Extension' (The Hague: Institute of Social Studies Working Paper No. 8).

—— (1985): 'The Problem of Balance in the Peripheral Socialist Economy', in *World Development* (forthcoming).

Flichman, G. (1982): *Renta de Suelo y Económia Internacional* (Amsterdam: CEDLA).

Irvin, G. (1978): *Modern Cost-Benefit Methods* (London: Macmillan).

JGRN (1981): *Ley de Reforma Agraria* (Managua: Junta de Gobierno de Reconstrucción Nacional).

Kalecki, M. (1972): *Selected Essays on the Economic Growth of the Socialist and Mixed Economy* (Cambridge: Cambridge University Press).

—— (1976): 'Hypothetical Outline of the Five-Year Plan 1961–65 for the Cuban Economy', in his *Essays on Developing Economies* (Hassocks, Sussex: The Harvester Press).

Lis, C. & H. Soly (1979): *Poverty and Capitalism in Pre-Industrial Europe* (Atlantic Highlands NJ: Humanities Press).

MIPLAN (1980): *Programa de Reactivación Económica en Beneficio del Pueblo, 1980* (Managua: Ministerio de Planificación).

—— (1981): *Programa Económica de Austeridad y Eficiencia 1981* (Managua: Ministerio de Planificación).

Noyola, J. F. (1978): *La Económia Cubana en los Primeros Años de la Revolucion* (Mexico City: Siglo XXI).

Preobrazhensky, E. (1965): *The New Economics* (Oxford: Oxford University Press; originally published in Russian, Moscow 1926).

World Development (1981): *Socialist Models of Development* (special issue), Vol. 9, Nos 9–10.

Wuyts, M. (1981): 'The Mechanization of Present-Day Mozambican Agriculture', in *Development and Change*, Vol. 12, No. 1, 1–27.

VIII

CRISIS AND REFORM IN JAMAICA: SOME ECONOMIC LESSONS

Richard Bernal

I. INTRODUCTION

The Manley Adminstration's attempts to implement a democratic socialist development strategy were essentially confined to the period 1977–80. Moreover, full evaluation of this experience is complicated by the impact of IMF programmes which undermined the Government's economic strategy, as well as by the often contradictory policies adopted. Such inconsistent policies reflected conflicts between the different interest groups represented in the PNP, which became increasingly acute as the Government crisis developed.

In Section II below, we attempt a brief characterisation of the main structural features of dependent capitalism in Jamaica. The balance of payments, critical to understanding the experience of the Manley Government, is then analysed in some detail in Section III. Finally, in Section IV, the policies of the Manley Government are critically analysed and their results assessed.

II. STRUCTURAL FEATURES OF THE JAMAICAN ECONOMY

Dependent capitalist reproduction on an extended scale takes place in response to global capital accumulation, the dynamic of which is provided by developed capitalist nations. The 'natural' tendency of dependent capitalist economies is towards crisis and stagnation; i.e. a structural crisis of accumulation and reproduction. Dependent capitalist economies can be thought of as passive participants in the global accumulation process. They are not integral to the process but are periodically integrated into, or marginalised from, the process depending on their ability to provide commodities needed for such accumulation. The fragility of capital accumulation in dependent capitalist economies derives from their disarticulated and externally dependent structure which causes accumulation to be determined by, and vulnerable to, exogenous factors.

Moreover, just as the requirements for global accumulation change over time, so too must the ability of an individual country to supply the commodities required. However, the structural rigidities and distortions of dependent economies limit their capacity for change, and the small size of the economy further compounds its vulnerability and constrains its adaptability. If development is to be achieved, a transitional period is required in which structural transformation and re-articulation of the economy to the world market takes place. This entails internal economic and social change, complemented by a break in the traditional form of insertion into the global capitalism.

Jamaica's experience is interesting because the country went through quite distinct phases of development in the 1960s and 1970s. The first phase, corresponding to the 1960s, may be characterised as that of 'underdevelopment with growth'; i.e. integration in the world economy under favourable circumstances which offset the tendency to crisis and generated growth, though not self-sustained capital accumulation and development. The second phase, characteristic of the 1970s, is that of 'underdevelopment with stagnation'; i.e. marginalisation from the process of global accumulation, but without structural transformation or growth. It was during this second phase that the Manley Government attempted to initiate a new development strategy, the tenets of which were neither capitalist nor communist.

The Jamaican economy is small, with a land area of 4,411 square miles, a population of 2.2 million, and a gross domestic product which in 1980 was J\$4.73 billion (US\$2.65 billion). Though small size is not a cause of underdevelopment, it can act as a constraint on development in the sense that the availability and range of domestic resources is limited and the size of the domestic market is insufficient to support economic production-runs for most capital goods. The Jamaican economy also exhibits a high degree of openness; i.e. international trade is large in relation to total economic activity. In the 1970s, the share of imports in GDP averaged just under 30 percent and the share of exports fluctuated between 34 percent and 39 percent. Exports were concentrated in the extractive sector (bauxite/alumina), while imports were primarily of capital goods, energy, raw materials and, to a lesser extent, consumer goods and food.

A further characteristic of this type of economy is the relative absence of inter-sectoral linkages. The main export sectors (plantation agriculture and mineral extraction) are highly dependent on imported inputs. This is especially true in capital-intensive branches such as bauxite, but also true of labour-intensive service branches such as tourism whose import content is over 40 percent. Equally, in the case of manufacturing for the home market, the ratio of imported materials to the gross value of output has been estimated to be in the range of 43–57 percent.

Another key structural feature of the economy is the concentration of ownership of the means of production (often in foreign hands) and the attendant highly-skewed nature of income distribution. In 1968 some 295 owners of farms of over 500 acres held 45 percent of total farming land, while nearly 150,000 owners farmed less than 5 acres, or 15 percent of total farming land. The richest 4 percent of households received 30 percent of total income while, at the other extreme, 60 percent of households received 19 percent. The core of the capitalist class consisted of 21 families, closely knit by intermarriage and interlocking asset ownership and control.

The economy has traditionally been dominated by foreign capital, with US direct investment being particularly important since 1945. US direct private investment in Jamaica amounted to US$654 million in 1975, of which US$390 million was in the bauxite/alumina industry. Canadian direct investments stood at C$112 million in 1977. Foreign capital dominates the most important sectors; e.g. bauxite/alumina, manufacturing, tourism, export-agriculture and banking.

Finally, the Jamaican economy does not produce its own capital goods; in Marxist terminology, there is no Department I. The absence of a Department I means that the openness of the economy is qualitatively different from that of a developed economy in the sense that the supply of capital goods, and hence the potential for expanded reproduction, depends directly on the external balance. Moreover, this problem must be understood in relation to the role of national and transnational capital. Circuits of national capital are distinguished by the fact that the money capital advanced is locally owned while transnational circuits of capital involve money capital which comes from abroad, though both types of capital may produce either for the national or the world market. The common feature of both circuits of capital in a disarticulated economy is that they cannot be operationalised and completed without foreign exchange. For extended reproduction to take place, import capacity must be growing; i.e. there must be growing real export earnings and/or capital inflows.

III.   EVOLUTION OF THE BALANCE OF PAYMENTS 1960–1980

Below, we first examine the period 1960–1970 which we have characterised as one of 'underdevelopment with growth'. During the decade of the 1960s, although the average rate of growth of GDP was 4.5 percent, the economy had a negative trade balance in every year except 1963. After 1966, the size of the trade deficit increased significantly from J$5.7 million in 1966 to J$89.2 million in 1970. The value of imports increased much more rapidly than export earnings, with imports rising from J$142 million in 1963 to J\$374.3 million in 1970. Exports during the same period increased from J\$148.8 million to J\$285.1 million. While exports covered imports in 1963, in 1964 exports paid for 85.8 percent of imports and, by 1970, exports covered only 76.2 percent of imports. The principal exports were all primary products: bauxite and alumina, raw sugar, molasses and bananas. Exports of bauxite/alumina became increasingly more important during the decade, accounting for 66.2 percent of total exports by 1970. Raw material and food exports, taken together, accounted for 89.5 percent of total receipts between 1964 and 1970. The bulk of exports was destined to three principal markets: the United States, the United Kingdom and Canada, respectively accounting for shares of 38.9 percent, 26.5 percent and 18.0 percent. The main export products were sold through negotiated preferential marketing arrangements; e.g. sugar and bananas were handled by multinational corporations (Tate and Lyle, Elders and Fyffes), while bauxite/alumina exports were intra-firm transfers as opposed to conventional international trade transactions, and prices were set by multinational corporations rather than by the market. Agreed export quotas for the period 1966–1969 were revised in 1970 when a new tax agreement was concluded between the Government and the aluminium multinationals.

The value and volume of imports increased significantly during the decade of the 1960s. The value of imports increased almost three-fold over the period, while the volume of imports nearly doubled. The volume of raw materials and capital goods imports during the period increased by 274 percent, faster than consumer goods declining from 41 percent of the total to 30.9 percent, while capital goods increased their total share from 27.2 percent to 39.9 percent (Gaffer & Napier 1978: 103).

The relatively slower growth in the volume and value of imports of consumer goods reflects the emergence of a manufacturing sector as part of an import-substitution industrialisation strategy. Growing imports of capital goods were largely the result of expansion of productive capacity in the bauxite/alumina industry (Ibidem: 138).

The net terms of trade fluctuated from year to year but declined from 123.2 in 1955 to 98.2 in 1970; i.e. by 25 percent. For the decade of the 1960s as a whole, net terms of trade deteriorated by 12.7 percent. The price of imports exceeded that of exports over the period, despite increases in the price of the principal export after 1964 (Bank of Jamaica 1971: Table 10).

The growing deficit on visible trade account during the 1960s was accompanied by a similar growth in the deficit for services from J\$12.0 million in 1960 to J\$52.6 million in 1970. Receipts from an expanding tourist industry provided a positive balance on foreign-travel account (which increased from J\$24.2 million in 1960 to J\$91.4 million in 1970), but this was offset by the increased outflow of investment income, especially after 1964. This outflow rose from J$33.8 million in 1964 to J$95.4 million in 1970, just over 90 percent of repatriated income coming from direct, as opposed to portfolio, investments. The increase in these payments was directly associated with foreign investment in bauxite/alumina, public utilities, tourism and manufacturing. The result was that net investment income, which amounted to J$21.8 million in 1960, rose to J$81.8 million in 1970. Net unrequited transfers showed a positive balance throughout the decade due to large remittances from Jamaicans residing overseas.

In summary, over the period 1960–1970, there was a deficit on current account in every year except 1963. The size of this deficit increased from J$16.6 million in 1960 to J$127.2 miliion in 1970. However, a positive balance on capital account more than offset the current account deficit, resulting in a small surplus in every year except 1964, 1965 and 1969. Net capital movements increased from J$17.0 million in 1960 to J$134.1 million in 1970. Nearly all capital inflows were private as official capital inflows remained small, and indeed were negative in 1961, 1962 and 1970. The net inflow of private capital was an autonomous variable which during the 1960s favourably affected the balance of payments and provided impetus for economic growth. Private capital flows consisted principally of direct private foreign investment to augment productive capacity in the bauxite/alumina industry and, of the J$664 million invested over the period of 1953–1972, J$497 million flowed in after 1966. Moreover, foreign investment had a dual effect, both offsetting the current deficit and permitting a higher level of total investment; on average, overseas investment accounted for 32 percent of total investment over the period 1953–1972.

Foreign investment on a scale sufficient to ensure a balance of payment surplus (or a deficit which can comfortably be financed by drawing down foreign reserves) permits a higher level of imports. Larger volumes of imports permit capital accumulation on a more extended scale and increase profits. Not surprisingly, the years of highest real growth are those in which the import bill rises steeply. In 1964, the real rate of growth of GDP was 6.9 percent and the increase in the import volume was 24.6 percent, while in 1965 GDP grew in real terms at 8.0 percent while total import volume increased by 10.7 percent; similarly, in 1968, real GDP growth was 6.2 percent and import volumes increased by 26.2 percent (Jefferson 1972: 45; Gaffer & Napier 1978: 121, 125).

Turning to the period 1970–1980, two major exogenous factors had a serious and deleterious impact on the Jamaican balance of payments. First, there was a marked slowdown in the rate of growth of the world economy. World trade grew, on average, at only 5.7 percent per annum in the 1970s as compared to nearly 8 percent annually over the previous decade. Reduced rates of growth were compounded by rising rates of inflation, spurred on by a four-fold increase in the price of oil in 1973–74. Second, direct foreign investment declined very sharply in the period 1972–74, and was actually negative in 1975 and 1976. The external balance, which in 1970 had registered a surplus of J$12.2 million, by 1972 was showing a deficit of J$35.9 million which further increased to J$231.3 million by 1976. In March 1976 a negative figure was registered for foreign reserves.

The trade deficit widened from J$89.2 million in 1970 to J$161.2 million in 1973 and remained in the red for the rest of the decade with the exception of 1977–78. The increasingly adverse trade balance reflected the rapid rate of growth of imports which outstripped that of exports. Price inflation was a major influence on the growing value of imports since the volume actually declined by 24.3 percent between 1972 and 1974, and by a further 14.6 percent between 1974 and 1976. While the import volume was the same in 1975 as it had been in 1970, unit costs had increased by 152 percent. Interestingly, export prices increased throughout the decade so that the commodity terms of trade did not deteriorate; however, export volumes remained virtually unchanged between 1970 and 1978, and for certain key lines of production, actually fell. Production in the bauxite/alumina industry was reduced, partly in response to the recession in the United States which led to declining demand for aluminium products, and partly because of intrafirm reloca- tion of raw material sources undertaken by transnational corporations in response to the imposition of a production levy by Jamaica in 1974. For bauxite, there was a shift away from Jamaica to Guinea, while for alumina there was a shift towards Australia. Declines in production were also experienced in sugar and bananas, mainly due to technological obsolescence, disease and increased domestic consumption.

Over the decade, the increasing deficit on services account, combined with the visible trade deficit and the stagnation of net transfers from abroad, resulted in a sizeable increase in the overall current account deficit. The deficit, which in 1970 had stood at J$145.4 million, by 1975 totalled J$280.8 million. Although the deficit was reduced somewhat in the period 1976–78, it increased sharply once more in 1979–80. Underly- ing the deficit was a decline in earnings from tourism and sharp increases in the outflow of profits from investment. Tourist arrivals fell by 30 percent between 1975 and 1977, with tourist occupancy falling from 43.5 percent to 28.9 percent and tourist expenditure falling from J$116.8 million to J$95 million, or by roughly 19 percent over the period. Outflows of investment income increased from J$52.8 million in 1973 to J$416.3 million by the end of the decade.

Whereas in the decade of the 1960s current account deficits had been offset by capital inflows, during the 1970s the net capital inflow figure declined from a peak of J$221.1 million in 1974 to J$41.5 million in

1976, a drop of J$180 million in just two years, and the decline continued until the end of the decade. The decrease in overall net capital movements reflected a sharp reduction in net private capital movements which fell from J$28.1 million in 1974 to a negative figure of J$28.1 million in 1976. Again, during the two year period 1978–1979, private capital outflows exceeded inflows by J$298.9 million. As capital inflows failed to keep up with capital outflows during the decade, so too overseas public debt and publicly guaranteed private debt increased in importance. Hence towards the end of the 1970s, the burden of debt-service grew.

The external payments deficits reflect the structural vulnerability of the economy and the paramount importance of exogenous factors in determining capital accumulation. Stagnating export volumes and falling compensatory net capital inflows, together with deteriorating international terms of trade, reduced Jamaica's import capacity. By 1976, not only were consumer and raw material import volumes down, but capital goods import volumes had fallen to less than half the level of 1970, while by 1978 capital goods import volumes were less than one-third their 1970 level. The contraction in import volume resulted in a general contraction of the economy as circuits of capital were retarded both in scale and turnover time.

The Jamaican economy clearly illustrates the crisis of disarticulated reproduction, where growth is a function of import volume which in turn is a function of the quantum of available foreign exchange. The fragility of the balance of payments inherent in the structure of dependent capitalism was, during the 1960s, masked by compensating inflows of direct foreign investment, enabling higher import volumes to be financed and facilitating relatively high rates of economic growth. In the 1970s, however, private capital outflows increased, new capital became more difficult and more expensive to obtain and had to be underwritten by Government. The resulting decline in net capital inflows made it impossible to continue financing the growing current account deficit. Under conditions of worsening international terms of trade, import volumes contracted, particularly for capital goods, thus undermining the accumulation process.

IV.   THE 1970: ECONOMIC STRATEGIES AND ATTEMPTED REFORM

Broadly speaking, two different economic strategies have been applied in Jamaica. The one, which we shall term the 'dependent capitalist growth strategy', is associated with the *Jamaican Labour Party* (JLP) which ruled fom 1962 to 1972 and is once more in power. The other, which may be termed the 'democratic-socialist development strategy', was pursued by the *People's National Party* (PNP) between 1974 and 1980.

The former views 'development' as an evolutionary trajectory from an original state of underdevelopment to a state of development. Since domestic income is low, domestic savings are low, and the 'vicious circle of poverty' can only be broken by an injection of foreign capital requiring, *inter alia*, a close political alliance with the capitalist world, particularly the United States, in order to obtain official aid and guarantee a favourable climate for private overseas investment. In this scheme, the private sector constitutes the engine of growth of the economy with the State fulfilling a complementary and subsidiary role, mainly that of financing economic and social infrastructure. The present Prime Minister, Mr Edward Seaga, summarised this view succinctly at the Commonwealth Ministers Meeting in 1969:

The first essential is that developing countries should ensure that a favourable climate exists for foreign investment [and] the second essential is the establishment of the necessary institutional framework to facilitate foreign private investment. (Seaga 1969: 8)

Although Jamaica experienced an annual rate of growth of GDP of 3.6 percent between 1960 and 1968, it is arguable whether the country achieved significant economic development. Unemployment increased from 13.5 percent in 1960 to 23.6 percent in 1972. Income distribution worsened; it is estimated that between 1958 and 1968 the share in earned income of the poorest 40 percent of the population declined from 7.2 percent to 5.4 percent. Absolute poverty grew during the same period; average per capita income of the poorest 30 percent fell from 32 US cents to 25 US cents per capita (at constant 1958 prices) and, in 1968, roughly 65 percent of the employed labour force was earning less than US$25 per week (Girvan, Bernal & Hughes 1980: 113–115).

In February 1972, the *People's National Party* (PNP) led by Michael Manley formed a new Government committed to a policy of growth with redistribution. From 1972–1974, the policy of the Manley Administration consisted largely of implementing social programmes aimed at alleviating the worst aspects of poverty and, to a lesser extent, effecting a redistribution of income through improved employment and social security. However, in September 1974, the PNP declared itself to be committed to Democratic Socialism. Manley warned that 'the capitalist economic system does not possess the kind of dynamic which can resolve the basic contradictions which exist in the Jamaican economy' (Manley 1977: 5). The fundamental factor conditioning the attempt to implement a Democratic Socialist development strategy by the Manley Government was political. True, there were serious underlying economic problems in this period, but the policies adopted and their means of implementation were politically conditioned by three main sets of forces: that of opposing class forces and intra-class divisions within the country itself; external political pressures brought to bear by the US Government and in particular by the IMF; and ideological divisions within the ruling party which formed the government coalition.

The expansion of the State in managing and planning the economy, as well as its participation in production and distribution, was seen as central to the construction of a mixed economy. Social ownership of the means of production was extended by means of a significant increase in the number of state enterprises. By 1979, 185 state enterprises had been brought into existence and by 1980, the State owned all utilities, the largest commercial bank, 51 percent of the bauxite mining operations of the multinationals, 75 percent of sugar output, 48 percent of hotel capacity and had established a State Trading Corporation. Gross assets of these enterprises amounted to approximately J$4.4 billion. Acquisition of these enterprises was not based on profitability considerations; rather, most acquisitions were 'salvage' operations aimed at bailing out bankrupt capitalists and preventing the laying-off of workers.

One of the most important sectors taken over by the state was the bauxite/alumina industry, accounting for over 60 percent of exports. The oil-price increase of 1973–74, which aggravated an already serious balance of payments situation, provided the occasion for State intervention. At the meeting of the International Bauxite Association in March 1974, Jamaica imposed a production levy of 7.5 percent of the average delivery price of primary aluminium in the United States. The royalty on mined bauxite ore, whether exported or processed locally, was doubled from 25 US cents to 50 US cents per ton. Minimum levels of production for each multinational company were stipulated, and an overall total annual production target was set of 14 million tons. The effect of these measures was to increase the State's tax receipts from bauxite/alumina from J$41 million in 1973 to J$174.9 million in 1974. The Jamaican Government announced its intention to purchase 51 percent of the assets of the bauxite/alumina companies operating in Jamaica, assets totaling US$1 billion. Keyser, Reynolds, Alcoa, Alpart and Alcan all negotiated separate agreements with the Jamaican Government. These agreements had in common that: (a) the State purchased 51 percent of the mining operations at their 'book value'; (b) the State purchased all land owned by the Companies; (c) the Companies were guaranteed a 40 year supply of bauxite; and (d) a production tax of 7.5 percent was fixed for 8 years. The Companies responded during and after the takeover negotiations by cutbacks in production, by challenging the constitutionality of the production levy, by seeking the assistance of the *International Centre for the Settlement of Investment Disputes* (an agency of the World Bank), and by lobbying the US State Department to take action against Jamaica. The companies threatened to use more aluminium recovered from scrap, and disclosures were made about new discoveries of bauxite deposits in countries that were not members of the IBA (International Bauxite

Agreement). The Ford Administration, through its trade strategist, William D. Eberle, warned bauxite producing countries that: 'if they act responsibly on supplies and prices we will give them access to our market. If they are not responsible, we reserve the right to take any action to limit them in the future' (Daily Gleaner, 26.11.1974).

As a precaution against such measures, Jamaica made a determined effort to diversify markets in which it sold bauxite. Export diversification was also undertaken to reduce the level of dependency on the US market. The need for diversification became clear in 1975 when Jamaica's bauxite exports fell by 19 percent as a result of a decline in the US demand. Jamaica undertook joint ventures with Mexico and Venezuela, and with Trinidad and Guyana, in setting up two new aluminium smelters. Both projects failed to materialise, the former because of US pressure on Mexico initiated by the aluminium multinationals, and the latter because of disagreements with Trinidad's Prime Minister, Eric Williams. Sales of bauxite to the Soviet Union were also initiated in 1979.

In the field of promoting social ownership, an important measure undertaken by the Manley Government was to convert sugar plantations into workers' cooperatives. During 1974 and 1975, some 5,265 workers on 29, 379 acres of land were formed into 20 cooperatives. The Government assisted the cooperatives in securing bank loans for capital investment, but the cooperatives experienced severe difficulties, in part because of obsolete equipment, but more generally because of a breakdown in labour discipline. Once the threat of unemployment was removed, productivity tended to fall. Unions fought for higher wages even after workers had become the new owners. The State initiated a programme of establishing *Community Economic Organisations*, a form of cooperative in which ownership was not vested in individuals but in the community (PNP 1979). The CEOs, along with the Community Councils, were intended to form the economic base of self-reliant communities which would then constitute the basis for a more self-reliant economy. The PNP left office, however, before this programme could be implemented on a significant scale.

Despite the creation of state enterprises and of a socially-owned sector, the capitalist mode of production remained essentially intact and dominant. Production, distribution and international trade continued to be controlled by private enterprise, making it difficult for the State to implement plans effectively. Planning was constrained, moreover, by the openness of the economy and the disarticulated nature of the economic structure; planning was essentially 'indicative' since the National Planning Agency was not empowered to enforce implementation. If in the early stages, a 'planning strategy' could be said to exist at all, the subsequent requirements of the IMF, to which we return below, further undermined attempts at planning.

In a two-party parliamentary democracy in which unemployment is 25 percent, the pressure for the State to alleviate poverty through social programmes is extremely acute. It strongly influences all political decisions, and the PNP, as a party in transition from populism to democratic socialism, was highly suceptible to these demands. Moreover, the PNP Government was caught in a classical 'fiscal crisis'; i.e. increasing State budgetary expenditure is required to sustain capitalist development, but increased tax revenue requires fiscal reform which capitalists, as a class, are unwilling to accept. Factors which led to a substantial increase in budget expenditure included the rapid expansion of social programmes and the funding of provisions for employment creation. Expenditure on labour-intensive projects increased by 66 percent in 1972 and by 1974–75 the employment content of the budget had risen to 110,200 man-years, of which 29 percent was in the form of temporary employment. The intensification of the crisis generated compelling social and political pressures to expand these programmes. Indeed, Prime Minister Manley described these programmes as 'the price of survival of the democratic system' (Manley 1972: 6). Moreover, given declining foreign investment and domestic private sector investment, the public sector response was to expand capital expenditure through foreign borrowing. In 1973, a decision was taken to finance only normal operational and maintenance of services out of central government revenue, all forms of productive expenditure being financed from loans. Even contributions to international institutions such as the World Bank were to be financed by means of international loans on the grounds that these were contributions to future economic projects. The inadequate and inefficient system of financial accounting in the state bureaucracy compounded the tendency toward excessive expenditure. A crude indicator of such excesses is the difference between original approved estimates of recurrent expenditure and final outturn. Outturn exceeded estimates by 10 percent in 1973/74 and by 20 percent in 1974/75. Inflation, which was 26.9 percent in 1973 and 20.6 percent in 1974, added considerably to the cost of operating the State apparatus. Moreover, high inflation generated mounting demands for compensatory wage increases. Indeed, in 1975, the Minister of Finance stated that 'the unprecedented increase in wages and salaries that occurred in both the private and public sectors over the past two years were, to a considerable extent, an inevitable consequence of a response to these inflationary pressures' (Coore 1975: 17). Government current expenditure tripled between 1971 and 1975 mainly as a result of wage increases, the special employment programmes and a reclassification of the civil service.

Total revenue grew between 1972/73 and 1975/76, but declined thereafter until 1978. Government's ability to raise revenue was adversely affected by the stagnation of the economy; the quantitative restrictions

on imports and the deteriorating foreign exchange situation caused a
decline in tax revenue from international transactions: from J$55.8
million in 1973/74 to J$32.4 million in 1977/78. Although the Govern-
ment imposed new taxes (the production levy on bauxite and alumina
brought in J$128.7 million per annum in its first four years) and increas-
ed already existing taxes (on land, retail sales and specific consumption
items), the increase in revenue was not sufficient. Increased local and
foreign borrowing were required to finance the resulting deficit.

In addition to increased Central Government borrowing, State-owned
institutions also borrowed heavily abroad and loans were secured by
Government guarantees. In 1972, for example, the electricity and
telephone companies announced expansion programmes costing J$280
million over ten years and J$80 million over five years, respectively.
Some State-owned companies required massive recapitalisation; e.g. the
Jamaica Omnibus Service. Government guarantees were provided for
foreign loans to State-owned financial institutions, such as the Jamaica
Development Bank and even for loans to foreign investors in the tourist
industry: e.g. the Bank of Nova Scotia Euro-dollar loan to Rose Hall
Intercontinental Hotels Limited.

In the five year period 1971–1976, the external public debt quadrupled
from US$142.9 million to US$488.6 million. Loans from transnational
commercial banks (Bernal 1981) grew faster than any other type of
foreign borrowing, increasing from US$29.0 million in December 1972
to US$256 million in December 1975. This represented a nine-fold
increase in a three-year period. But by 1976, the balance of payments
crisis had become so acute that transnational commercial banks stopped
lending. The Government resorted to loans from the IMF, but IMF 'con-
ditionality' entailed a major change in economic strategy, one which
stood in contrast to the original promises made by the Manley Administration (Girvan & Bernal 1982).

In December 1976, the Government opened discussions with IMF
(Girvan, Bernal & Hughes 1980) and in June 1977 agreed on a two-year
stand-by arrangement. In September 1977 the first drawing was made,
and in December of the same year, Jamaica failed the 'net domestic
assets test' when the ceiling of J$355 million was exceeded by 2.6 percent.
The IMF terminated the agreement and negotiations began on a new
IMF agreement. In May 1978, the Government agreed to an External
Fund Facility (EFF) which would provide US$240 million over three
years. This was increased to US$429 million in 1979, but in December
of that year, Jamaica failed to meet the stipulated target again when the
ceiling on net international reserves was exceeded. The IMF suspended
the EFF agreement, having dispersed only US$172 million. This failure
was due primarily to exogenous factors, namely, increased oil prices,
increased world inflation, increased interest rates and flood rains.

For one-and-a-half years, between May 1978 and December 1979, Jamaica fulfilled all the requirements of the IMF's Extended Fund Facility Programme, but there was no growth and no improvement in the balance of payments. Real GDP declined by 1.7 percent in 1978 and 2.2 percent in 1979. The balance of payments deficit increased by US$40 million in 1978 and by a further US$78 million in 1979. The Government, after six months of discussions with the Fund, decided in March 1980 not to seek a new IMF agreement but to pursue a 'non-IMF path'.

The policies prescribed by the IMF agreements were as follows. Jamaica was to devalue in order to discourage imports and make exports more competitive. Wage increases were to be minimised in order to reduce aggregate demand, and therefore import demand, and to reduce costs of production and, therefore, cost-push inflation. Price controls, subsidies, exchange controls, import licencing and import restrictions were to be removed, and Government expenditure was to be reduced generally in order to eliminate the budget deficit. As part of the same logic, State enterprises were to be eliminated gradually, as well as programmes supporting non-capitalist forms of production. Restrictive monetary and credit policies were to be introduced, involving money-supply targets, higher interest rates and cash limits on borrowing by the State enterprises. In general, such measures were designed to enhance the profitability of the private capitalist sector through a reduction in real wages and the elimination of price controls; to reduce the ability of the State to undertake production; to establish free markets as the only mechanism of resource allocation; and to increase the openness of the economy, permitting full integration into the world capitalist economy and facilitating foreign capital penetration. In short, the IMF provided a comprehensive prescription for preserving dependent capitalism (Bernal 1984a) in Jamaica which the PNP's democratic socialism had sought to reform and, potentially, to transform.

All of this took place against a background of growing conflict within the party which increasingly curtailed the PNP's ability to direct the State apparatus. These ideological differences, best illustrated by the split between left and right over the IMF programmes, were rooted in the multi-class character of the Party and were particularly pronounced at the level of Party leadership. Moreover, by the time the decision was taken to follow a path independent of the IMF, a general election was less than a year away. Hence, by mid-1980, the Government had retreated on nearly every one of its major policy goals, social unrest was rising, the economy was in crisis, and the Party was deeply divided. The social and political effects of economic policies entailed in the IMF programmes had a major impact on dismembering the class alliance which supported the PNP (Bernal 1984b).

V. LESSONS

In this paper we have argued that the crisis of dependent capitalism is structural in character, and its tendency to stagnation is inherent in its disarticulated economic structure. The process of capital accumulation is itself dependent and even when extended reproduction takes place it does not provide a basis for self-sustaining development. Development requires structural transformation which is difficult, in particular when the economy is in crisis. While structural transformation is being effected, it is necessary both to secure sufficient foreign exchange to sustain capital accumulation, and for the State to expand its role, quantitatively and qualitatively, in order to direct structural transformation. However, the state is constrained by 'fiscal crisis' and hence expansionary expenditure policies tend to aggravate balance of payments deficit. The Manley Administration's attempt to implement a Democratic Socialist development strategy was very limited and, essentially, confined to the period 1977–80. An evaluation of the experience is made difficult by the impact of IMF programmes which diverted the government's economic strategy.

There are two sets of lessons to be learned from the Jamaican experience. First, at the technical level, there is the problem of securing sufficient foreign exchange to maintain capital accumulation during structural transformation. The Manley Government did not succeed but became heavily indebted to transnational banks and hence submitted to IMF discipline. Second, the implementation of a Democratic Socialist development strategy requires the state to be an instrument of structural transformation, but this can only take place if there is a unified political leadership with a clear ideological position. Sadly, the PNP's internal class conflicts and ideological disputes in the end paralysed the regime.

REFERENCES

Bank of Jamaica (1971): *Balance of Payments of Jamaica, 1964–1970* (Kingston: Bank of Jamaica).
Bernal, R.L. (1981): 'La Banca transnational, el Fondo Monetario International y la crisis capitalista de Jamaica', in J. Estevez & S. Lichtensztenjn (eds): *Nueva fase del Capital Financiero; Elementos Teóricos y experiencias en America Latina* (Mexico City: Editorial Nueva Imagen).
—— (1984a): 'The IMF, Economic Policy and the Preservation of Dependent Capitalism in Jamaica', in J. Torrie (ed.): *Banking on Poverty: The IMF, World Bank and the Global Economy* (Toronto: Between the Lines).
—— (1984b): 'IMF and Class Struggle in Jamaica, 1977–80' (Paper presented at the 10th World Congress of Sociology, Mexico City, 16–21 August; forthcoming in *Latin American Perspectives*).
Coore, Hon. D. (1975): *1975–76 Budget Speech*, 15 May (Kingston: API).

Gaffer, J. & W.J. Napier (1978): *Trends and Patterns of Commonwealth Caribbean Trade 1954–1970* (University of West Indies: ISER).

Girvan, N., R. Bernal & W. Hughes (1980): 'The IMF and the Third World: The Case of Jamaica 1974–1980', in *Development Dialogue*, No. 2, 113–115.

Girvan, R. & R. Bernal (1982): 'The IMF and the Foreclosure of Development Options: The Case of Jamaica', in *Monthly Review*, Vol. 33, No. 9, 34–48.

Jefferson, O. (1972): 'The Post-War Economic Development of Jamaica' (University of West Indies: ISER).

Manley, Hon. M. (1972): *Budget Debate Speech*, 1 May (Kingston, Government Printer).

—— (1977): 'A People's Plan' (Transcript of Address to Parliament, 22 April; Kingston: Agency for Public Information).

People's National Party (1979): 'Principles and Objectives' (Kingston: PNP).

Seaga, Hon. E. (1969): 'Development Strategy for the Next Decade' (A submission made to the meeting of Commonwealth Finance Ministers, 26 September).

IX

TRANSNATIONAL BANKS AND FINANCIAL CRISIS IN THE CARIBBEAN

Hillbourne Watson

Hillbourne Watson

I. CARIBBEAN INDUSTRIALISATION AND THE TRANSNATIONAL BANKS

The Caribbean region consists mainly of pre-industrial and semi-industrial economies which have been integrated into the international division of labour through production of primary commodities for the world market.[1] Production and circulation of commodities obey the law of value and the character of private accumulation is imprinted upon the class nature of the state. Within this reality, however, there is considerable diversity both in economic structure and in the organisation of political power around the state. The range is from extreme political authoritarianism in Haiti, which borders on a neo-colonial variant of fascism, to (until recently) revolutionary nationalism with a socialist orientation in Grenada. In between these are forms of post-colonial capitalism, generally highly conservative, found in Barbados, Jamaica, and Trinidad and Tobago, and the perverse authoritarian state capitalism of Guyana. In none of these countries has there been any marked success in building social democracy.

Foreign capital predominates in the national life of these systems and, for the most part, these economies are highly open. Since the late 1960s, moreover, the Caribbean has been strongly affected by the capitalist world economic crisis. Throughout the region, the crisis of capital accumulation has assumed diverse forms: production crises, foreign exchange crises, unemployment crises, inflation crises, balance of payments and debt crises, and in general priorities have been severely distorted.[2] Transnational banks operating in the Caribbean may therefore be said to be functioning in an environment that is characterised by economic crisis and political instability. The banks have chosen to continue their operations, which suggests that the crisis has not undermined their profitability. Their lending activities are for the most part relatively risk-free and yield quick returns. Most of these activities are in themselves the expression of what can be called 'perverse' development.

During the past two decades various studies have been carried out by
Caribbean scholars and researchers on the specific monetary and financial relationship between Caribbean economies and international
capitalism.[3] These include studies by Thomas (1965, 1972), McClean
(1971) and Miller (1971). Common to most is evidence of the pervasive-
ness of financial and monetary dependence as a function of broader
structural economic dependence. Odle (1981) has contributed significantly to this theme within the tradition of the critique of political
economy. Certain earlier studies have provided useful insights towards
understanding the objectives and operational mechanisms of transnational banks in the relatively early phase of post-war industrialisation
in the English-speaking Caribbean. Thomas (1972), Bourne (1974), and
Odle (1981) have shown how difficult it is to attempt to build independent
monetary and financial institutions in peripheral economies that are fully
integrated into the capitalist world economy, and which reproduce all the
features of structural dependence. The weakness and ineffectiveness of
traditional institutions and instruments of monetary policy has been
demonstrated by McClean (1971) and Thomas (1972). Jefferson (1972:
241–42), and Girvan (1971: 172–78) and Miller (1971: 200–201) have
shown that the basic pattern of commercial bank lending in Jamaica has
consistently reflected the dominant position of foreign capital in the
'real' sector and import dependence in consumption patterns. A decade
later, Odle demonstrates that very little has changed.

How do banks contribute to 'perverse' industrialisation in periphery
countries? Odle states the argument this way:

Capitalism has a tendency not to focus its production on those goods which many consider
as basic needs (but rather for profits based on the market votes of those consumers with
the most spending power) and banks are an integral part of this process of unequal
provision and unequal consumption. (Odle 1981: 77)

In other words, bank profits thrive on existing patterns of income
distribution in the peripheral economy, and in this way reinforce prevailing distortions in resource allocation and demand patterns.

Frobel, Heinrichs and Kreye support this argument in concluding that:

... export oriented industrialization manifestly perpetuates the historical process of
dependent development in the underdeveloped countries ... It restricts industrial development to non-complex, horizontally disintegrated, partial operations which result in an
extraordinary unbalanced manufacturing structure. This export-oriented industrialization
is the form of the development of structurally dependent industry which produces structurally dependent uneven development. (1978: 26)

The banks have not disputed these claims. In fact, according to Chase
National Bank, its lending priorities are to finance short-term trade in US
exports and the subsidiaries of US-based multinationals, and export-
oriented production in borrowing countries. The lowest priority is

Table 1 Incidence of Branches, Subsidiaries and Affiliates in each Caribbean Host Country Disaggregated According to the Multinational Host Country

CARIBBEAN	(B)	(S)	(A)	Total MWB Units	Canada (B,S,A)	USA (B,S,A)	Britain (B,S,A)	France (B,S,A)	Germany (B,S,A)	Holland (B,S,A)	Italy (B,S,A)	Switzerland (B,S,A)	Japan (B,S,A)	Other Developed (B,S,A)	Under Developed (B,S,A)
Antigua	5	1		6	3(3,0,0)	1(1,0,0)	2(1,1,0)								
Anguilla	1			1		1(1,0,0)									
Bahamas	48	28	18	94	4(3,8,3)	53(40,9,4)	8(2,3,3)	1(0,0,1)		1(0,0,1)	4(0,4,0)	8(1,2,5)		3(1,1,1)	2(1,1,0)
Barbados	7	4		11	6(3,3,0)	3(3,0,0)	2(1,1,0)								
Belize	3	1		4	2(2,0,0)	1(0,1,0)	1(1,0,0)								
Bermuda		1	16	17	2(0,0,2)	1(0,1,0)	10(0,0,10)			2(0,0,2)			1(0,0,1)		1(0,0,1)
Cayman Isl.	26	18	17	61	8(3,4,1)	32(19,8,5)	9(1,2,6)	2(0,0,2)	1(1,0,0)		1(0,1,0)	1(0,1,0)		4(1,1,2)	3(1,1,1)
Dominica	1			1	1(1,0,0)										
Grenada	5	1		6	3(3,0,0)	1(1,0,0)	2(1,1,0)								
Guadeloupe	3			3	1(1,0,0)	1(1,0,0)		1(1,0,0)							
Guyana	4	1		5	3(2,1,0)	1(1,0,0)	1(1,0,0)								
Jamaica	3	15	1	19	8(1,7,0)	10(2,7,1)	1(0,1,0)								
Neth. Antilles	3	16	3	22	4(1,2,1)	6(2,3,1)	1(0,1,0)	1(0,1,0) 1(1,0,0)	1(0,0,1)	6(0,6,0)			2(0,2,0)	1(0,1,0)	
Martinique	4			4	1(1,0,0)	2(2,0,0)									
Montserrat	3	1		4	1(1,0,0)	1(1,0,0)	2(1,1,0)								
St Kitts	3	1		4	1(1,0,0)	1(1,0,0)	2(1,1,0)								
St Lucia	5	1		6	3(3,0,0)	1(1,0,0)	2(1,1,0)								
St Vincent	4	1		5	3(3,0,0)		2(1,1,0)								
Suriname	1	5	1	7	1(0,0,1)				6(1,5,0)						
Trinidad	6	8	1	15	9(3,6,0)	4(3,1,0)	2(0,1,1)								
Turks and Caicos Is.	1			1			1(1,0,0)								
Virgin Isl.	8			8	3(3,0,0)	4(4,0,0)	1(1,0,0)								
Dom. Rep.	6	3	3	12	3(2,0,1)	6(3,2,1)	2(1,1,0)								
Haiti	5			5	2(2,0,0)	2(2,0,0)		1(1,0,0)							1(0,0,1)

(B)—Branches
(S)—Subsidiaries
(A)—Affiliates
Source: Odle 1981: 41–42 (Table 2.3)

assigned to loans to finance balance of payments deficits (US Senate Sub-committee on International Finance 1977: 144).

One reason the banks are in a position to follow these policy prescriptions is that they generally enjoy a monopoly position. It can be seen from Tables 1 and 2 how dominant the foreign banks have become in the Caribbean, from Jamaica to Guyana. In most instances, one or two transnational banks have dominated banking activity in each country. Barclays Bank and The Royal Bank of Canada were the leading banks in the Commonwealth Caribbean in 1974. In 1976, as Table 2 shows, Barclays' financial power was exclusive in its Caribbean branches and subsidiaries and was significant in its affiliates. Table 3 summarises information on the spread of transnational banking activity in the Caribbean in 1977–78, and it can be seen that Canadian, US and British banks dominate banking activity throughout the region. The presence of other European banks is primarily a result of the growth of offshore banking which is a product of the rapid expansion of the Eurocurrency markets. The Bahamas, Bermuda, Cayman Islands and the Netherlands Antilles are the offshore banking enclaves of international finance in the region. The expansion of branches, subsidiaries and affiliates has also been most rapid in these offshore banking centres.

The financial side of the picture of offshore banking centres in the Caribbean is presented in Table 4. Obviously, not all the countries listed are offshore banking centres, but it is clear that the Caribbean has

Table 2   *Operations of Barclays in Caribbean by Function and Percentage Ownership, 1976*

Branches	%	Subsidiaries	%	Affiliates	%
Territory		*Name of Corporation*		*Name of Corporation*	
Bahamas	100	Banco Barclays-Netherlands Antilles	53.33	Bahamas Trust-Bahamas	26.00
Barbados	100	Barclays-Jamaica	100.00	Barclays-Trinidad	49.00
Belize	100	Barclays Finance-Bahamas	100.00	Bermuda Provident-Bermuda	32.33
Cayman Islands	100	Barclays Finance-Barbados	100.00	Cayman Trust-Cayman Islands	26.00
Guyana	100	Barclays Finance-Grand Cayman	100.00	Export Leasing-Bermuda	33.33
Leeward and Windward Islands (Caribbean)	100	Barclays Finance-Trinidad	100.00	International Trust-Bermuda	20.00
Turks and Caicos Islands	100	Barclays Finance-Leeward & Windwards	100.00		
Virgin Islands	100	Barclays Finance-Jamaica	100.00		

Source: Odle 1981: 22, and author.

Table 3 *World Ranking, Hierarchical Position Within Respective Host Countries, and Oligopolistic Share of Deposits, Multinational Banks in the Caribbean*

1974	Barclays	Royal	Imperial	Scotia	Montreal	Chase	Citibank	FNB of Chicago	America	Citizens	Baroda	Virgin Is.	Neth. Antilles
MNB Rank Within World	12	23	30	55	51	6	2	49	1	225	300+	300+	300+
Guyana % Share Rank Within Country	40.1% (2)	44.6% (1)	—	3.3% (5)	—	8.4% (3)	—	—	—	—	3.5% (4)	—	—
Jamaica % Share Rank Within Country	30.7% (2)	11.5% (3)	6.8% (4)	39.0% (1)	1.8% (7)	—	5.3% (5)	1.0% (8)	—	3.7% (6)	—	—	—
Trinidad % Share Rank Within Country	39.8% (1)	16.5% (3)	13.9% (4)	19.5% (2)	—	4.3% (6)	6.1% (5)	—	—	—	—	—	—
Antigua % Share Rank Within Country	31.2% (1)	22.9% (3)	9.2% (5)	26.8% (2)	—	—	—	—	—	—	—	9.4% (4)	0.5% (6)
Dominica % Share Rank Within Country	60.4% (1)	39.6% (2)	—	—	—	—	—	—	—	—	—	—	—
Grenada % Share Rank Within Country	42.4% (1)	13.6% (2)	13.6% (3)	8.1% (4)	—	4.3% (5)	—	—	—	—	—	—	—
Montserrat % Share Rank Within Country	27.7% (2)	52.4% (1)	—	—	—	19.8% (3)	—	—	—	—	—	—	—
St Kitts % Share Rank Within Country	52.1% (1)	22.6% (3)	—	—	—	—	—	—	25.3% (2)	—	—	—	—
St Lucia % Share Rank Within Country	39.8% (1)	19.5% (3)	10.8% (4)	22.9% (2)	—	7.0% (5)	—	—	—	—	—	—	—
St Vincent % Share Rank Within Country	56.1% (1)	25.9% (2)	18.1% (3)	—	—	—	—	—	—	—	—	—	—

Source: Odle 1981: 55 (Table 3.2).

Table 4   *External Positions in Domestic and Foreign Currencies of Banks and of Certain Offshore Branches of US Banks Operating in the Caribbean (million US$, year end)* *

Country	1976 Liabilities	Assets	1977 Liabilities	Assets	1978 Liabilities	Assets
Bahamas (JU)**	16,656	34,682	19,887	40,154	28,809	47,303
Barbados	37	646	76	21	74	41
Bermuda (J)	3,300	893	3,034	1,072	5,739	2,010
Cayman Is.	6,079	5,970	12,710	14,546	20,715	21,051
Cuba (JU)	84	1,007	260	1,278	272	1,478
Dom. Republic	7	153	10	203	93	321
Guyana	35	39	43	47	65	107
Haiti	13	13	9	15	30	22
Jamaica	68	394	52	305	91	527
Neth. Antilles (U)	1,711	1,421	2,311	1,960	3,593	3,205
Trinidad & Tobago	398	24	759	166	959	255
West Indies (UE)	599	332	880	514	221	180
Residual (MCJU)	4,935	9,839	3,539	5,162	1,800	2,827
Total	33,922	55,413	43,570	65,443	62,461	79,327

* Available data for years after 1978 (i.e. 1979–1981) are not broken down on a per country basis. All offshore and non-offshore banking centres in the Caribbean are reported together with Hong Kong, Lebanon, New Hebrides, Panama and Singapore. See Annual Reports of the Bank for International Settlements for years 1979–1981.
** JU = Japan, USA; J = Japan; U = USA; UE = USA, European; MCJU = Mixed Canadian, Japanese, USA.
Sources: for 1976–77 BIS 1977; 112; for 1977–78 BIS 1978; 94; for 1978–79 BIS 1979: 112.

become a major outpost for sheltering vast sums of money, mainly held by American banks. Ironically but not surprisingly, most of these sums have little direct impact upon the internal operations of the offshore banking havens. Between 1976 and 1978 the liabilities of the offshore banks rose by 84 percent while assets grew by 55 percent: from US$33.9 billion to US$62.5 billion and from US$55.4 billion to US$79.6 billion respectively. Most of the loans are made to borrowers outside the Caribbean.

It is partly the kind of evidence presented in Tables 1–4 that prompted Odle to conclude that:

The consortia banks represent the ultimate penetration of the periphery and the final culmination of multinational bank capital. They are essentially offshore operations with all the benefits and none of the disadvantages (such as taxing of interest and constraints on repatriation of income and capital) of an onshore activity; they wield tremendous authority, power and influence ... the bank consortia are nothing short of a Board of Directors running a comprador state. (Odle 1981: 180)

Indeed, as argued below, the influence and power of these banks in the Caribbean is not restricted to the regular commercial banking activities in which they engage. Their influence reflects the position they have acquired in multinational capitalism especially during a period of crisis and instability of the world economy.[4] The transnational banks' disregard of basic development needs of the Caribbean is a function of their own assumed role and the Caribbean's assigned role, in the international division of labour and the general accumulation process. These banks do not have to conspire against meeting those needs. It is the Caribbean ruling classes who are the major 'conspirators'. Such an assertion does not fit in well with conventional nationalistic ideology.

For what purposes do the foreign commercial banks make loans in the Caribbean? They lend to branches of other multinational enterprises; they finance the distributive sector (mainly import distribution activity); they lend to a range of professionals who produce services; they lend for private consumption (again mainly imports) and to the public sector. Details of bank lending activities by country are provided in Tables 5–8 for Jamaica, Barbados, and Trinidad and Tobago and by group for the Leeward and Windward Islands. Economic scale and the degree of industrial development are significant factors influencing the allocation of loans to construction, manufacturing and mining activity. As a result Trinidad and Tobago (Table 6) and Jamaica (Table 5) show significant outlays to these areas. For example, in 1973, $155.8 million or 24 percent of all funds was loaned to manufacturing, construction, and mining sectors in Trinidad and Tobago out of a total of $636.1 million in loans to all sectors/borrowers. In 1980, the corresponding amount was $893.1 million, or 77 percent of a total of $1,153.6 million.

Table 5 *Jamaica: Commercial Bank Loans and Advances 31 December 1972–1980 (million US$)*

Sector	1972	1974	1976	1978	1980
Agriculture & Fishing	12.9	26.6	82.4	81.9	117.8
Mining	8.1	6.2	6.4	5.7	6.2
Manufacturing	85.9	112.8	123.0	132.8	213.9
Construction & Land Development	72.3	125.4	126.8	127.8	127.3
Credit & Other Financial Institutions	12.9	18.1	19.9	32.7	23.1
Public Utilities	26.6	27.6	43.2	70.3	149.6
Government Services	14.7	18.1	16.1	27.8	23.5
Distribution	69.8	85.5	107.6	80.7	89.6
Tourism	12.3	16.1	13.0	25.8	60.3
Entertainment	3.7	4.7	4.2	6.8	12.1
Professional & Other Services	15.5	33.0	44.7	55.9	76.7
Personal	83.5	105.1	112.9	116.9	185.9

Sources: 1972–1978: Department of Statistics 1979; 1979–1980: National Planning Agency 1981.

Table 6   *Trinidad & Tobago: Commercial Banks, Quarterly Analysis of Loans and Advances (year end) (million US$)*

Sector	1973	1976	1978	1979	1980
Government & Other Public Bodies	89.1	50.3	81.2	117.9	238.7
Financial Institutions	23.7	16.6	59.0	72.7	79.3
Manufacturing	126.8	182.1	416.9	41.06	499.4
Construction	19.1	84.7	100.4	248.3	329.0
Mining & Refining	15.9	46.4	79.0	103.8	64.7
Agriculture	16.8	27.2	59.9	51.1	90.9
Distributive Trades	111.8	137.5	318.4	389.1	453.6
Transportation	12.5	22.0	56.5	97.1	132.6
Professional Services	15.0	27.7	111.1	144.1	154.9
Entertainment & Catering	4.0	7.0	14.7	22.3	32.6
Miscellaneous	12.2	30.1	11.1	12.3	50.8
Individual (Non-Business Firms)	195.2	554.1	952.7	977.9	1,152.6

Sources: Central Bank of Trinidad and Tobago (various years, 1974–1981).

For Jamaica (Table 5), the same sectors accounted for 58 percent of all loans in 1972 and 31 percent in 1980. Distributive trades, professional loans and personal loans to individuals accounted for 50 percent of all loans made by commercial banks in Trinidad and Tobago in 1973, compared with 53 percent in 1980. Loans for similar purposes in Jamaica represented 40 percent of all loans made in 1972 and 32 percent in 1980. In both countries, as well as in Barbados, foreign bank loans to agriculture were quite low. In 1974, loans for distribution, professional

Table 7   *Barbados: Commercial Banks Credit by Sector 1972–1980 (million Bds dollars)* *

Sector	1972	1974	1976	1978	1980
Agriculture	15.2	11.9	14.6	15.6	19.9
Fisheries	0.4	8.7	11.6	4.4	0.3
Manufacturing	16.7	26.9	24.9	38.8	94.6
Distribution	49.2	55.2	52.0	68.5	87.6
Tourism	22.9	27.3	41.6	46.9	62.3
Public Utilities	10.1	7.8	19.5	18.3	30.4
Construction	25.5	35.4	35.4	36.1	39.5
Government	9.8	16.0	13.6	20.4	9.5
Professional & Other Services	0.0	9.2	10.1	14.5	23.2
Miscellaneous	24.4	11.9	18.0	25.2	44.4
TOTAL	174.2	210.3	241.3	288.7	411.7

* Figures for 1973–80 include overdrafts that averaged roughly 50 per cent of credit per year for those years. See Central Bank of Barbados 1980: Tables B7 and B8.

Table 8 *ECCA Area Quarterly Analysis of Banks' Loans and Advances (thousands Eastern Caribbean dollars)*

Sector	Dec. 1974	Dec. 1975	Dec. 1976	Dec. 1977	Dec. 1978
Agriculture	21,144	23,371	25,001	20,445	28,317
Manufacturing	13,793	20,806	30,543	37,224	48,498
(1) Food and Non-Alcoholic Beverages	2,359	2,635	4,508	8,259	12,643
(2) Alcoholic Beverages and Tobacco	856	5,756	6,347	8,670	9,924
(3) Clothing and Accessories	1,760	3,194	2,218	4,549	4,336
(4) Other Industries	8,818	5,221	17,470	15,746	21,595
Distributive Trades	61,596	65,114	70,166	87,743	83,158
Tourism	25,602	24,308	25,858	26,933	32,624
Transport	16,270	15,658	15,301	20,392	30,697
Public Utilities (gas, electricity, telephone)	5,109	3,959	5,179	5,522	7,084
Building and Construction	30,690	28,772	27,574	27,561	33,985
Government & Other Statutory Bodies	35,993	40,954	44,782	51,090	51,090
Personal	59,481	61,431	69,402	96,962	114,878
Other advances	18,027	18,010	15,783	20,630	33,935
Total Loans & Advances	301,498	319,189	360,132	431,726	512,764
% of Long Term Loans to Total Loans	31.6	31.4	32.8	34.0	33.9

Source: East Caribbean Currency Authority 1978: 20, and 1979: 19.

and personal purposes accounted for 56 percent of all loans advanced by the foreign banks in Barbados, compared with 44 percent in 1980. The lending pattern of banks in the Windward and Leeward Islands for 1974 and 1978 suggests a similar situation (Table 8): distribution and personal loans accounted for 42 percent of all loans in both these years. Long-term loans were 31.6 percent of all loans made in 1974, and 33.9 percent of all loans advanced in 1978 (Table 8).

In 1970 and 1981, respectively, manufacturing activity provided 41 percent and 56 percent of the value-added contributed by wholesale and retail trade in Barbados. Corresponding figures for Guyana were 106 percent and 229 percent; 103 percent and 82 percent for Jamaica, and 50 percent and 57 percent for Trinidad and Tobago (Inter-American Development Bank 1982: 355,357). While the capitalist fractions which dominate internal trade in these Caribbean countries (whether in the state sector or private sector) may no longer be defined as purely 'comprador', this aspect of their activity, which provides surplus for productive investments in other areas and countries, has the effect of reproducing neo-comprador features within the internal market.

In general it can be argued that, today, both multinational enterprises and multinational banks decisively shape the new international division of labour. The lending patterns of transnational banks in Caribbean countries merely reflect a more general phenomenon. Productive enterprises operating in the Caribbean, including 'export market-oriented enterprises and manufacturers producing for the local market under various forms of (socially subsidised) incentives' apply labour-saving technologies which have the effect of reinforcing unemployment (Watson 1981: 56; Girvan 1976: 22–23). During the 1970s in particular, new forms of foreign capital entered the region under subcontracting and licensing arrangements – the Caribbean version of partial industrial relocation.

Although this development is not novel, 'it reflects the crystallization of the new international division of labour and its institutionalization throughout much of the periphery now that it has become possible to establish Free Production Zones (FPZs) and World Market Factories (WMFs) on those sites (FPZs) in order to produce commodities for export to the core economies' (Watson 1981: 59). This new reality is largely the result of the existence of large reserves of readily available cheap labour, or the ease with which capital can intensify the production process by speeding up production and lengthening the working day; it is also indicative of the ability of capital to simplify and standardise complex technologies and production processes (Watson 1981: 59).[5] WMF export commodities which are produced or assembled in Caribbean FPZs include garments, metal goods, electronics, toys, sporting goods, pharmaceuticals, eyeglass frames, textiles, leather products, furniture, dental products, fishing rods, plastic and rubber products, office machines, and automobiles (Watson 1981: 73–74a; Frobel, Heinrichs & Kreye 1980: Table III).

For most of these commodities inputs are imported, and very limited benefits accrue to the local economy through net value transfers. The banks find these export-oriented assembly industries attractive targets for loans because they are generally owned or controlled by foreign enterprises with access to markets in the core economies. In addition, they are low risk ventures: the loans advanced are generally short-term loans that carry high interest rates, in association with commodity stocks that can be readily liquidated (Odle 1981).

Odle (1981) has also noted that the output of assembly operations destined for local consumption bears a distinct class bias, as reflected by prevailing income distribution and related demand patterns, and the nature and type of production that is carried out. The production of luxury and semi-luxury goods ignores the broad needs of the popular masses (Amin 1976; Odle 1981). The skewed pattern of consumption and output reinforces the 'blockage to transition' and has important consequences. The market is narrow; the volume of production tends to be low; excess production capacity is reinforced by applied technology biases;[6] production cost tends to be high relative to output; diseconomies of scale exist in production and distribution; inefficiency tends to be widespread; and structural unemployment remains high.

The irony is that both large-scale reserves of cheap labour and capital-intensive technologies continue to co-exist. When bank lending for export-oriented assembly production is linked to lending to the distributive sector and the professional and personal category, it can be seen that there is a financial bias against the development of a manufacturing base appropriate for local industrialisation (Odle 1981: 50). The main beneficiaries of this process, which reinforces structural disarticulation, are the banks which profit from the loans and the producers who make the commodities. For the working classes it is a quite different reality.[7]

Working conditions which represent a synthesis of Manchester capitalism and the forms of capitalist organization of work of the last quarter of the twentieth century compel the labour force in free production zones and world market factories in the underdeveloped countries, on the one hand, to achieve levels of productivity and intensity of labour which correspond to the most advanced current levels in the world, and on the other hand, to tolerate wage levels which are not much higher than those which prevailed in Manchester capitalism's heyday. (Frobel, Heinrichs & Kreye 1980: 360)

Increasing class polarisation and deepening inequality in income distribution accompany this form of pseudo-industrialisation. One of the consequences of this phenomenon is to increase the hostility of workers toward a state that is eager to appease foreign capital and imperialism.

Hitherto, what has been stressed is that the profit objective and risk-avoiding policies of the banks combine with international economic and financial structures to reinforce 'perverse' industrialisation. International and regional political factors must also be considered. These include the consequences of America's declining hegemony, growing political radicalisation and the move toward greater autonomy of states in parts of the periphery. What is of particular importance, however, is the way core states have deliberately lent political support to pseudo-industrialisation policies in the Caribbean at the expense of fomenting an autonomous process of growth. One should not disregard the importance of the role of extra-economic factors in the shaping of significant economic decisions.

The decade of the 1970s was rich in useful illustrations although one could draw many illustrations from the 1960s as well. Acheson (1966); Baldwin (1966); Javits (1950); Watson (1975) and Griffith (1983) have all drawn attention to the role of international political factors and considerations in influencing Third World and/or Caribbean industrialisation options. There is no need to retrace these steps here. The production crises which Jamaica and Guyana experienced in the second half of the

1970s was not unrelated to United States policy toward the Caribbean. The economic proposals contained in the Caribbean Basin Initiative provide a clear illustration of this principle. The United States recognises the principle of comparative advantage for Caribbean economies only in the area of primary commodities. Even in this area, obtaining access to US markets has depended on the relative strategic importance of commodities such as bauxite and oil. Any attempt to explain the Caribbean industrialisation crisis of the 1970s which excludes an account of the interests of the USA is conceptually, methodologically and empirically incomplete.

Griffith (1983) has noted that, during the 1970s when Jamaica's and Guyana's production crises developed, Barbados was experiencing significant industrial expansion, rapid growth of export receipts from tourism and a relative increase in foreign capital inflows. Griffith attributes this largely to political factors; i.e. to the role Washington had assigned to Barbados in the Eastern Caribbean, a role consistent with perspectives and objectives of ruling class interests in Barbados. In short, although transnational banks play a role in reproducing perverse industrialisation, their role is not sufficient to explain the problem. At this stage, however, it is useful to return to other general issues about the nature of the global crisis.

II. TRANSNATIONAL BANKS AND SOVEREIGNTY

The disintegration of the US post-war 'imperial order' has produced widespread anarchy in inter-state relations. This is revealed in the absence 'of a world political authority capable of pursuing the general capitalist interest' (Arrighi 1982: 90) The dominance of the 'private money market' under the leadership of the transnational banks is clearly a temporary adjustment mechanism for dealing with such anarchy. As Aglietta (1982: 20) has argued, 'the ensuing rise of the Eurodollar radically altered the postwar international monetary system based upon central bank preponderance and symmetrical balance of payments constraints'. The appropriate context in which to situate the relationship between the peripheral state and the transnational bank is precisely that of the growing dominance of private money capital in the crisis-ridden capitalist world economy.

Chick has noted that the dominance of private capital has received little attention from most international relations experts who continue to assume:

that nation states can still exercise the decisive influence on the construction and operation of the international monetary system, while in tact, transnational enterprise at once is able to function substantially independently of the monetary regime and is a source of conflict in reform negotiations. (Chick 1979: 131–132)

This new reality, according to Chick, means that the

autonomy of nations has been substantially curtailed while the TNCs display considerable ability to circumvent any adverse effects of policy changes including exchange rate policies and capital controls. (Ibidem)

In fact the Subcommittee on MNCs of the US Senate Foreign Relations Committee (1975) concluded that the transnationalisation of economic organisation, production and distribution – the new international division of labour within multinational capitalism – has ruptured nation state boundaries and considerably weakened the ability of the state to exercise direct influence over trade via tariffs, exchange rates policies, exchange controls, fiscal and monetary measures.

The conduct of transnational banks' offshore activities outside the jurisdiction of any single nation state is also indicative of the growth of the power of private capital. Capital has also been able to exploit the structural asymmetry of power that exists within the global state system: between major powers; between major powers and small nation states; between transnationals and nation-states, especially small states; and the conditions that require transnationals and core states to maintain a cooperative relationship.

A discussion of the contending perspectives of instrumentalism and structuralism within the Marxist theory of the state will be avoided here because, while they are plausible descriptions, they fail to address the complexities of the state-capital relationship under contemporary capitalism. The state serves to reproduce the social order in which capital predominates. It plays a balancing role vis-à-vis all fractions of capital which compose the capitalist class. In its representation and mediation function, the state must consider the interests of non-capitalist classes and, in seeking to reproduce the capitalist order, incorporate and redefine the problematic of the exploited classes in ways that do not disrupt the integrity of the social order. In this way the state is neither above classes nor outside the class struggle (Therborn 1980a).

To what extent, if any, do transnational banks exercise political power in peripheral economies? It has already been suggested that they have acquired power partly as a result of the anarchy that exists in the international economy and the instability of the international state system. At the level of relations between private capital and the peripheral state, a much more concrete level of analysis is required. In the case of the Caribbean, external assistance strategies such as the one proposed by the Caribbean Group for Cooperation and Economic Development (CGCED) set up in 1978 (Watson 1979), and more recently in the Caribbean Basin Initiative (Watson 1982), suggest that finance capital in general, and transnational banks in particular, are becoming more 'politicised'. Both the above strategies were destined to produce 'divide and rule' effects in the Caribbean. The funding of activities under such US-sponsored projects has had to rely mainly on private bank capital, and recipient states have had to meet criteria established by private banks, bilateral and multilateral agencies, and the USA.

The details of the strategic and political objectives of the Caribbean Basin Initiative (CBI) have been provided elsewhere by the author (1982) and there is no need to repeat that discussion here. The decision to exclude Nicaragua, Grenada and Cuba from the CBI programme and to disqualify any state that nationalises foreign capital and refuses to adopt policies acceptable to Washington amounts to an act of political interference in the internal affairs of Caribbean Basin states. Clearly, then, governments such as those of Manley, Bishop and Burnham, which adopted radical nationalist, state-capitalist and/or socialist-oriented policies, have had to contend with the reactions of core states and core capital.

Transnationals, including transnational banks, are disposed to play political roles in these societies because they have a great deal at stake in terms of their dominant financial and economic interests. Valdez argues as follows:

As opposed to the nationalist tendencies expressed in the political processes . . ., transnational corporations represent an entirely opposite phenomenon: the internationalization of capitalist production and domestic markets. Transnational corporations therefore represent a structurally adverse position to that of the regimes confronting them. In economic and political terms, the ability of TNCs to adopt macro-decisions at a global level competes with that of the regimes, and thus makes them a political force. The domination by TNCs of some important markets in the functioning of the system, as well as their insertion in the dominant social structure allows them to exert effective political pressure within the host society. (Valdez 1978: 3)

Transnationals may therefore be said to exercise political power when they attempt to alter the behaviour of the state in a host country. The political support provided by core states to banks which face localisation, regulation or nationalisation by peripheral states represents a political act.[8] The ability of transnational banks to utilise their financial power to affect monetary and/or fiscal policy, the level of output, foreign exchange receipts, employment, and general financial and monetary stability are acts which have profound political implications and consequences, as shown by Jamaica's experience with the IMF and the transnational banks under the Manley Administration (Manley 1982: 165; US Senate Subcommittee on Foreign Economic Policy 1977: 62–65).

The power which the transnational banks exercise derives from their class position, their links to local capital in the periphery, their relationship with the core states, and their relationship to multinational agencies such as the IMF. The IMF is charged with guaranteeing financial stability of the capitalist world economy, pending the reconstitution of the system. The relationship between the transnational banks and the IMF is crucial. As Crough and the US Senate (Committee on Foreign Relations), Subcommittee on Foreign Economic Policy (1977: 62–65) point out:

> For the banks there would be certain advantages in having closer ties with the official lending institutions. Such linkage would enable them to keep their highly profitable lending to deficit countries at [acceptable levels] while the IMF and its member governments take on much of the risk involved in those new loans. In addition the IMF will have the burden of imposing economic reforms on individual countries to insure that the loans the banks have already made will be repaid. Thus, just as the oil producers have interposed the private banks as a buffer against the risks of recycling petrodollars, the banks would now be able to interpose the IMF between themselves and debtor countries. (Crough 1979: 203)

The IMF is, in short, the primary agency of supranational capital. Payer (1974) clarifies the nature of the relationship between the IMF and transnational capital as a whole. Measures to which peripheral economies such as Jamaica (1974–80) have resorted in order to cushion the effects of the world crisis are systematically dismantled under the Fund's scrutiny and supervision. The most common IMF prescriptions include the following: dismantling foreign exchange and import controls, devaluation, adoption of anti-inflationary policies in order to control money supply, reductions in government spending especially for social programmes, abolition of price controls, implementation of wage controls, and liberalisation of foreign investment codes. These measures are the bearers of profound political leverage as Hayter (1971) has demonstrated.

Transnational banks also exercise power at the level of ideology. The power of ideology is revealed in its class reinforcing dimensions (Therborn 1980b). The banks, by virtue of their dominant position in the financial and monetary sectors of these countries, are able to impose their rules of conduct as the norm. Bank employees throughout the banking system, including the local banking subsector, adopt values that are consistent with those of the transnational banking institutions. This includes values related to lending and the setting of criteria for credit-worthiness (Odle 1981: 149). The absence of strong and independent local banking and capital market institutions in the Caribbean also means that there are no competing or alternative monetary systems to rely on. The very nature of the economic systems means that all local banking norms and criteria are geared toward satisfying capitalist objectives. This reinforces the structural dominance exercised by the transnational banks. Client governments, and Guyana is a prime example, perceive themselves as being incapable of confronting the power of corporate finance. When Guyana nationalised bauxite and export agriculture, it did not touch the foreign commercial banks. The 'myth of resource insufficiency' feeds on the ideology of capital scarcity which is largely a product of the practice of exporting surplus value. The latter practice is partly a function of foreign domination and unequal exchange. The banks are powerful indeed, and the sources and forms of their power must therefore be sought within the capitalist world system which they dominate through their hegemony over the private capital market.

III. BANKS, STATE AND THE DEBT PROBLEM

The external debt problem of peripheral economies, including the form, extent and management of this debt, is another expression of the collapse of the Bretton Woods monetary and financial system: the disintegration of the post-war 'international monetary system based upon central bank preponderance and symmetrical balance of payments constraints' (Aglietta 1982: 20). The growth of the credit and debt economy around the private capital market means that the transnational banks (TNBs) are in the strategic position to influence the financial, monetary and general economic wellbeing of all countries.

The foreign exchange crisis of the periphery is the expression of the over-production crisis in the capitalist world economy. The synchronisation of the industrial cycle within the international division of labour has aggravated the crisis while the differential incidence of crisis in central and peripheral countries is partly determined by the transfer pricing mechanism of multinational enterprises. The growth of current account deficits in peripheral economies has become impossible to control by recourse to traditional adjustment mechanisms provided under Bretton Woods arrangements. That is why the peripheral economies have turned increasingly to the enormous surpluses created by the recycling of Eurodollars and petrodollars. The current account deficits of peripheral economies, which began to grow in the 1970s, have resulted from several factors that were aggravated but not caused by the oil crisis: retardation of structural transformation, inability to penetrate core markets for manufactured goods, location in the international division of labour, leakage of surplus due to dominance of foreign capital, change in demand patterns for peripheral exports, policies and practices of TNBs in the periphery, measures taken by core states and the IMF to correct foreign exchange and balance of payments problems, and the collapse of the Bretton Woods system.

By the time TNBs began to respond to the demand from peripheral economies for loans, the banks had already staged their 'coup' with the help of the United States authorities. The fact that traditional lending institutions were no longer in a position to meet the loan requirements of the periphery was confirmation that the Bretton Woods system was experiencing its 'death agony'. It was also evidence that the US position had finally won out: borrowing countries should turn to the private capital markets for necessary loans, and restrict the role of the state sector by adopting austerity measures which would ultimately reduce the need to borrow in the capital markets (Wachtel 1977: 15)

The adverse conditions experienced in the Caribbean during the last decade are not totally attributable to the international crisis although, as already observed, the synchronization of the circuits – commodity, finance and industry – of capital has led to the transfer of crisis effects with a vengeance. Steps taken by leaders such as Burnham (1972–78) and Manley (1974–80) to give neocolonial economies an independent economic basis had the effect of playing into the hands of imperialism. In fact, the radicalisation of populist rhetoric in these two countries, whether in the form of 'statism' or 'pseudo-socialism', was essentially an indication of America's weakening hegemony: in this context the Caribbean class struggles were calling into question the foundations of neocolonialism.

The expansion of the public sector through debt mortgaging increased neocolonialism's susceptibility to external pressure. Both Jamaica and Guyana experienced real production crises starting in the middle of the 1970s (Watson 1980; Manley 1982). High interest rates, inflation and foreign exchange shortages were compounded by decapitalisation in the industrial sector and illegal expatriation of foreign exchange. In 1977 alone, at least $300 million were illegally exported from Jamaica. Declining production and declining imports, when added to these problems, increased the propensity to borrow. One should not forget that there was also the ongoing problem of surplus leakage in the form of repatriated profits and capital transfers by the banks.

Tables 9 and 10 reveal the extent of private overseas direct investment in the Caribbean. Levels of investment also reflect the expansion of offshore banking in the Caribbean. Investment levels rose from US$3.3 billion at the end of 1967 to US$6.09 billion at the end of 1978, an increase of 82 percent. The figures for 1978 exclude the assets of offshore banking institutions held in Bermuda and the Bahamas. The extent of US direct investment in selected Caribbean countries is shown in Table 10. The level of investments grew from US$1.54 billion in 1971 to US$5.40 billion in 1981, an increase of 349 percent. US investment in the Caribbean grew much faster than total foreign investment in the region. This level and extent of foreign investment means that foreign capital now occupies a strategic position in areas such as mining (e.g. bauxite and petroleum), smelting and refining, agriculture, manufacturing, trade, public utilities, transport, commercial banking, tourism, insurance, offshore banking, etc.

Table 9   *Private Overseas Direct Investment (PODI) in Caribbean Countries 1967–1978 (year end, selected years) (million US$)*

Country	Total Private Overseas Investments[1]						
	1967 (1)	1971 (2)	1972 (3)	1973 (4)	1975 (5)	1976 (6)	1978 (7)
British West Indies[2]	1,109.7	1,650.0	1,800.0	2,230.0	5,650.0	610.0[3]	710.0
Dominican Republic	157.9	280.0	315.0	360.0	350.0	350.0	390.0
Guyana	189.0	135.0	135.0	140.0	180.0	190.0	210.0
Haiti	36.2	50.0	55.0	57.0	70.0	70.0	80.0
Jamaica	670.9	1,000.0	1,100.0	1,200.0	970.0	870.0	900.0
Netherlands Antilles	381.5	600.0	800.0	1,100.0	1,400.0	1,610.0	2,500.0
Surinam	99.6	120.0	120.0	130.0	330.0	—	—
Trinidad & Tobago	686.8	1,000.0	1,100.0	1,140.0	1,200.0	1,200.0	1,300.0
Total	3,331.6	4,835.0	5,425.0	6,357.0	10,150.0	4,900.0	6,090.0

1. PODI mainly in petroleum and related activities, mining and smelting, agriculture, manufacturing, trade, public utilities, transport, banking, tourism, other.
2. Includes Barbados, Trinidad, and Leewards Islands, Bahamas and Bermuda.
3. Excludes Bahamas and Bermuda which accounted for US$5340 offshore banking centres in 1976 and US$6360 in 1978.
Source: taken from Watson 1981: 42.

Guyana and Jamaica were the only two countries in this group to register a decline in the volume of direct investments. However, if one looks at external indebtedness (Table 11), it can be readily seen that these two countries experienced a massive expansion of their external debt: Guyana's public external debt rose from $123 million (1970) to $743 million (1980), an increase of 604 percent, while Jamaica's external public debt rose from $192 million (1970) to $1,697 million (1980), or by 883 percent. The Dominican Republic was another country with a major debt problem by the end of 1980. Correspondingly, service payments on

Table 10   *US Direct Investments in Selected Caribbean Countries 1971–1981 (year end) (million US$)*

Country	1971	1973	1975	1977	1979	1981
Bahamas	450	632	763	997	2,262	2,987
Barbados	12	20	19	26	32	31
Dominican Republic	155	181	222	243	251	373
Guyana	35	n.a.	22	3	7	10
Haiti	14	14	13	14	20	31
Jamaica	618	618	654	378	308	385
Trinidad & Tobago	262	433	656	971	930	932
West Indies (UK)				381	736	646

Sources: US Department of Commerce 1978: Tables 5–10; *US Direct Investment Abroad* (1983).

Table 11 *External Public Debt of Selected Caribbean Countries 1970–1980*

	(1) External Public Debt Outstanding (billions of dollars)			(2) Service Payments on External Public Debt			(3) External Public Debt Service % Value of Exported Goods and Services (Percentages)		
Country	1970	1975	1980	1970	1975	1980	1970	1975	1980
Bahamas	50	59	88	7	16	15	n.a.	2.7	1.3
Barbados	16	55	154	1	4	14	1.0	1.8	2.5
Dominican Republic	290	656	1,750	12	51	157	4.7	5.0	12.8
Guyana	123	399	743	5	16	69	3.4	4.3	16.9
Haiti	45	106	366	4	8	13	7.5	7.5	4.5
Jamaica	192	885	1,697	14	81	201	2.7	7.4	13.1
Trinidad & Tobago	122	217	723	15	27	80	4.4	2.2	3.1

Sources: Column 1: Inter-American Development Bank 1982b: Table 55; Column 2: Ibid: Table 60; Column 3: Ibid: Table 61.

the external debt (column 2) and the ratio of debt service to the value of exports of goods and services (column 3) rose significantly for all countries, but massively for these three countries in particular: debt service payments rose by 1,308 percent for Guyana, and 1,435 percent for Jamaica. For the Dominican Republic this represented an increase in debt service ratio of 8.1 percent over 1970; for Guyana it was an increase of 13.5 percent, and for Jamaica a 10.4 percent increase. The situation in Trinidad and Tobago is somewhat different largely because of petrodollars, though it shares all the characteristic features of underdevelopment.

For all these countries the banks are the major lenders and therefore the holders of their debt: a total of $5,521 million at the end of 1980. The level of US direct investments in these same countries, including off-shore bank assets, was US$5,405 million at the end of 1981. For these economies, the pressure of foreign capital is perhaps the central feature of their present reality and predicament. The extent of control by bank capital can be more readily appreciated by examining the structure of the external public debt. As can be seen from Table 12, by 1981 private banks had significantly increased their holdings of Caribbean countries' debt compared to the 1970 level. Multilateral assistance is still relatively important, and while bilateral aid has not disappeared, it has fallen off considerably, partly as a result of the expansion of bank lending.

Earlier it was argued that banks are disposed to lend mainly on a short-term basis. The picture of external indebtedness, seen in terms of loan maturities, suggests that short-term lending (up to five years) is on the increase (Table 13). For other maturities of above five years the data picture is incomplete and it is not possible to be conclusive. Odle (1981), Crough (1979), and several US congressional committees have discussed at length the problem of gaining access to data on banking activities. No doubt banks have much to hide from the public, including the governments of the countries in which they conduct business. Powerful institutions are generally reluctant to release information that could compromise their power. While the growth of consortia banking activities enables the transnational banks to spread their risks and diversify the structure of their liabilities, it also reflects the crisis proportions of the present international debt economy. The contradictory features are evident: the major banks now hold billions of dollars of periphery debt. The banks form consortia groups to protect themselves: if the borrowers default, all the participating banks will lose money. However, borrowers do not confront the banks alone; they also confront the power of the states in which the banks are based as well as the power of the multilateral agencies and, in particular, the IMF. This overall situation clearly demonstrates that the entire system is at stake and shares a common interest, best articulated by the IMF, in acting to avoid disaster.

Table 12   Structure of Selected Caribbean Countries' External Public Debt by Types of Credit 1970, 1981* (percentages)

Country	Official Multilateral		Official Bilateral		Suppliers		Private Banks		Other Creditors	
	1970	1981	1970	1981	1970	1981	1970	1981	1970	1981
Bahamas	—	9.7	38.0	3.1	18.0	0.4	44.0	86.4	—	0.4
Barbados	—	44.7	18.8	18.1	—	—	—	37.2	81.2	—
Dominican Republic	9.6	38.2	74.5	36.2	9.0	0.6	6.9	25.0	—	—
Guyana	10.6	35.4	76.4	41.4	—	2.8	—	11.8	13.0	8.6
Haiti	2.2	62.1	64.5	22.6	24.4	1.7	—	13.6	8.9	—
Jamaica	24.0	27.8	24.0	43.9	—	0.6	8.8	24.3	43.2	3.4
Trinidad & Tobago	34.4	10.2	20.5	25.8	3.3	—	12.3	59.0	29.5	5.0

*Based on total outstanding debt at year end.
Source: Inter-American Development Bank 1982: Table 13.

Table 13   *Structure of Selected Caribbean Countries' External Public Debt by Maturities, 1970, 1981* (percentages)*

Country	Up to 5 years		More than 5 and Up to 10 years		More than 10 and Up to 15 years		More than 15 Years	
	1970	1981	1970	1981	1970	1981	1970	1981
Bahamas	n.a.	38.5	n.a.	58.4	n.a.	2.7	n.a.	0.4
Barbados	n.a.	30.7	n.a.	36.0	n.a.	19.5	n.a.	13.8
Dominican Republic	20.6	38.6	23.1	19.2	18.8	13.1	37.5	29.1
Guyana	n.a.	32.9	n.a.	22.5	n.a.	16.2	n.a.	28.4
Haiti	n.a.	13.1	n.a.	15.4	n.a.	12.1	n.a.	58.4
Jamaica	40.0	41.9	27.1	23.5	20.0	13.7	12.9	20.9
Trinidad and Tobago	30.6	49.9	32.9	38.8	14.9	6.7	22.4	4.6

* Based on total outstanding debt at year end.
Source: Inter-American Development Bank, 1982: Table 14.

IV. CONCLUSION

Throughout this paper it has been argued in the tradition of Arrighi (1978) and Aglietta (1982), and to some extent of Baran and Sweezy (1968) and Sweezy (1972), that a theory of multinational (enterprise) capitalism is central to explaining the crisis of world capitalism and multinational banking. By means of an analysis of the role of banking policies and activities of transnational banks in the Caribbean, it has been concluded that TNBs contribute to perverse industrialisation in the region. This is not an original conclusion. Odle (1981), for example, has reached this same conclusion for the Third World as a whole.

It is not argued that TNBs create perverse industrialisation. To do so would be to adopt a methodologically misleading framework. The problem of underdevelopment is a problem of the forms and processes of capitalism in the periphery. The uneasy co-existence of pre-capitalist and capitalist modes of production in the social formations of peripheral capitalism reproduces crisis within unequal accumulation. It is the relationship of these social formations to the capitalist world economy as a whole which yields what is called underdevelopment. Clearly, no alternative path within imperialism is open to these economies. The development of the wage labour-capital relation in the periphery, which reflects the articulation/disarticulation of the law of value under those conditions, produces the context in which bank capital operates. The banks merely contribute to this process.

This study has shown that the basic lending strategies of the banks advance the crystallisation processes within the new international division of labour. It has also been shown that the forms of industrialisation pursued correspond to, and reflect, the concerns of core capital given the instability in the world economy at large and in the periphery in particular. The decline of private overseas direct investment in the periphery is an indicator of this instability. The growth of subcontracting, licensing, and the spread of world market factories are the present forms of industrial relocation. These are all adjustments to the accumulation crisis. The banks fund these activities because they have the available capital in the form of recycled petrodollars and Eurodollars. The banks are not interested in volatile and unstable regimes, in markets that are unpredictable, and in products that have no 'clout' in the world market. Their strategies in the periphery are, in part, a response to the protectionist and deflationary policies of the core economies.

The question of how TNBs exercise power in the Caribbean has been discussed in some detail. It was suggested that the banks exercise power in peripheral countries by virtue of their class position, location in the world financial system, and by virtue of their relationship to core states and the agencies of supranational capital. The banks are pivotally situated, particularly given the collapse of the Bretton Woods system. They dominate the international debt economy through their control of international capital markets, and the policies of the core states have contributed to this development. It has also been shown that the banks have become financially dominant in the Caribbean economies, making it difficult for there to be sound and effective monetary policy in these economies. Massive external debt, including private debt, must be guaranteed by the peripheral state. Financially, these economies are in a bind. But the banks also have a great deal at stake; they simply cannot allow the debt economy to collapse for that would mean their own ruin.

The Europeans and Japanese are looking to the United States to lead the way towards world economic recovery, but the United States is acting to promote its own national interests. The Caribbean Basin Initiative (CBI), though presented as the US economic recovery programme for the Caribbean, is essentially a military-strategic programme for overcoming the challenges to America's weakened hegemony in the region: as such it is a reflection of the strategy of 'resurgent America' on the move. This point is made precisely because the Caribbean has also been looking to American leadership and capital to provide opportunities for economic recovery. Mr Seaga's attempt to resuscitate the discredited Puerto Rican model in Jamaica seems destined to fail because there is no impetus for its potential success outside of the realities that exist in the international economic, financial, monetary and credit spheres.

One may conclude that the banks will continue to play a dominant role and that current patterns of 'perverse' industrialisation will continue. Whether the Reagan Administration succeeds in transforming Jamaica and Barbados into show pieces depends not so much upon industrialisation as on the momentum of class struggles in the region and the geopolitical and strategic-military objectives of the US in the area. Barring revolutionary transformation, it is likely that, unless a new world political authority emerges capable of providing a new set of institutional mechanisms for directing the world capitalist economy, very little improvement will occur.

NOTES

1. The data base for this study includes countries within the English-speaking Caribbean, Haiti and the Dominican Republic. The analysis will be developed around selected English-speaking countries.
2. For details on the performance of the Caribbean economy between 1960 and 1979, including GDP, trade, capital flows, external debt etc., see Watson 1981: esp. 24–52.
3. See Watson 1975. A discussion of some of the philosophical and theoretical problems associated with monetarism is provided as they bear upon the Commonwealth Caribbean.
4. The relationship of Eurodollars and petrodollars to offshore banking has been discussed and analysed by a number of researchers. See especially Odle 1981, Crough 1979,

Gorostiaga 1978, Bank for International Settlements' Annual Reports for various years, US Congress, Joint Economic Committee 1971, and Wachtel 1977.

5. Data on average working hours and hourly wages in manufacturing (1974–76) in selected Caribbean countries, including Barbados, Dominican Republic, Netherlands Antilles, Haiti, Jamaica, St Lucia, and Trinidad and Tobago, are provided in Watson (1981: 62) and Frobel, Heinrichs & Kreye (1980: 351–54).

6. The question of appropriate technology in economies characterised by backward capitalism requires closer attention and study. In such economies merchant and agrarian capital tend to predominate in the domestic sector of the economy. These forms of capital tend to rely on the application of backward pre-industrial techniques of production which are incapable of reproducing labour power, value and capital accumulation on an expanded scale. This is the result of the fact that modern industry has neither developed nor captured the home market. Production based upon 'absolute surplus value' predominates. When modern technology based upon 'relative surplus value' enters these economies it produces contradictions between the pre-industrial and the industrial sectors of the economy. The idea of the 'modern technology bias' tends to obscure this reality. Modern capital and modern industry relies on relative surplus value in order to reproduce labour power, value and capital consistent with the needs of capital accumulation. Merchant capital and pre-industrial agrarian capital obstruct this necessary rationalising process of modern capitalism.

7. A study conducted by the US Tariff Commission on productivity in US-owned firms that produce in Caribbean-based world market factories (WMFs) has concluded that Caribbean workers in the garment industry tend to be as productive as comparable US workers and that in other industries such as electronics, foreign workers work harder and longer. They are said to be more productive than US workers in firms associated with the production of toys, sports goods, scientific instruments, etc. See Frobel, Heinrichs & Kreye 1980: 360.

8. Steps to reduce the perverse effects of transnational bank dominance in the Caribbean were taken by Jamaica in 1973. Manley attempted to regulate the banks in order to strengthen the position of local banks and to increase the local regulation of banking activities. In Guyana and Trinidad & Tobago measures taken included preventing TNBs from lending to other TNBs in order to increase the volume of bank assets available to local borrowers. Attempts to increase the scope of local banking were used in Guyana, Trinidad & Tobago, Jamaica and Dominica. The process of localisation went furthest in Trinidad & Tobago and Jamaica. TNBs did not find these measures acceptable and took a variety of measures to pre-empt any restructuring of their profit-making activity. The banks were able to combat localisation, nationalisation and other measures. In the end they found that they could reduce their overall risk while at the same time increasing their profits. They are adept at transforming disadvantages into assets. See Odle (1981) and Watson (1975: 597–602).

BIBLIOGRAPHY

Books and Articles

Acheson, Dean (1966): 'Economic Policy and the ITO Charter' in David Baldwin (ed.): *Foreign Aid and American Foreign Policy: A Documentary Analysis* (New York: Praeger).

Aglietta, Michel (1982): 'World Capitalism in the Eighties', *New Left Review*, 136, November-December.

Amin, Samir (1976): *Unequal Development* (New York: Monthly Review Press).

Arrighi, Giovanni (1978): *The Geometry of Imperialism: The Limits of Hobson's Paradigm* (London: New Left Books).

—— (1982): 'A Crisis of Hegemony' in Samir Amin, Giovanni Arrighi, Andre Gunder Frank & Immanuel Wallerstein: *Dynamics of Global Crisis* (New York: Monthly Review Press).

Baldwin, David (1966): *Economic Development and American Foreign Policy* (Chicago: University of Chicago Press).

Baran, Paul & Paul Sweezy (1968): *Monopoly Capital* (New York: Monthly Review Press).

Bourne, Compton (1974): 'The Political Economy of Indigenous Commercial Banking in Guyana', *Social and Economic Studies* (March).

Chick, Victoria (1979): 'Transnational Corporations and the Evolution of the International Monetary System' in G.J. Crough: *Transnational Banking and the World Economy* (Sidney: University of Sidney Press).

Crough, G.J. (1979): *Transnational Banking and the World Economy* (Sidney: University of Sidney Press).

Davis, Mike (1978): '"Fordism" in Crisis: A Review of Michel Aglietta's *Regulation et Crisis: L'experience des Etats-Unis'*, *Review*, 2, 2 (Fall).

Dixon, Marlene (1983): 'The Trojan Horse: Transnational Banks and The International Debt Crisis', *Our Socialism* 1, 3 (May).

Fitch, R. & M. Oppenheimer (1971): 'Who Rules the Corporations', *Socialist Revolution*, 1, 4–6.

Frobel, F., J. Heinrichs & O. Kreye (1978): 'Export-Oriented Industrialization of Underdeveloped Countries', *Monthly Review*, 30, 6 (November).

—— (1980): *The New International Division of Labour* (New York: Cambridge University Press).

Girvan, N. (1971): *Foreign Capital and Economic Underdevelopment in Jamaica* (Mona: Institute of Social and Economic Research, University of the West Indies).

—— (1976): *The Impact of Multinational Enterprises on Employment and Income in Jamaica* (Preliminary Report; Caribbean Center for Corporate Research, Mona, Jamaica. Prepared for the ILO World Employment Programme Research Working Papers.

Gorostiaga, Xabier (1978): *Los Centros Financieros Internacionales en Los Paises Subdesarrollados* (Mexico City: Instituto Latino-Americano de Estudios Transnacionales [ILET]).

Griffith, Winston (1983): 'Post World War II Industrial Development in the Commonwealth Caribbean: Some Neglected Issues' (Paper Presented at the Caribbean Studies Association Meeting in Santo Domingo, Dominican Republic, 25–28 May).

Hayter, Teresa (1971): *Aid as Imperialism* (Harmondsworth: Penguin Books).

Hilferding, Rudolph (1923): *Finance Capital – The Latest Phase of Capitalism* (Vienna: Voorwarts).

Javits, Benjamin (1950): *Peace by Investment* (New York: Funk and Wagnalls).

Jefferson, Owen (1972): *The Postwar Economic Development of Jamaica* (Mona: Institute for Social and Economic Research, University of the West Indies).

Lenin, Vladimir (1916): *Imperialism: The Highest Stage of Capitalism* (Moscow: Progress Publishers, 1975).

Lipietz, Alain (1982): 'Towards Global Fordism?', *New Left Review* (March-April).

Mandel, Ernest (1978): *The Second Slump* (London: New Left Books).

Manley, Michael (1982): *Jamaica: Struggle in the Periphery* (London: Third World Media Limited in Association with Writers and Readers Publishing Cooperative Society Ltd).

McClean, Wendell (1971): *Money and Banking in the East Caribbean Currency Area* (Unpublished M.Sc. Thesis. University of the West Indies).

Miller, Nugent (1971): *Organization and Structure of Commercial Banking in Jamaica* (Mona: Institute of Social and Economic Research. University of the West Indies).

Muller, R. & R. Cohen (1977): 'US Banking and Economic Instability: A Systematic Dilemma', *Executive*, 3, 2 (Winter).

Odle, Maurice (1981): *Multinational Banks and Underdevelopment* (New York: Pergamon Press).

Payer, Cheryl (1974): *The Debt Trap: The IMF and the Third World* (New York: Monthly Review Press).

Sweezy, Paul (1972): 'The Resurgence of Finance Capital', *Socialist Revolution*, 2, 8 (March–April).

Therborn, Goran (1980a): *What Does the Ruling Class Do When It Rules?* (London: Verso Books).

—— (1980b): *The Ideology of Power and the Power of Ideology* (London: Verso Books).

Thomas, Clive (1965): *Monetary and Financial Arrangements in a Dependent Monetary Economy. A Study of British Guyana. 1945–1962* (Mona: Institute of Social and Economic Research, University of the West Indies).

—— (1972): *The Structure, Performance and Prospects of Central Banking in the Caribbean* (Mona: Institute of Social and Economic Research, University of the West Indies).

Valdez, Juan (1978): *Political Regimes and Transnational Corporation in Conflict: Case Studies on Latin America and the Caribbean* (Mexico City: Instituto Latinoamerica de Estudios Transnacionales).

Wachtel, H.M. (1977): *The New Gnomes: Multinational Banks in the Third World* (Washington DC: Transnational Institute, Institute for Policy Studies).

Watson, Hillbourne (1975): *The Political Economy of Foreign Investment in the Commonwealth Caribbean Since World War II* (Unpublished Ph.D. Dissertation, Howard University, Washington DC).

—— (1979): 'External Resources in the Financing of Development in the Caribbean: Underdevelopment and World Accumulation' (Paper presented to the Panel on Financing of Development in Latin America at the Annual Meeting of the American Society for Public Administration. Baltimore, April 2–5).

—— (1980): 'Metropolitan Influence on Caribbean State Systems and Responses of Selected Caribbean States' (Paper presented at the Caribbean Studies Association Meeting, Curacao, Netherlands Antilles, May 25–28).

—— (1981): 'International Migration and Unequal Exchange: The United States and the West Indies' (Paper presented at the Symposium on International Relations and International Migration sponsored by the Instituto de Investigaciones Sociales, National Autonomous University of Mexico, Mexico City, October 26–30).

—— (1982): 'The Caribbean Basin Initiative: Consolidating American Hegemony', *TransAfrica Forum*, 1, 2 (Fall).

Official Publications

Bank for International Settlements (1977): *Forty-seventh Annual Report for the Year 1976–77* (Basle: Switzerland; see also Reports for 1977–78 through 1978–79).

Central Bank of Barbados (1980): *Statistical Digest* (Bridgetown, Barbados).

Central Bank of Trinidad and Tobago (1974–1981): *Statistical Digest* (Various Issues; Port of Spain, Trinidad and Tobago).

East Caribbean Currency Authority (1978, 1979): *Economic and Financial Review,* 9, 1 (June); 9, 4 (March).

Government of Jamaica, Department of Statistics (1979): *Monetary Statistics, 1978* (Kingston).

National Planning Agency (1981): *Economic and Social Survey of Jamaica. January–June 1981* (Kingston).

Inter-American Development Bank (1982a): *Annual Report* (Washington DC).

—— (1982b): *Economic and Social Progress in Latin America. The External Sector 1982* (Washington DC).

United States Department of Commerce, Bureau of Economic Analysis (1978): *Selected Data on U.S. Direct Investments Abroad 1966–76* (Washington DC).

—— (1983): *U.S. Direct Investment Position Abroad 1977–1981* (Washington DC).

United States Congress, Joint Economic Committee (1976): *Some Questions and Brief Answers About the Eurodollar Market* (Washington DC: United States Government Printing Office).

——, House of Representatives Committee on Banking Currency and Housing (1976): *Financial Institutions and the Nation's Economy*, Book II, Part 4 (Washington DC: United States Government Printing Office; FINE Report).

——, Senate Committee on Banking, Housing, Urban Affairs, Sub-Committee on International Finance (1977): *International Debt* (Washington DC: United States Government Printing Office).

——, Senate Committee on Foreign Relations, Sub-Committee on Multinational Corpora-
tions (1975): *Multinational Corporations in the Dollar Devaluation Crisis. Report on a
Questionnaire* (Washington DC: United States Government Printing Office).
——, Senate Committee on Foreign Relations, Sub-Committee on Foreign Economic Policy
(1977): *International Debt, The Banks and U.S. Foreign Policy* (Washington DC: United
States Government Printing Office).

X

AGRARIAN TRANSFORMATION AND FOOD SECURITY IN THE CARIBBEAN BASIN

Solon Barraclough and Peter Marchetti

I. INTRODUCTION

Although the Caribbean region has the highest levels of malnutrition of any major region of Latin America, agrarian transformation and food security are neither featured in the US Caribbean Initiative nor given prominence during United Nations or *Contadora* Group discussions. Increasing violence in Central America and the broader Caribbean Basin[1] is ascribed, *inter alia*, to the widespread poverty and social injustice long endured by the region's people. Yet there exists little understanding that a crucial aspect of that poverty and social injustice is food insecurity and malnutrition associated with archaic and lopsided land tenure systems, stagnant agricultural production for home markets, and food distribution systems that increasingly provide entitlements to food only to those with incomes to purchase it.

Section II of this paper describes the main characteristics of the Caribbean Basin and Central American food systems. Section III examines a series of dilemmas which arise amidst revolutionary efforts to bring about rapid agrarian transformation and establish a food system which would increase national food security. Reflections are primarily derived from recent experiences in Nicaragua. It is argued that only a significant change in the socioeconomic power structures of these societies can open the way for an agrarian transformation leading to food security for all.

What exactly is meant by agrarian transformation and food security? In its broadest sense, agrarian transformation may be defined as far-reaching qualitative and quantitative changes in the social relations, market structures and technologies affecting agriculture.[2] It involves a sweeping revision of the food system, i.e. of the whole complex of relationships determining the production, marketing, processing, distribution, consumption, import and export of food.

A food system is a much more extensive sub-system than agricultural production, and in many poor agrarian societies covers almost the entire social system. Understanding how it works leads to a better comprehension of the dynamics of the overall social structure, including existing and potential mechanisms for economic accumulation. A food system meets or fails to meet two basic societal needs by, firstly, providing a level of food security or insecurity as the case may be; and second, by serving as a kind of trampoline, both in terms of supply of food (the basic consumer or wage good) and demand (for non-food products and services), for the development of each country or region's industrial system.

Food security signifies an assured supply of food sufficient in quality and quantity to meet the nutritional needs of all.[3] In the opinion of the authors, any society (even after having undergone agrarian transformation) which fails to provide food security for all its members is inherently unstable. Thus, a national development strategy should attach high priority to a food system that would permit simultaneous achievement of both national and individual food security.

Alejandro Schejtman (1983) has indicated five essential attributes of a food system offering food security. These are:

1. *Sufficiency*, meaning the system's capacity to generate a sufficient internal food supply (via national production or imports) to meet expanding demand and the basic food needs of all.[4]
2. *Reliability*, signifying control of food system mechanisms, so that seasonal and cyclical production fluctuations, especially of staple food crops, are minimised; increasing the reliability and lessening the importance of seasonal (non-irrigated) crops; eliminating the often erratic effects of food subsidies; and improving transport storage, distribution, etc.
3. *Autonomy or self-determination* of a food system, requiring maximum reduction of its vulnerability to the uncertainties of the international market place (hence rendering it more dependable). But autonomy in no way signifies autarky or complete self-sufficiency. On the contrary, specialisation (at the local level) and regional trade should be stimulated. The preconditions for specialisation and comparative advantage, however, cannot be dictated solely by market considerations.[5]
4. *Long-term stability*, meaning a food system's ability to provide sufficiency, reliability and autonomy without destroying the base of agriculture: the eco-system. Agricultural modernisation (with the US serving as a model) is, in terms of long-term stability, a chimera. It has been estimated that, in the US, over nine calories of fossil energy are needed to produce one calorie of food. Although the corresponding ratio for France, estimated at 5.5 to 1, is lower, world fossil

energy resources would not permit widespread imitation of either model (Steinhart & Steinhart 1974).

5. *Equity*, which is the final and perhaps most important attribute of a food system offering acceptable levels of nutritional security. Though difficult to define, it involves, as a minimum, access to sufficient food by all social groups and individuals. This implies that the food system is shaped in part by the interests of the majority. In poor countries, it also means curbing the luxury consumption that could sabotage meeting the first four goals (see UNRISD 1979: 13)

II. THE CHARACTER OF FOOD SYSTEMS IN THE CARIBBEAN BASIN

In a real sense, there is no such thing as a regional food system in the Caribbean Basin, a key factor that any analysis of its national food systems must take into account. The salient characteristic of the region's different food systems is their increasing interaction with the economies of developed industrial countries, combined with particularly low levels of national and regional market integration. It is as if the nations of the Caribbean Basin were sets of puppets each independently connected to the developed world (especially the US).[6] Thus, any study of regional food security should start with an analysis of the food system in each individual country.

The Central Contradiction of Caribbean Basin Food Systems

The attunement of these food systems to the outside world has been modified by three decades of sweeping agrarian transformation associated with the rapid development of export-oriented, agriculture-based economies.

External demand from the world market is the motor which drives this type of economy. Within present frameworks, however, this demand enters into systematic conflict with a relatively stagnant smallholder economy producing mainly for the home market. Land tenure arrangements, usurious credit systems, exploitative marketing structures, low levels of investment in infrastructure and technical assistance, and pricing policies all work against the smallholder and, together, ensure that peasant producers cannot accumulate. As a result impoverished families are forced to sell their labour cheaply to the agro-export entrepreneurs, who usually manage to reap stable profits despite fluctuating international commodity prices and ever-costlier imported inputs. With investment potential blocked for the vast majority of smallholders but stimulated for the export sector, overall accumulation has been highly unstable, depending as it does on the cyclical nature of inter-

Table 1   *Latin America: Estimated Arable and Irrigable Lands 1970–75 (millions of hectares)*

Countries	A Cultivated land	B Arable land	C % Arable land cultivated	D Irrigable land	E D as % of B
Argentina	33.9	73.9	46	3.9	5
Brazil	61.9	308.6	20	4.2	1
Mexico	27.2	37.7	72	6.4	17
Andean Pact Nations	24.8	106.7	23	9.6	9
Other Countries*	16.7	35.5	47	3.6	10
Central America	5.3	13.5	39	2.7	20
Latin America	169.8	575.9	29	30.4	5

* Includes Caribbean
Source: IDB (1982: 32–33)

national prices within the context of externally-determined terms of trade.

Levels of malnutrition associated with this development model, as noted above, are among the highest in Latin America. Although the region possesses some of the continent's best land and water resources (see Table 1), Central America and the Caribbean were the only parts of Latin America where rates of population increase between 1950 and 1975 were estimated to have outstripped rates of growth in home-market agriculture (Leon 1981). Although the region has a greater irrigation potential (20 percent of its arable land) than anywhere else in Latin America, it has lagged significantly behind Argentina, Mexico and other countries in percentage of arable land actually under cultivation. Moreover, per capita arable land resources in Central America stand at approximately 2.0 hectares. This is higher than in most European countries and much higher than in China (including Taiwan) with 0.4 hectares per capita, South Korea with 0.6 hectares, and Japan with 0.7 hectares. Yet these latter countries have eliminated the malnutrition still prevalent in the Caribbean Basin. Abundant resources and systematic restriction of agricultural production for domestic consumption provide the backdrop for the type of repressive political regime that characterises the region.

Regional Food Systems' Linkages with Industry and Other Economic Sectors

The positive impact of boom years on the agro-export business, import substitution programmes, and past and present regional integration efforts, have been nullified by a series of economic problems closely associated with the stagnation of home-market agriculture. Two of these problems are of special importance.

Lack of purchasing power

Partly because the mass of peasants are prevented from developing national agriculture and livestock production they are largely excluded, as consumers, from the internal market which has remained extremely narrow. Over half the industrial plant of Central America stood idle in the mid-1970s for lack of effective demand. This was not a problem of scarcity of capital but rather of inadequate purchasing power in home markets.

Lack of integration of agriculture with rest of economy

Export agriculture's integration with industry, construction and other sectors of the economy is weak, which prevents self-reinforcing multiplier effects. Moreover, the attempt to graft an import substitution strategy on to the agro-export model (a full three decades after such strategies had been initiated throughout the rest of Latin America) only increased the economy's outward orientation. Table 2 shows growth rates for the various sectors of the Central American economy during the 1960s, the decade of attempted import substitution. Whereas import substitution occurred in Argentina, Brazil and Chile during a period of recession in the metropolitan economies, in Central America it took place at a time of growth and increasing penetration of the periphery by the metropole.

Table 2   *Central America: Cumulative Growth Rates by Sector 1960–1970*

Sector	Rate of Growth %
Metal and mechanical industry	17.2
Intermediate industry	15.6
Agro-industry	8.5
Agriculture	4.4

Source: IDB (n.d.).

Investments in intermediate industry and metal-finishing, 75 percent of the inputs of which were imported, merely served to link Central America's productive structure more closely to developed industrial economies rather than to increase inter-sectoral links. Moreover, an analysis of net foreign exchange earned by the various sectors reveals that agriculture and agro-industry were far more efficient than the newly-created intermediate industries (which, in effect, tend to function more as part of commerce than of industry because of the small proportion of value added). Nevertheless, agro-industry, which accounted for 76 per cent of Central America's industrial structure, remained primarily concentrated in the rudimentary elaboration of coffee, sugar and meat. Cotton, for instance, was exported raw rather than in the form of thread; sugar and cocoa likewise, instead of as chocolate or candies. The outward-orientation of industry and agro-industry was matched by patterns in the agricultural sector, where growth occurred overwhelmingly in the modernising agro-export sector, which depends heavily on imported inputs and tends to generate less employment than home-market agriculture.

Regional Food Dependence

In the Central American and Caribbean region as a whole, an ever-deepening reliance on food imports[7] has increased the drain of scarce foreign exchange. Total food system imports (including inputs of fertilisers, machinery, etc.) for the region's principal countries, excluding Cuba, jumped from $306 million in 1960 to about $3,434 million in 1980 in current dollars (from 260 million to about 568 million in 1970 dollars). Table 3 gives a breakdown in current dollars for the 1960-1980 period and Table 3a in constant (1970) dollars, for selected countries. Increasing dependence on cereals (essential to the diet of the poor) is shown in Table 4. The Caribbean countries, which have traditionally suffered from grain dependence, imported 58 percent of their cereals in 1970; this rose to 69 percent in 1980. The corresponding increase for the Central American countries was from 15 percent to 23 percent.

Table 5 indicates one of the possible complementary trade links within the Caribbean Basin. Among cereal imports wheat plays a principal role, as can be seen from Table 6. In some countries, the growing dominance of wheat occurred gradually; in others it was abruptly introduced. In Nicaragua, for instance, mills were burned down during the Somoza period in order to pave the way for increased US imports. Television and radio stations for years extolled the merits of bread over maize *tortillas*. Yet the region is poorly suited for wheat production and, moreover, the nutritional value of mass-produced bread (which now dominates much of the region) is far lower than that of maize tortillas.

Table 7 shows imports of another important food staple, pulses. Other main food imports (poultry, eggs, meat and milk) are detailed respectively in Tables 8, 9, 10 and 11. Table 12 lists trade in miscellaneous foods and Table 13 shows animal feed imports. All cover the period 1965–1980.

Table 3   Food Systems Imports Selected Central American and Caribbean Countries 1960–1980 (millions of current US$)

Countries	1960 Food* & Ag. Prod.	1960 Agric.** Inputs + Forestry Fishery	1960 Total Food System	1970 Food & Ag. Prod.	1970 Agric. Inputs + Forestry Fishery	1970 Total Food System	1978 Food & Ag. Prod.	1978 Agric. Inputs + Forestry Fishery	1978 Total Food System	1980 Food & Ag. Prod.	1980 Agric. Inputs + Forestry Fishery	1980 Total Food System
Guatemala	31.4	11.8	43.2	32.1	24.4	56.5	120.1	106.2	226.3	128.5	184.6	313.1
El Salvador	19.1	2.6	21.7	30.8	43.6	74.4	119.9	103.8	223.7	172.7	78.6	251.3
Honduras	9.0	0.4	9.4	25.7	27.6	53.3	78.8	86.9	165.7	139.4	87.3	226.7
Nicaragua	5.7	1.0	6.7	19.9	14.5	34.4	60.5	65.0	125.5	144.8	91.7	236.5
Costa Rica	14.6	0.7	15.3	35.0	39.3	74.3	91.4	96.4	187.8	146.1	167.4	313.5
Panama	15.4	0.7	16.1	28.3	27.6	55.9	72.9	61.3	134.2	120.0	69.7	189.7
Sub total	95.2	17.2	112.4	171.8	177.0	348.8	543.6	519.6	1063.2	851.5	679.3	1530.8
Jamaica	44.0	9.9	53.9	84.8	40.5	125.3	212.8	77.0	289.8	226.2	74.0	300.2
Dominican Republic	7.9	0.9	8.8	36.0	26.9	62.9	134.1	125.7	259.8	217.1	148.8	365.9
Cuba							840.7	401.4	1242.1	1093.2	383.8	1477.0
Haiti	45.3	6.3	51.6	13.1	1.4	14.5	63.2	11.3	74.5	118.7	11.8	130.5
Trinidad & Tobago	20.6	0.7	21.3	60.0	17.9	77.9	212.8	77.0	289.8	346.2	132.2	478.5
Bahamas	14.9	2.0	16.9	63.0	13.1	76.1	58.6	8.2	66.8	99.4	8.9	108.3
Barbados	18.3	2.4	20.7	27.3	7.9	35.2	68.9	23.3	92.2	83.6	31.3	114.9
Guadalupe	17.9	2.5	20.4	29.0	8.0	37.0	103.5	19.0	122.5	171.9	28.0	199.9
Martinique				31.6	10.6	42.2	113.8	28.4	142.2	165.6	39.9	205.5
Sub total	168.9	24.7	193.6	344.8	126.3	471.1	967.7 (1808.4)	369.9 (771.3)	1337.6 (2579.7)	1428.7 (2521.9)	475.0 (858.8)	1903.7 (3380.7)
Total	264.1	41.9	306.0	516.6	303.3	819.9	1511.3 (2352.0)	889.5 (1290.9)	2400.8 (3642.9)	2280.2 (3373.4)	1154.3 (1538.1)	3434.5 (4911.5)

* Food & other Agricultural Products.

** Agricultural Inputs and machinery, fish and forest products.

N.B. Sub-total and total figures for 1978 and 1980 do not include Cuba in order to keep the figures comparable with previous years. The sub-total and total including Cuba are given in brackets.

Source: FAO (1971, 1980), FAO (1971a, 1981a).

Table 3a *Food Systems Imports Selected Central American and Caribbean Countries 1960–1980 (millions of constant 1970 US$)*

Countries	1960 Food* & Ag. Prod.	1960 Agric.** Inputs + Forestry Fishery	1960 Total Food System	1970 Food & Ag. Prod.	1970 Agric. Inputs + Forestry Fishery	1970 Total Food System	1978 Food & Ag. Prod.	1978 Agric. Inputs + Forestry Fishery	1978 Total Food System	1980 Food & Ag. Prod.	1980 Agric. Inputs + Forestry Fishery	1980 Total Food System
Guatemala	33.8	12.7	46.5	32.1	24.4	56.5	65.9	58.4	124.3	63.6	91.4	155.0
El Salvador	19.9	2.7	22.6	30.8	43.6	74.4	68.9	59.7	128.6	89.9	40.9	130.8
Honduras	12.0	0.5	12.5	25.7	27.6	53.3	53.6	59.1	112.7	87.6	54.9	142.5
Nicaragua	6.9	1.1	8.0	19.9	14.5	34.4	31.0	33.3	64.3	66.1	41.8	107.9
Costa Rica	15.9	0.8	16.7	35.0	39.3	74.3	47.6	50.2	97.8	68.2	78.2	146.4
Panama	17.9	0.8	18.7	28.3	27.6	55.9	42.9	36.0	78.9	63.8	37.1	100.9
Sub total	106.4	18.6	125.0	171.8	177.0	348.8	309.9	296.7	606.6	439.2	344.3	783.5
Jamaica	56.4	12.7	69.1	84.8	40.5	125.3	74.3	30.2	104.5	75.4	24.6	100.0
Dominican Republic	10.0	1.1	11.1	36.0	26.9	62.9	75.3	70.6	145.9	109.6	75.1	184.7
Cuba	—	—	—	—	—	—	486.0	232.0	718.0	617.6	216.8	834.4
Haiti	—	—	—	13.1	1.4	14.5	25.3	4.5	29.8	41.2	4.1	45.3
Trinidad & Tobago	48.7	6.7	55.4	60.0	17.9	77.9	117.6	42.5	160.1	172.2	65.8	238.0
Sub total	115.1	20.5	135.6	193.9	86.7	280.6	778.5	379.8	1158.3	1016.0	386.4	1402.4
Total	221.5	39.1	260.6	365.7	263.7	629.4	1088.4	676.5	1764.9	1455.2	730.7	2185.9

* Food and other Agricultural Products.
** Agricultural Inputs and Machinery, Forest and Fish Products.
Sources: FAO (1971, 1980), FAO (1971a, 1980a).

Table 4 Net Cereal Imports Central American and Caribbean Countries 1965–1980 ('000 metric tons)

	1965		1970		1978		1980	
	Net cereal imports	% apparent consumption*	Net cereal imports	% apparent consumption	Net cereal imports	% apparent consumption	Net cereal imports	% apparent consumption
Central America	290	14.6	433	14.9	760	18.8	957	22.9
Caribbean	2026	69.5	1724	57.8	2881	67.6	3201	68.5
Total Region	2316	42.1	2157	36.6	3641	43.9	4158	47.0

* Apparent consumption = production + net imports.
Source: FAO (1971, 1980), FAO (1971a, 1980a).

Table 5 *Cereal Production and Apparent Consumption Selected Central American and Caribbean Countries 1965–1980 ('000 metric tons)*

Countries	Cereal Production				Net Cereal Imports				Imports as % of Apparent Consumption			
	1965	1970	1978	1980	1965	1970	1978	1980	1965	1970	1978	1980
Guatemala	721	810	1058	1186	93	113	204	247	11.4	12.2	16.1	17.2
El Salvador	325	554	720	727	68	61	224	105	17.3	9.9	23.7	12.2
Honduras	397	401	526	410	—	59	115	159	—	12.8	17.9	27.9
Nicaragua	222	394	403	360	16	46	92	118	6.7	10.5	18.5	24.7
Costa Rica	132	136	312	295	74	110	79	143	35.9	44.7	20.2	27.8
Panama	201	183	227	219	39	44	46	108	16.3	19.4	15.4	33.5
Sub total	1998	2478	3246	3197	290	433	760	957	12.7	14.9	18.8	22.9
Jamaica	8	5	10	6	199	285	428	478	96.1	98.3	97.7	98.7
Dominican Republic	112	255	413	482	60	53	263	364	34.9	17.2	38.9	43.0
Cuba	342	456	554	594	1549	1155	1871	1907	81.9	71.7	77.2	76.7
Grenada	—	—	1	1	8	9	6	5	100.0	96.6	85.7	83.3
Haiti	455	530	375	376	61	61	109	177	11.8	10.3	22.5	32.0
Trinidad & Tobago	13	12	26	31	149	161	204	236	92.0	93.1	88.6	78.4
Sub total	930	1258	1379	1490	2026	1724	2881	3201	68.5	57.8	67.6	68.5

Sources: FAO (1971, 1980), FAO (1971a, 1980a).

Table 6 *Net Wheat Imports* Selected Central American and Caribbean Countries 1965–1981 (metric tons)*

Countries	1965		1970		1978		1980		1981	
	Net Wheat imports	% apparent consumption	Net Wheat imports	% apparent consumption	Net Wheat imports	% apparent consumption	Net Wheat imports	% apparent consumption	Net Wheat imports	% apparent consumption
Guatemala	84,900	72.6	88,615	74.1	109 986	64.7	108,020	63.4	107,917	62.8
El Salvador	49,800	100.0	60,407	100.0	116 148	100.0	116,497	100.0	106,440	100.0
Honduras	32,800	97.0	47,665	99.4	63 275	99.5	71,010	100.0	78,403	100.0
Nicaragua	35,200	100.0	37,548	100.0	56 162	100.0	52,361	100.0	37,056	100.0
Costa Rica	60,700	100.0	68,716	100.0	85 198	100.0	103,851	100.0	96,056	100.0
Panama	35,000	100.0	42,298	100.0	57 296	100.0	47,260	100.0	62,035	100.0
Sub total	298,400	89.9	345,249	91.5	488 065	88.9	498,999	90.7	487,907	88.2
Jamaica	142,400	100.0	175,923	100.0	169 818	100.0	201,967	100.0	187,023	100.0
Dominican Republic	55,400	100.0	78,834	100.0	159 612	100.0	158,349	100.0	197,710	100.0
Cuba	1054,100	100.0	732,370	100.0	1123 679	100.0	1228,175	100.0	1244,140	100.0
Grenada	6,800	100.0	7,640	100.0	5 556	100.0	1,342	100.0	1,940	100.0
Haiti	61,100	100.0	61,341	100.0	88 419	100.0	149,496	100.0	198,919	100.0
Trinidad & Tobago	92,100	100.0	85,984	100.0	105 838	100.0	120,954	100.0	103,545	100.0
Sub total	1411,900	100.0	1142,092	100.0	1652 922	100.0	1860,283	100.0	1933,277	100.0
Total	1710,300	98.1	1487,341	97.9	2140 987	97.2	2359,282	97.9	2421,184	97.4

* Wheat and wheat flour equivalent.
Sources: FAO (1971, 1972, 1980, 1981), FAO (1971a, 1972a, 1980a, 1981a).

Table 7 Net Pulse Imports Selected Central American and Caribbean Countries. 1965–1981 (metric tons)

Countries	1965 Net Pulse imports	1965 % apparent consumption	1970 Net Pulse imports	1970 % apparent consumption	1978 Net Pulse imports	1978 % apparent consumption	1980 Net Pulse imports	1980 % apparent consumption	1981 Net Pulse imports	1981 % apparent consumption
Guatemala	4,120	8.3	2,697	4.1	6,603	6.9	100	0.1	160	0.2
El Salvador	17,240	55.4	6,279	17.3	1,268	2.9	885	2.2	3,000	7.5
Honduras	160	0.7	65	0.1	195	0.4	2,771	7.2	—	—
Nicaragua	410	1.0	1,834	3.8	118	0.2	12,767	17.6	10,000	14.3
Costa Rica	2,760	12.7	16,292	64.4	605	6.4	13,041	52.1	13,070	52.1
Panama	3,270	35.3	4,796	40.7	4,040	40.2	3,753	38.5	5,500	44.0
Sub total	27,960	14.1	31,963	12.4	12,829	5.0	33,317	12.1	31,730	11.3
Jamaica	3,010	60.0	2,903	42.1	615	3.9	430	5.1	600	6.3
Dominican Republic	2,220	4.9	5,370	8.8	3,305	5.2	5,463	6.9	117	0.2
Cuba	61,730	64.5	33,489	60.4	106,011	80.9	104,237	80.0	110,000	80.9
Grenada	—	—	—	—	—	—	—	—	—	—
Haiti	—	—	—	—	320	0.3	1,200	1.5	600	0.7
Trinidad & Tobago	5,750	100.0	9,745	88.8	14,724	96.6	13,799	74.2	13,414	77.0
Sub total	72,710	42.8	51,516	28.9	125,590	38.7	125,129	39.0	124,731	38.2
Total	100,670	27.3	83,479	19.2	138,419	23.7	158,446	26.5	156,461	25.8

Sources: FAO (1971, 1972, 1980, 1981), FAO (1971a, 1972a, 1980a, 1981a).

Table 8 Net Poultry Imports* Selected Central American and Caribbean Countries 1965–1981 (metric tons)

Countries	1965 Net Poultry imports	1965 % apparent consumption	1970 Net Poultry imports	1970 % apparent consumption	1978 Net Poultry imports	1978 % apparent consumption	1980 Net Poultry imports	1980 % apparent consumption	1981 Net Poultry imports	1981 % apparent consumption
Guatemala	—	—	—	—	110	0.4	644	1.3	674	1.4
El Salvador	1	0.03	1	0.02	30	0.2	255	1.7	300	2.1
Honduras	89	3.1	32	0.8	2	0.02	4	0.04	—	—
Nicaragua	16	1.1	59	1.9	295	4.0	3,384	25.3	3,100	25.6
Costa Rica	1	0.05	49	1.0	45	0.8	20	0.3	—	—
Panama	45	1.8	55	0.8	124	1.1	246	1.9	500	3.5
Sub total	152	0.8	196	0.5	606	0.8	4,553	4.4	4,574	4.3
Jamaica	1,979	35.5	6,320	29.6	19,627	44.0	22,992	45.1	24,822	46.1
Dominican Republic	73	—**	170	0.7	46	0.1	6,075	8.4	1,095	1.4
Cuba	—	—	—	—	10,291	13.3	20,036	21.5	25,000	25.0
Grenada	212	100.0	320	100.0	—	—	1,100	100.0	1,200	100.0
Haiti	—	—	—	—	19	0.4	160	2.6	230	3.7
Trinidad & Tobago	550	—**	187	1.4	1,257	5.9	4,243	16.8	4,200	16.7
Sub total	2,814	8.2	6,997	7.5	31,240	16.8	54,606	22.0	56,547	21.5
Total	2,966	5.6	7,193	5.7	31,846	12.1	59,159	16.8	61,121	16.6

* Poultry meat, excluding figures for poultry liver and edible offal.
** No data available on production for calculation of apparent consumption.
Sources: FAO (1971, 1972, 1980, 1981), FAO (1971a, 1972a, 1980a, 1981a).

Table 9 Net Egg Imports* Selected Central American and Caribbean Countries 1965–1981 (metric tons)

Countries	1965 Net Egg imports	1965 % apparent consumption	1970 Net Egg imports	1970 % apparent consumption	1978 Net Egg imports	1978 % apparent consumption	1980 Net Egg imports	1980 % apparent consumption	1981 Net Egg imports	1981 % apparent consumption
Guatemala	153	0.6	684	2.4	18	0.05	27	0.1	27	0.1
El Salvador	321	2.1	86	0.4	39	0.1	99	0.3	100	0.3
Honduras	347	3.3	788	6.2	1	0.01	151	1.3	—	—
Nicaragua	219	2.4	101	0.9	384	1.4	1611	5.2	1600	5.1
Costa Rica	54	0.6	1434	9.9	128	0.8	422	2.4	420	2.4
Panama	21	0.4	125	1.8	226	1.3	56	0.7	83	0.5
Sub total	1115	1.5	3218	3.2	796	0.5	2366	1.6	2230	1.4
Jamaica	408	9.1	913	7.1	1690	10.4	1662	9.7	1663	9.4
Dominican Republic	27	0.2	819	4.1	395	1.7	1434	4.7	663	0.02
Cuba	1	0.01	—	—	—	—	—	—	—	—
Grenada	—	—	—	—	—	—	—	—	—	—
Haiti	—	—	—	—	54	2.0	170	5.5	170	5.4
Trinidad & Tobago	659	18.7	559	6.6	1744	17.7	2117	22.5	2422	24.5
Sub total	1095	1.5	2291	2.0	3883	2.8	5383	3.2	4918	2.9
Total	2210	1.5	5509	2.5	4679	1.6	7749	2.4	7148	2.2

* Hen eggs in the shell
Sources: FAO (1971, 1972, 1980, 1981), FAO (1971a, 1972a, 1980a, 1981a).

Table 10 Net Meat Imports* Selected Central American and Caribbean Countries 1965–1981 (metric tons)

Countries	1965 Net Meat imports	1965 % apparent consumption	1970 Net Meat imports	1970 % apparent consumption	1978 Net Meat imports	1978 % apparent consumption	1980 Net Meat imports	1980 % apparent consumption	1981 Net Meat imports	1981 % apparent consumption
Guatemala	0.0	0.0	0	0.0	2,408	2.7	0	0.0	0	0.0
El Salvador	999	3.8	0	0.0	0	0.0	0	0.0	0	0.0
Honduras	x	—	0	0.0	0	0.0	0	0.0	0	0.0
Nicaragua	x	—	0	0.0	0	0.0	0	0.0	0	0.0
Costa Rica	x	—	0	0.0	0	0.0	0	0.0	0	0.0
Panama	x	—	0	0.0	0	0.0	0	0.0	0	0.0
Sub total	999	0.5	0	0.0	2,408	0.6	0	0.0	0	0.0
Jamaica	2,919	18.3	6,892	36.5	6,951	24.9	1,778	7.2	2,834	12.3
Dominican Republic	x	—	0	0.0	1,056	1.7	0	0.0	2,751	5.5
Cuba	0	0.0	1,000	0.5	2,400	1.1	0	0.0	0	0.0
Grenada	0	0.0	0	0.0	0	0.0	0	0.0	0	0.0
Haiti	0	0.0	0	0.0	0	0.0	0	0.0	0	0.0
Trinidad & Tobago	4,076	67.1	5,458	84.5	8,547	68.1	6,228	55.5	9,878	66.4
Sub total	6,995	3.2	13,350	5.2	18,954	5.1	8,006	2.2	15,463	5.7
Total	7,994	2.0	13,350	2.5	21,362	2.8	8,006	1.0	15,463	2.5

* Includes beef and veal, buffalo meat, mutton and lamb, goat meat and pig meat Imports have been calculated as net imports of fresh, chilled or frozen meat plus the difference between slaughterings of indigenous animals and total slaughterings. In some cases the figures given for slaughterings of indigenous animals were greater than the total. This has been indicated by a cross (x).

Sources: FAO (1971, 1972, 1980, 1981), FAO (1971a, 1972a, 1980a, 1981a).

Table 11 Net Milk Imports* Selected Central American and Caribbean Countries 1965–1981 (metric tons)

Countries	1965 Net Milk imports	1965 % apparent consumption	1970 Net Milk imports	1970 % apparent consumption	1978 Net Milk imports	1978 % apparent consumption	1980 Net Milk imports	1980 % apparent consumption	1981 Net Milk imports	1981 % apparent consumption
Guatemala	3,480	1.8	3,548	1.3	6,250	2.0	9,313	2.8	8,230	2.5
El Salvador	6,100	3.9	5,840	3.1	11,634	4.4	13,124	4.5	13,757	4.5
Honduras	1,930	1.5	3,895	2.2	3,785	1.8	6,851	3.2	6,700	3.1
Nicaragua	2,140	1.3	2,472	1.2	1,620	0.4	3,344	2.0	5,600	3.5
Costa Rica	1,570	1.1	1,945	0.8	6,069	2.0	6,146	1.9	3,703	1.2
Panama	1,180	1.8	3,212	3.7	3,018	2.6	8,664	7.5	3,944	3.5
Sub total	16,400	1.9	20,912	1.8	32,376	1.9	47,442	3.3	41,934	2.9
Jamaica	6,760	14.5	10,253	17.0	15,651	16.5	11,802	13.5	13,964	15.3
Dominican Republic	5,490	2.9	12,600	4.3	8,400	2.4	10,873	2.5	8,191	2.2
Cuba	42,920	9.9	79,907	12.7	51,999	4.1	59,626	4.5	52,200	3.9
Grenada	810	—**	900	—**	680	25.4	1,446	42.0	1,940	49.2
Haiti	2,990	15.0	4,643	7.7	9,858	16.8	10,800	19.4	7,660	14.0
T-inidad & Tobago	11,030	40.8	11,546	50.1	19,054	79.1	20,975	82.1	22,349	82.6
Sub total	70,000	9.7	119,849	11.2	105,642	5.9	115,522	6.0	106,304	5.6
Total	86,400	5.9	140,761	6.3	138,018	4.0	162,964	4.8	148,238	4.4

* Including fresh, evaporated, condensed and dried milk (whole, skimmed, buttermilk and whey).
**= No data available on production for calculation of percentage of apparent consumption.
Source: FAO (1971, 1972, 1980, 1981), FAO (1971a, 1972a, 1980a, 1981a).

Table 12 *Trade in Miscellaneous Foods Selected Central American and Caribbean Countries 1965–1980 ('000 US$)*

Countries	1965		1970		1978		1980	
	Imports	Exports	Imports	Exports	Imports	Exports	Imports	Exports
Guatemala	2,100	700	2,873	3,235	2,407	7,640	1,500	8,000
El Salvador	300	900	1,307	1,665	7,063	2,802	8,592	1,266
Honduras	2,400	400	3,411	1,115	7,964	853	8,940	1,179
Nicaragua	800	—	3,562	30	6,218	23	6,896	128
Costa Rica	800	700	1,778	3,852	3,803	6,609	5,894	10,114
Panama	1,800	200	809	48	2,546	2,192	3,413	3,276
Sub total	8,200	2,900	13,740	9,945	30,001	20,119	35,235	23,963
Jamaica	2,700	200	2,933	210	2,877	1,518	2,410	2,150
Dominican Republic	1,300	600	2,424	166	8,733	4,086	14,516	5,682
Cuba	—	—	—	—	—	—	62,573	—
Grenada	—	—	—	—	—	—	—	—
Haiti	3,000	—	3,092	—	3,019	—	2,470	—
Trinidad & Tobago	—	—	2,787	2,787	7,389	2,706	11,170	3,263
Sub total	7,000	800	8,449	3,163	22,018	8,310	93,139	11,095
Total	15,200	3,700	22,189	13,108	52,019	28,429	128,374	35,058

Source: FAO (1971a, 1972a, 1980a, 1981a).

Urban-Rural Problems

Historical growth patterns have generated a swollen tertiary sector made up of government administration, commerce, and a myriad of informal, small-scale, urban economic activities. The tertiary sector, which largely serves as an economic refuge for migrants unable to find work in rural areas, has not lessened in importance despite twenty years of attempted industrialisation (see Table 14). On the contrary, agricultural modernisation and the concentrated character of industrial development have kept it at slightly over half the GNP. Continued activity in this tertiary sector, combined with rapid urbanisation, absorbs a disproportionate amount of scarce foreign exchange. The latter could in theory be better invested to increase production rather than to subsidise commercial activities, luxury imports and urban growth.

Obviously, the type of sweeping agricultural transformation that has occurred as a consequence of agro-exports-plus-import-substitution has not increased regional food security. Less obvious, but equally relevant, are the cases of Mexico and Cuba, where radical agrarian transformations followed national revolutions. In Mexico, such transformation did not eliminate rural/urban polarisation. Since the mid-1960s, after three decades of rapid agricultural growth, Mexico has become increasingly dependent on the USA for grain and many other basic consumer needs (Hewitt de Alcantara 1976). Although Cuba's agrarian transformation has broken through rural/urban polarisations, contributing to a major redistribution of income, it has not reduced that country's dependence on imports of many basic consumer foods, as can be seen from Tables 5, 6, 7 and 8. Tables 15 and 16 show food systems imports as a percentage of GNP and per capita in 1970 dollars for selected countries for 1960–1980. These data suggest growing food system dependency. Food security for all Cubans has, however, been achieved.

What type of agrarian transformation can best provide the framework for national economic accumulation and adequate levels of food security? This is the subject of the next part of this paper.

III. SOCIAL TRANSFORMATION AND NATIONAL AGRARIAN STRATEGY

The following reflections are principally concerned with the national agrarian strategy and the social transformation programme set in motion by the Sandinista revolution in Nicaragua. Nevertheless, an attempt has been made to locate the Sandinista experience within the broader context of the region and of problems faced by other countries which have attempted a programme of social transformation. One common problem is that food shortages or scarcity appear in the wake of revolutionary change and are intensified if this is preceded by armed conflict.

Table 13 Trade in Animal Feedstuffs Selected Central American and Caribbean countries 1965–1980 ('000 US$)

Countries	1965		1970		1978		1980	
	Imports	Exports	Imports	Exports	Imports	Exports	Imports	Exports
Guatemala	2,100	2,200	2,355	2,212	5,435	5,447	5,857	8,238
El Salvador	2,300	3,800	1,605	2,009	6,329	408	7,198	804
Honduras	200	200	819	208	3,164	932	4,817	848
Nicaragua	400	1,000	429	2,959	2,004	14,445	453	2,506
Costa Rica	1,400	—	2,612	308	10,532	805	11,374	1,337
Panama	1,500	900	1,192	—	3,951	23	6,683	584
Sub total	7,900	8,100	9,012	7,696	31,415	22,060	36,382	14,317
Jamaica	2,500	100	740	126	7,275	30	6,059	94
Dominican Republic	600	600	20	1,178	8,620	33	10,714	1,642
Cuba	—	—	—	—	—	—	40,971	—
Grenada	100	—	—	—	—	—	—	—
Haiti	—	—	—	—	399	—	440	2,500
Trinidad & Tobago	3,700	200	4,242	703	17,710	286	26,473	17
Sub total	6,900	900	5,002	2,007	34,004	349	84,657	4,253
Total	14,800	9,000	14,014	9,703	65,419	22,409	121,039	18,570

Source: FAO (1971a, 1972a, 1980a, 1981a).

Table 14 Sectorial Distribution of GNP Selected Central American and Caribbean Countries 1960–1981

Countries	GNP (million of 1980 $)		Primary Sector		Secondary Sector*		Tertiary Sector	
	1960	1981	1960 %	1981 %	1960 %	1981 %	1960 %	1981 %
Costa Rica	1,106.3	3,284.0	26.0	19.0	19.7	29.9	54.3	51.1
El Salvador	1,409.3	2,998.2	31.0	25.8	18.5	22.1	50.5	52.1
Guatemala	2,855.2	8,518.3	30.5	25.5	15.6	21.3	54.9	53.2
Honduras	933.3	2,354.9	35.0	30.5	17.0	21.7	48.0	47.8
Nicaragua	981.9	2,204.1	24.5	24.8	17.8	30.3	57.7	44.9
Panama	1,088.5	3,846.5	23.3	13.3	20.6	22.3	56.1	64.4
Sub total	8,374.5	23,206.0	28.8	23.0	17.7	23.7	53.5	53.3
Cuba	6,487.3	15,477.0	18.9	13.7	31.1	45.8	50.0	40.5
Dominican Republic	1,781.6	5,895.9	34.4	21.3	18.7	26.5	46.9	52.2
Haiti	836.6	1,381.2	44.1	33.0	15.7	21.6	40.3	45.4
Jamaica	2,001.1	3,107.5	18.5	16.9	28.6	23.5	52.9	59.5
Trinidad & Tobago	1,155.7	3,128.8	14.5	12.7	31.0	21.9	54.5	65.4
Sub total	12,262.3	28,990.4	22.3	16.4	27.8	35.9	49.9	47.7
Total	20,636.8	52,196.4	25.0	19.3	23.7	30.4	51.3	50.3

= Manufactures, Electric Energy, and Construction.
Source: Brundenius (1983).

Table 15 *Food Systems Imports as % of GDP Selected Central American and Caribbean Countries (1960–1980)*

Countries	1960			1970			1978			1980		
	Food* & Ag. Prod.	Agric.** Inputs + Forestry Fishery	Total Food System	Food & Ag. Prod.	Agric. Inputs + Forestry Fishery	Total Food System	Food & Ag. Prod.	Agric. Inputs + Forestry Fishery	Total Food System	Food & Ag. Prod.	Agric. Inputs + Forestry Fishery	Total Food System
Guatemala	3.0	1.1	4.1	1.7	1.3	3.0	2.0	1.8	3.8	1.7	2.4	4.1
El Salvador	3.4	0.5	3.9	3.0	4.2	7.2	3.9	3.4	7.3	5.1	2.3	7.4
Honduras	2.6	0.1	2.7	3.6	3.8	7.4	4.3	4.8	9.1	5.4	3.4	8.8
Nicaragua	1.7	0.3	2.0	2.6	1.9	4.5	2.8	3.0	5.8	7.4	4.7	12.1
Costa Rica	3.0	0.2	3.2	3.6	4.0	7.6	2.6	2.7	5.3	3.0	3.5	6.5
Panama	3.7	0.2	3.9	2.7	2.6	5.3	3.0	2.5	5.5	3.7	2.1	5.8
Sub total	2.9	0.5	3.4	2.7	2.7	5.4	2.8	2.7	5.5	3.6	2.9	6.5
Jamaica***	6.7	1.5	8.2	6.0	2.9	8.9	8.7	3.5	12.2	8.5	2.8	11.3
Dominican Republic	1.1	0.1	1.2	2.4	1.8	4.2	2.9	2.7	5.6	3.6	2.5	6.1
Cuba	—	—	—	—	—	—	9.0	4.3	13.3	11.3	4.0	15.3
Haiti	—	—	—	4.0	0.4	4.4	6.0	1.1	7.1	9.6	9.5	19.1
Trinidad & Tobago	8.5	1.2	9.7	6.9	2.1	9.0	5.5	2.0	7.5	6.4	2.4	8.8
Sub total	5.1	0.9	6.0	5.2	2.3	7.5	6.8	3.1	9.9	—	—	—

* Food and other agricultural products.

** Agricultural inputs and machinery, forest and fish products.

*** In 1978 the value of the US dollar rose substantially against the Jamaican dollar. The new rate of exchange was used in calculating the GDP figure from Jamaican dollars from 1978.

Sources: FAO (1961a, 1971a, 1981a), UN (various years).

NB: The data in this table have been modified from an original to include Cuba and Haiti. Since the source of the 1980 GDP figures was not given, it has been impossible to give a percentage for the whole Caribbean area.

Table 16 Food Systems Imports Per Capita Selected Central American and Caribbean Countries 1960–1980 (millions of constant 1970 US$)

Countries	1960 Food* & Ag. Prod.	1960 Agric.** Inputs + Forestry Fishery	1960 Total Food System	1970 Food & Ag. Prod.	1970 Agric. Inputs + Forestry Fishery	1970 Total Food System	1978 Food & Ag. Prod.	1978 Agric. Inputs + Forestry Fishery	1978 Total Food System	1980 Food & Ag. Prod.	1980 Agric. Inputs + Forestry Fishery	1980 Total Food System
Guatemala	8.9	3.3	12.2	6.1	4.6	10.7	10.0	8.8	18.8	8.7	12.6	21.3
El Salvador	8.1	1.1	9.2	8.7	12.4	21.1	15.8	13.7	29.5	18.7	8.5	27.2
Honduras	6.5	0.3	6.8	9.7	10.5	20.2	15.6	17.2	32.8	23.7	14.9	38.6
Nicaragua	4.9	0.8	5.7	10.9	7.9	18.8	12.9	13.8	26.7	24.5	15.5	40.0
Costa Rica	12.7	0.6	13.3	20.2	22.7	42.9	22.3	23.6	45.9	30.3	34.8	65.1
Panama	16.8	0.8	17.6	19.8	19.3	39.1	23.4	19.7	43.1	34.7	20.1	54.8
Sub total	9.0	1.6	10.6	10.5	10.8	21.2	14.9	14.3	29.2	19.5	15.2	34.7
Jamaica	34.6	7.8	42.4	45.3	21.7	67.0	34.9	14.2	49.1	34.4	11.2	45.6
Dominican Republic	3.3	0.4	3.7	8.9	6.6	15.5	14.7	13.8	28.5	20.2	13.8	34.0
Cuba	—	—	—	—	—	—	50.2	23.9	74.1	62.8	22.1	84.9
Haiti	—	—	—	3.1	0.3	3.4	5.2	0.9	6.1	8.2	0.8	9.0
Trinidad & Tobago	58.6	8.1	66.7	58.2	17.4	75.6	104.1	37.6	141.7	151.1	57.7	208.8
Sub total	20.9	3.7	24.6	30.8	11.3	42.1	34.0	16.6	50.6	43.0	16.4	59.4
Total	12.8	2.3	15.1	18.7	11.0	29.7	24.9	15.5	40.4	31.5	15.8	47.3

* Food and other Agricultural Products.
** Agricultural Inputs and Machinery, Forest and Fish Products.
Sources: FAO (1971, 1980), FAO (1971a, 1980a).

Food *insecurity* can be expected to increase during rapid social transformation following a revolution as a consequence of: (i) disruption of agriculture (and hence of domestic farm output) due to the land having being used as a battlefield, and ruined infrastructure; (ii) a redistribution of national income quickly reflected in increased demand for foodstuffs, because of the higher food consumption propensities of low-income groups and also of the absence of other consumer goods on the market; (iii) inflation and speculation, which further erode productive capacity; (iv) flight of capital, contributing to a greater foreign exchange shortage (and hence reduced capacity to import essential inputs); (v) attempts to block foreign aid, trade and investment by interests opposed to the revolution. Evidently, an agro-export based economy cannot be expected to continue to function normally in such a situation.

In this abnormal climate, the need to undo old economic mechanisms and to respond to demands for increased consumption by the majority obliges the new government to intervene in the food system in various ways. First, popular-based governments are pushed towards land reform in response to long-repressed peasant pressure for land. Second, state controls over prices of basic foodstuffs often prove ineffective and gradually give way to a rationing system. Third, initially, food imports increase rapidly (as they did in Cuba, Chile and Nicaragua) and the government must also import industrial consumer goods in order to stimulate both rural and urban production. Further, the technical and economic basis for a firm worker-peasant alliance does not exist; industrial workers cannot produce sufficient consumer goods to stimulate increased peasant production, and without special incentives (e.g. better availability of consumer goods and more favourable terms of trade between city and countryside) the peasantry will not meet increased demand for food. As the shortage of foreign exchange makes itself felt and many imports become unavailable, the weakness of the worker-peasant alliance tends to become accentuated.

All these pressures lead to an unravelling and reshaping of the nation's economic structure, generating at least four basic policy dilemmas with regard to national agrarian strategy and efforts to increase food security. We use the term 'dilemmas' because policy-makers frequently do not have much choice – events beyond governmental control determine the outcome.

The Participation Dilemma

What form of leadership should be developed by the various social forces and to what degree should they participate in decision-making and implementation within the overall process of change?

Revolutionary change in many Third World countries is generally based on complex class alliances. Socio-economic transformation depends less on policy decisions by the state or the 'party' than on existing class structures and actual tendencies towards inter- and intra-class cooperation or conflict.[8]

Some idea of the wide differences in rural class structures within Central America can be obtained from Table 17. Clearly, Guatemala and El Salvador in the north of the Isthmus developed more polarised agrarian structures than Nicaragua and Costa Rica in the south. In the latter countries, commercial producers and family farmers were more numerous, but at the same time much less well-endowed economically than in Guatemala and El Salvador where wide gaps exist between a few large and medium-sized estates, a small group of relatively prosperous family farmers, and numerous impoverished small producers.[9]

Table 17 *Distribution of Economically-Active Population in Central America's Agrarian Sector 1965–1970 (% of economically active population)*

Countries	Large and medium producers; landed oligarchy (> 35 Ha.)	Family farmers (7–35 Ha.)	Minifundistas (0–7 Ha.)*	Landless labourers
Guatemala	2	7	74	17
El Salvador	2	6	76	17
Honduras	5	20	50	26
Nicaragua	15	19	35	31
Costa Rica	13	20	25	42

* Small Producers with or without land who may also sell their labour.
Source: Economic Commission for Latin America.

A seeming anomaly in Central America is that the more polarised societies have had lower levels of landlessness. In the 1960s, the percentage of the economically active population (EAP) in Nicaragua and Costa Rica who depended entirely on wage labour for their livelihood was about double that in the northern countries. This difference probably diminished during the 1970s but remained significant. One of the key factors determining the higher levels of polarisation in terms of land tenure in Guatemala and El Salvador was, as suggested in Table 18, demographic pressures on land. With a considerable amount of undeveloped land on the agrarian frontiers in Nicaragua and Costa Rica (and, to some extent, in Honduras), it was much more difficult for a few large commercial producers to monopolise resources. Consequently they were forced to gain control over labour supplies by offering wages higher

than peasants could earn as small producers. In fact, in Nicaragua
between 1950 and 1970, agricultural wages may well have risen more
rapidly than agricultural GNP. At the same time, overall agricultural
policy discriminated against peasant production, both in terms of credit
and of price policies.[10]

Table 18   *Demographic Pressure on the Land Central America 1980
(hectares per rural inhabitant)*

Countries	Arable and Permanent Cropland	Permanent Pasture	Forest and Woodland	Total land
Guatemala	0.5	0.2	1.1	1.8
El Salvador	0.3	0.2	0.1	0.6
Honduras	0.8	1.5	1.8	4.1
Nicaragua	1.4	3.0	4.2	8.6
Costa Rica	0.7	2.0	2.4	5.1

Source: FAO (1981).

In El Salvador and Guatemala, pressure on land and huge manpower
reserves made it possible for agribusiness to develop using
minifundistas[11] as agricultural labourers. In the southern countries,
economic growth based on export crops was along more classical lines,
generating conflicts between large commercial producers and landless
labourers. In parallel with this plantation-type agriculture, with its
highly-modernised production relationships, a broad swath of family
farms evolved in Costa Rica and to a lesser extent in Nicaragua.[12] Many
of these farmers, controlling small enterprises producing for the market,
depended to a much greater extent on a labour force made up of
minifundistas than did the dominant large producers. Moreover (and this
was particularly true of Nicaragua) small producers made up a significant
proportion of the total rural labour force.

The implications of the above for small commercial producers' and
peasants' participation in agrarian transformation are relatively clear. In
Nicaragua, the Sandinista insurrection won the support of vast numbers
of small and medium commercial producers who, under Somoza, had
been excluded from access to credit and infrastructure. After the revolution, policies favouring a mixed economy were a response to existing
class structures.

The two-year delay in implementing major land reform (other than
nationalisation of the Somoza properties) also indicates the importance
revolutionary leaders attached to gaining the support of small commercial producers and family farmers[13] as well as to keeping production
going on large private estates. The demands of the rural poor were met

with increased employment, higher money wages (although not for long in real-wage terms) and new forms of social benefits in the state farm sector (lands confiscated from those closely associated with the Somoza regime).[14] The needs of the minifundistas were met through rent mechanisms requiring that idle land be rented out to them at rates well below pre-revolution market values. During the first year-and-a-half, government leaders had favoured an integrated rural organisation that included workers and peasants. Nevertheless, after only a year of Sandinista government, all but the poorest peasant farmers were pressing for their own organisation to advance their interests as producers. Demands for land were coming as much from better-off peasant groups as from the poor. By the beginning of 1981, the Union of Farmers and Cattle-Raisers (UNAG) had already consolidated itself in local areas. The widely recognised effectiveness of this mass organisation was the result of its solid small commercial producer and family-farmer base. (One implication of this analysis is that the types of alliances among commercial farmers and farm workers which will accompany a revolution in El Salvador or Guatemala will be different from those that have developed in Nicaragua.)

Perhaps even more relevant to the participation of different social forces within a national strategy of agrarian transformation are regional variations in local power structures. This is so because the participation of the hitherto powerless always defines itself vis-à-vis particular socio-economic power structures at the local level. In Nicaragua, expropriation policy and cooperative development strategy are currently being formulated against the backdrop of five distinct power structures dominated by: (1) sugar, banana, rice, or tobacco enclaves; (2) large, modernised capitalist cotton and coffee plantations; (3) merchant capital intertwined with small farmer production for the national market; (4) *latifundios* dedicated to extensive cattle-raising and administered through *seigneurial* mechanisms; (5) peasant communities where these constitute the predominant local power structures.

The landed oligarchy, the peasantry and the rural working class are all abstract concepts requiring the character of local power structures to be specified. In practice, the results of an agrarian strategy will be measured against real transformation within given regional socio-economic power structures.[15]

Pressures from urban social forces often create tensions within the agricultural sector. Government subsidies for basic consumer items such as rice, maize, beans, sorghum, sugar, milk, etc. have grown steadily during the first four years of the Sandinista regime and currently total about seven percent of the national budget. For example, peasants are paid about US$0.10 for a pound of maize (i.e. roughly the international market value) but consumers buy the same amount for half the price.

Obviously, this creates problems. Farmers can buy grain at the sub-sidised price and resell it at double that amount on their farms. This weakens the incentive to produce. Such has been the case particularly with coffee and cattle producers who had previously grown maize and beans for their work force but now find it more profitable to buy state-subsidised grains.

Despite these problems, the government has continued to maintain the subsidies – which reflects the political importance given to urban low-income consumers who figured so prominently in the insurrection against Somoza. In fact, during 1981 and 1982, prices paid to maize producers were set somewhat below the international market value in order to minimise the gap between what went to the producer and what the con-sumer had to pay. Thus peasant interests and the social need to maintain and increase aggregate supply were being sacrificed to urban demands, as has happened in so many underdeveloped countries. As maize short-ages grew and imports rose, however, producer prices were increased in 1983 to world market levels.

It would, of course, be impossible to maintain these kinds of subsidies if the urban population were unorganised. In fact, distribution is ensured via an extensive network of locally-run urban neighbourhood organisa-tions, with approximately 100 families organised around a local mer-chant, who has a contract with the state to market a fixed amount of goods to those families for a small commission. This system has proved quite effective in controlling speculation and corruption; moreover, inflation for 23 basic consumer goods was only 9 percent during 1981–82, whereas that for the middle-class consumption bundle was nearly 60 percent. Overall inflation for the same period was around 25 percent. Popular participation has thus played an important role in the general success of the government in maintaining a proper macro-economic balance[16] by controlling both wages and prices.

The nature and quality of popular participation is determined largely by the ability of political leaders adequately to interpret these often conflicting interests and to respond to the economic interests of the different social forces. This complex dialectic often leads to unforeseen results that create new tensions among these same social forces. Moreover, the success of agrarian transformation strategy depends heavily on how political leaders deal with the other policy dilemmas discussed below.

The Accumulation Dilemma

To what extent should resources be assigned and priority given to capital-intensive agro-industry producing for export versus labour-intensive peasant production of food for the population? And to what extent should demand for increased consumption be sacrificed for longer-term productive investment? Possibilities for sustained accumulation in agro-export economies like those of the Caribbean Basin depend on the depth of the structural transformations attained, and on the success of their governments in breaking the vicious circle of underdevelopment: stagnation of home-market agriculture, outward orientation of the industrial base, and overall dependence on the more developed countries for finance, capital, technology and markets.[17] The following discussion emphasises agrarian transformation, food security and the consumer or wage-goods problems as they affect government efforts to overcome the above obstacles and open the way to steady economic progress.

The hypothesis presented here is that the mobilisation of the peasantry as a whole, and alliances with small commercial farm producers, are not incompatible with achieving long-term goals. They are in many respects crucial for overall economic accumulation.[18] Historically, the relationship between agrarian transformation and overall economic accumulation (investment) and development, has been extremely complicated and confused. For example, despite their widely different approaches to agrarian transformation, the Soviet Union, China, Yugoslavia and Poland, which were all substantial food exporters prior to their revolutions, all became in varying degrees dependent on food imports under 'socialism'.[19] While this can be explained in part by increased food consumption of low-income groups, especially the peasantry, clearly that is not the only factor involved. Selden (1982) has argued that failure to resolve the agrarian question is precisely what has bedeviled and weakened socialist accumulation. It is impossible here to attempt an analysis of the food problem under socialism. Suffice it to say that accepted doctrine on agrarian transformation seems to boil down to a sort of 'virility test'; i.e. whether a government is willing to pay the price deemed necessary for modernisation and development, at the heart of which lies the idea that squeezing the peasantry will provide a source of accumulation.[20]

The Soviet peasantry was in fact brutally squeezed under Stalin, although neither Marx nor Lenin had encouraged audacious or accelerated transformation of peasant production.[21] There seems to have been a considerable potential for increases in the latter which the leadership failed to perceive. But collectivisation proved incapable of providing a base for primitive accumulation and, moreover, with the heavy state subsidies needed, was often a drain on investment. One consequence was that agricultural productivity and total investment in agriculture were in many countries far below what they could have been under more flexible policies providing better incentives for the peasantry. The crucial issue in socio-economic transformation is to mobilise the social forces necessary to render a policy both possible and effective.

182 SOLON BARRACLOUGH AND PETER MARCHETTI

In any event, the problems of transformation in small peripheral agro-export countries like Nicaragua are vastly different from those faced by larger and more autonomous countries. Some analysts have rightly emphasised that the agro-export sector can substitute partially for capital goods industries in these small, vulnerable economies.[22] This crucial role of foreign trade has been analysed by various development economists during the post-war decades.[23] FitzGerald identifies the different types of consumer (wage) goods necessary for an agrarian transformation and the accumulation process, but over-stresses the importance of the external sector for national accumulation. This simplification obscures the great complexity of economic growth processes and can lead to unrealistic policy recommendations. Unlike capital-goods-producing sectors in more developed economies, the external sector of small export economies is connected directly to both productive and non-productive consumption. Prior to revolutionary change, these countries are usually dependent on imports for part of their supplies of basic foodstuffs, as well as for 'luxury' goods (including food) for urban high-and-middle in-come strata and for the multiple imported inputs required to maintain and expand urban infrastructure, industry and agro-exports.

Increasing the pace of economic growth will not occur merely by cutting back on luxury imports, necessary as this may be. Consumer trends – even among the popular classes – will probably come into conflict with the need for more constructive investment. But even if consumerism is quickly controlled and does not represent an added drain on foreign exchange earned through traditional exports, it should not be expected that higher real rates of accumulation will occur during the first years. Existing accumulation mechanisms are intimately woven into the foreign sector. Prospects for that sector, during the early years, are not particularly attractive for a variety of reasons. One of these is the need for economic restructuring; others include various elements which have negative effects on export earnings and prospects for investment capital and foreign aid, such as foreign hostility to the new regime, worsening terms of trade, etc.

Thus, even radical transformation of the foreign sector will not be enough to create a new surge of investment. Although more socially-oriented, more modern and more equitable management of agricultural export mechanisms is necessary for the small vulnerable economy, increased accumulation will depend primarily upon carrying out success-ful structural transformations. This in turn will require new social relations of production; new economic relations between city and countryside[24]; new inter-sectoral relationships in which production receives priority[25]; new patterns of income distribution; and, above all, a new relationship between the external and internal sectors. Only then can surplus from exports be more fully available for reinvestment in the home economy and for reinforcing complementary linkages between agriculture and other sectors of the economy.

It is unlikely that any of these transformations will bring about an immediate rise in GDP. Rather, they should be seen as the basis for sustained growth in the future. In this context, talk of a 'new axis [eje] of accumulation'[26] turns out to be rather confusing. In fact, the 'accumulation axis' metaphor may obscure more than it clarifies. It must be assumed that the image refers to an axis that dynamises the whole economy (e.g. it stimulates the growth and restructuring of a truly national and more autonomous input-output matrix). In this sense, however, 'axis' can have two meanings: (1) referring to a dynamic industry or activity that acts as a catalyst for the rest of the economy (i.e. investments that provoke and stimulate numerous other investments); and (2) a dynamic line of investment yielding higher levels of earnings, thus permitting direct reinvestment of those earnings in other sectors of the economy, but not necessarily having many direct linkages with other sectors. (The agro-export sector in Central America seems to fall more within this second category.)

In the final analysis, future development in Central America and the Caribbean depends on the establishment of integrated and relatively autonomous national economies that are also more regionally integrated and autonomous. One basic requirement, obviously, is the creation of a relatively autonomous national food system assuring food security for all individuals and social groups. Without sufficient food, no other activity can advance very far before its expansion is blocked by rising food prices, shortages and social tensions. But a sound and dynamic food system would have widespread multiplier effects and would facilitate the expansion of agro-industry and new lines of agro-exports.

Since the societies of Central America and the Caribbean are predominantly rural, their current integration in the world market depends on the export of primary products. Thus, land reform and rural transformation surface as principal mechanisms through which to attain strategic regional objectives seeking to establish viable accumulation models and new modes of insertion within the international division of labour. Such a rural transformation programme should begin with land reform, putting idle and under-utilised land into the hands of the peasantry, in order to strengthen the regional grain economy (which in 1980 in the Caribbean Basin region as a whole depended on the rest of the world, primarily the USA, for nearly half its grain consumption). The mobilisation of the peasantry to produce grains and other foodstuffs would fulfil three prerequisites for any new model of accumulation and growth: (1) better integration of agriculture with other sectors of the economy; (2) the saving of hundreds of millions of dollars in foreign exchange for food imports which could otherwise be used to buy in technology and other capital goods; and (3) the adjustment and improvement of working conditions within the existing export sector, in order to guarantee a flow of foreign currency sufficient for the acquisition of capital goods and technology and for energy needs that cannot at present be met within the region.

Major emphasis on the improvement of existing peasant technologies, as well as the development of new ones to meet their needs, is also implied in such a strategy. It promises, in addition, to stimulate peasant livestock production (especially milk, eggs, pigs, etc.); to give impetus to the construction industry, which now shows the greatest multiplier effects on the rest of the economy in Central America (through the construction of feeder roads, storage facilities, export infrastructure, irrigation canals, etc.); and to generate effective demand by the peasant producers for home-produced inputs, consumer goods and longer-term investments.

A policy of investment in peasant-based agro-industry and industrialisation of natural resources could generate higher overall rates of accumulation than one primarily emphasising import substitution through investment only in capital-intensive large enterprises (either private or public). It would result in more effective integration of diverse sectors of the national economy.[27] An effective agrarian transformation of this type, however, would depend on simultaneous efforts to produce and to import the consumer goods (wage goods) and inputs required to stimulate peasant food production (FitzGerald *supra*).

The accumulation dilemma for government planners in practice comes down to taking decisions on the types of investments to be made or encouraged by the state during the early transition years. At each stage, therefore, it is necessary to weigh carefully the priority and importance to be accorded: (a) to investment in modern capital-intensive agriculture versus investment in labour-intensive agricultural development; and (b) to investments in export agriculture versus investments in home market production.

In neither case should a zero-sum logic be employed; finding the proper value and effective bridges between micro-economic incentives and macro-economic growth is precisely what the art of agrarian transformation is about. The sum of small investments made by countless small producers may turn out to be as important for future growth as are the large development projects financed by the state or from other sources.

The Institutional and Equity Dilemma

What should be the relative importance given (in terms, for example, of land and capital allocated) to state farms, commercial agriculture, peasant production and cooperatives? And to what extent should popular aspirations for greater equity be subordinated to the need to maintain material incentives to increase production in the short run? Frequently, debate over agrarian strategy centres on the type and prevalence of institutional forms used to organise agricultural production. The principal socio-economic sectors that make up an agrarian institutional package are state farms, production cooperatives, credit and service smallholder cooperatives, independent peasant production units, and commercially-managed farms.

The more collectivised farms can guarantee greater equity among families and between sexes as well as permitting more rapid access to a series of social welfare services. If they are preceded by real agrarian reform and operate within the framework of a well-conceived national strategy, the more traditional forms of peasant organisation or cooperatives, however, tend to permit increased participation, wider local autonomy and, in practice, more rational use of resources. Above all, they offer a solution to the consumer goods problem, provided that government can find a way of combining micro-economic incentives with its overall macro-development plan.

The traditional concern has been that mobilising the peasantry could lead to their social differentiation into small entrepreneurs and wage labourers, thus creating new conflicts in the countryside and a potentially powerful opposition to a state concerned primarily with popular needs. However, if the government maintains control over fiscal affairs (including taxes) and the marketing system, there should be little to fear in this respect.[28] The Sandinista model of transformation, through control of finance and internal and external commerce, will be a crucial test of the possibilities of transforming an agrarian structure within a mixed economy. During the present period, international capital prefers to turn the risks over to independent farmers while maintaining control over inputs, finance and marketing. Why could not a progressive government do the same, while at the same time lowering the income differentials between the urban bureaucracy and the peasant producers? History shows that the main equity issue in 'socialist' transition is not the rise of small farm commercial producers but excessive power and privileges of urban bureaucracies, both public and semi-private.

Table 19 shows the amount of land controlled by the various sectors in Nicaragua in 1978 and 1982 as well as giving a projection for the end of the decade.

Much more important than the budget of each sector are the dynamics among them.[29] What is essential is that each sector make whatever contribution it can to broad-based, overall national development, and that there be greater equity in the distribution of benefits among sectors, regions, social classes and individuals. Perhaps the key reason why

Table 19   *Control of Agricultural Land – Nicaragua*

Socio-Economic Sector	1978	1982	1989
State farms	0	23	25
Production cooperatives	0	2	20
Credit and service cooperatives	1	8	20
Unorganised peasant producers	14	10	5
Large commercial producers (140 Has. or more)	55	31	10
Small commercial producers (35–39 Has.)	30	26	20
Total	100	100	100

Source: Estimates based on monthly reports of MIDINRA (Managua).

the Sandinista agrarian transformation has successfully increased agricultural production across the board, except for cotton and cattle, has been its flexibility in combining different forms of production.

The International Market Dilemma

On what terms can eventual re-insertion within the international division of labour take place, and how can markets for exports and imports be better diversified both immediately and in the future? The type of international re-insertion considered compatible with the existing situation in the Central American and Caribbean region is explained below.

It is proposed, in essence, that the region move up one step within the international division of labour: from being an exporter of mainly primary goods (commodities) it would become an exporter of processed foods and commodities, industrialise its natural resources base,[30] and develop its relatively stagnant home agriculture for an expanded home market. It would move away from dependence on US imports and would develop relative independence within a regional trading system linked to diversified international markets. In effect, re-insertion means 'de-linking' from the old production and trading system and finding a new place in the international division of labour. Doing this will require time: re-insertion will, inevitably, be gradual.

That diversifying international trade has been a gradual process for Nicaragua can be seen from Tables 20, 21, 22 and 23. Four years of Sandinista efforts to diversify exports and seek new trading partners have not overcome the country's dependence on trade with the USA for its exports of livestock and processed agricultural products (proposed growth areas), and for imports of machinery and such agricultural inputs as fertilisers and pesticides (which now, however, can be purchased elsewhere; e.g. Mexico or Brazil).

Although increased investment and re-insertion take time, Nicaragua has moved forward quickly within the realistic yet highly demanding

Table 20   *Export Markets Nicaragua 1978–82 (in millions of US $)*

Countries	1978	%	1982	%
United States of America	150.8	23	96.5	24
Japan, Western Europe, Canada	245.8	38	175.9	43
COMECON	1.1	0	31.3	7
Third World Countries	248.4	39	104.1	26
Total	646.1	100	407.8	100

Sources: Ministry of Foreign Affairs Bulletins (Managua).

re-insertion programme defined above. As can be seen from Table 24, between 1978 and 1982 (a period of international recession), Nicaraguan imports of capital goods for agriculture and agro-industry climbed steadily, whereas those of Costa Rica and Guatemala declined sharply.

Industrialisation of natural resources will lead to new levels of self-determination. At present 40 percent of foreign earnings are consumed by petroleum imports. Investments in hydroelectric and geo-thermal projects could make Nicaragua a net exporter of energy by 1990. Other projects which tap marine resources and renew woodlands are also key elements in resource industrialisation strategy.

Agro-industrialisation means tying agriculture and industry more closely together. Nicaragua's principal export crop in value terms is cotton, which was previously exported raw only to be reimported as thread for the country's small textile industry. International economic advisers attached little importance to the irrationality of this loss of value-added to a major export. At present, a new thread-manufacturing industry is being constructed in Nicaragua with COMECON aid. Perhaps the most crucial investment, in terms of food security, is the gigantic irrigation project going forward in the rich western plains area. This investment provides a basis for regional re-insertion, permitting increased trade with the Caribbean Basin; i.e. to start basic grains flowing from Central America to the Caribbean islands and certain minerals and manufactured goods in the opposite direction.

Table 21   *Sources of Imports Nicaragua 1978–82 (in millions of US $)*

Countries	1978	%	1982	%
United States of America	186.1	31	147.4	19
Japan, Western Europe, Canada	146.3	25	172.8	22
COMECON	3.6	1	89.1	11
Third World Countries	257.9	43	366.2	47
Total	593.9	100	775.5	100

Sources: Ministry of Foreign Affairs Bulletins (Managua).

Table 22 *Export Markets by Product Nicaragua 1982 (in millions of US $)*

Countries	Coffee and Cotton		Non-traditional Agricultural Exports*		Meat and Fish**		Industrials		Gold and Silver	
	$	%	$	%	$	%	$	%	$	%
United States of America	22.9	1	34.1	62	46.8	83	12.7	18	0	
Japan, Western Europe, Canada	153.3	73	4.7	9	2.9	5	0		15.1	100
COMECON	24.9	12	2.3	4	6.4	11	4.3	6	0	
Third World Countries	30.1	14	14.1	26	0.2	0	52.8	76	0	
Total	231.2	100	55.2	100	56.3	99	69.8	100	15.1	100

* Banana, sesame and sugar.
** Lobster, shrimp and fish included.
Sources: Ministry of Foreign Affairs Bulletins (Managua).

Table 23 *Source of Imports by Product Nicaragua 1982 (in millions of US $)*

Countries	Petroleum and Oil $	%	Raw Materials $	%	Chemical Products $	%	Manufactured Products $	%	Machinery and Equipment $	%	Transport Equipment $	%
United States of America	4.7	3	6.9	64	30.8	42	22.4	15	41.3	31	4.3	9
Japan, Western Europe, Canada	0.3	0	1.6	15	25.8	34	38.6	25	38.9	30	11.4	24
COMECON	0	0	0	0	2.7	3	2.1	1	22.8	17	23.5	50
Third World Countries	171.8	97	1.3	21	15.7	21	90.2	59	28.5	22	7.8	17
Total	176.8	100	9.8	100	75.0	100	153.3	100	131.5	100	47.0	100

Source: Banco Central (1982).

Table 24 *Imports of Capital Goods for Agriculture 1978–1982 (millions of constant 1978 US $)*

Years	Agricultural GNP (1)	Imports of Capital Goods (2)	Imports as % of GNP (2/1) (3)	Index of Imports as % GNP Base 1978 (4)
		Guatemala		
1978	998	35	3.5	100
1980	847	19	2.2	63
1981	858	16	1.9	54
1982	841	13	1.5	43
		Costa Rica		
1978	831	37	4.4	100
1980	850	23	2.7	61
1981	860	13	1.5	34
1982	861	11	1.2	27
		Nicaragua		
1978	312	13	4.2	100
1980	238	24	10.1	240
1981	262	30	11.5	274
1982	268	45	16.8	400

Source: CEPAL (1982).

IV. CONCLUSION

The pattern of economic growth based on the export of a few agricultural commodities and other primary products that has been dominant in most of the Caribbean Basin countries has been accompanied by social and economic polarisation, deplorable social conditions, and high levels of dependency, primarily on the USA, for finance capital, technology, markets, food and other consumer goods. There has been minimal integration of national economies and practically none regionally. Food systems in the region have become particularly dependent and have generally failed in their basic function of providing food security for the whole of the population. Profound agrarian transformation must be a key element in the region's future development and integration.

The above dilemmas represent only a fraction of the complexities faced during a process of profound agrarian transformation. The basic contention of this paper is that mobilisation of the rural masses with the aim of achieving national food security is not only a vital component of this transformation but also a major and necessary step in the direction of sustained economic growth. Moreover, peasant and rural worker mobilisation is vital for consolidating the political support of the rural population against outside attempts to destabilise the nascent processes of national sovereignty and non-aligned economic growth designed to meet popular needs and aspirations.

Agro-export growth and industrial policy during the past three decades, far from serving to dismantle colonial class relations, have served to instrumentalise them in ever-increasing integration within the international market.

NOTES

1. In this paper we use the term Caribbean Basin to include all Central American countries and Caribbean islands. Data are available, however, only for some of them.
2. These are closely related to developments in industry and international trade.
3. National food security means that the supply of food necessary to satisfy effective demand is assured; individual food security that access to foods essential for meeting biological needs is guaranteed to the entire population – i.e. not just to those able to translate their food needs into effective market demand.
4. Although the cumulative agricultural growth rate in Latin America during the past two decades has been more than 3 percent and that of agro-industry nearly 6 percent, over 62 percent of the rural population and 26 percent of the urban apparently have a food consumption level below recommended minimal biological norms. See Altimair (1979).
5. For example, most European countries (and Japan) are at present heavily subsidising their agriculture in order to reduce vulnerability to international competition and the vagaries of international market prices and supplies.
6. Instead of, as they should be, a grid or network of stable market mechanisms integrating national and regional economies.
7. Tables 3 through 12 present the best information available on national food net imports. The tables at best indicate general trends due to often inadequate country data submitted to the FAO.
8. Marx believed that the industrial proletariat would be the leading force in changing the capitalist structure of the economy; Lenin insisted on an alliance between proletariat and peasantry; Amilcar Cabral stressed the role of the national petty bourgeoisie and urban middle strata. Orlando Nuñez, to explain popular participation in Nicaragua's massive revolt against Somoza, developed the concept of the 'third force', i.e. Cabrera's middle sectors, those engaged in tertiary-sector informal commerce and, especially, youth, an important force in the Third World today.
9. Small producers in Nicaragua and Costa Rica were also impoverished, but the gap between them and family farmers and most commercial producers was less marked.
10. For a description of the type of controls exercised by the Somoza regime on small peasant production, see: IFAD (1980), and Barraclough (1982). For a historical analysis of how commercial producers used the wage mechanism for recruiting labour in Nicaragua, see Levy (1976: pp. 385–387).
11. The term *minifundista* is used here to denote small producers who often work for wages to supplement their meagre farm earnings. They are often described as 'semi-proletarians'.
12. Small commercial producers and independent peasants in Costa Rica controlled more highly developed production units than their counterparts in Nicaragua because of the more democratic economic development in that country.
13. The rich and middle peasantry is referred to here.
14. It is probable that overall employment dropped for full-time rural wage earners because of rapid declines in both cotton and cattle prices.
15. It is for this reason that national class analyses should always be based on sub-national regional analyses.
16. This conservatism was a conscious attempt by leaders to avoid the types of problems faced by the *Unidad Popular* in Chile during the Allende years.

17. Clearly, the outward orientation of the industrial base in these economies is markedly different both with regard to internal multiplier effects and the international terms of trade than it is in manufacturing export-platform economies like Korea, Taiwan, Singapore and Hong Kong. In the agro-export economy of the Caribbean region, dependence carries with it a dynamic quite distinct from that at work in the Pacific Basin.

18. This depends on the capacity of the government to control finance, inputs, marketing price and tax mechanisms in such a way as to give high priority to the interests, potentially conflicting, of both workers and peasants.

19. We use the term 'socialism' in the vulgar sense, meaning those states commonly regarded as having adopted 'socialist systems' and described in the UN literature as 'centrally planned economies'. We do not imply any historical judgment about whether or not they may be approaching a 'socialist mode of production'.

20. The validity of this proposition has been increasingly questioned for a number of reasons. Not the least of these is that the belief that fragmented forms of peasant production would be swept away by the development of modern production forces has been challenged by the surprising vigour and resilience of peasant and informal artisan economies, both in developed capitalist and in socialist countries.

21. Selden (1982: 6–7) indicates that almost no thinking or planning had been done on collectivisation during the years preceding the revolution and that it was, in fact, a desperate measure.

22. See FitzGerald's Kaleckian reinterpretation of Marx's departments in the present volume.

23. See for example Balassa (1971) and Maizels (1968). Arthur Lewis, on the other hand, emphasises the need of a prior agricultural revolution before income from trade can be expected to contribute to dynamic growth. See W. Arthur Lewis (1977).

24. What is vital here is increasing control by peasant producers through production cooperatives (and by the state sector) over the production of their inputs and over the elaboration and marketing of their products either through takeover of existing input and food processing industries or through the creation of new industries by those cooperatives.

25. In Nicaragua, giving priority to production over commerce involves the mobilisation of the 'third force' (informal urban commerce and youth) towards productive activity. Because of the social weight of this third force, mere restrictions on commerce will be of little avail and maintaining youth (who represent 40 per cent of the entire population) as passive consumers is hardly advisable.

26. The metaphor is used in two different variants in Latin America: 'eje de acumulacion' or 'axle of accumulation' implying support for a process, and 'axis' which connotes a line of investments. The English metaphor 'engine of growth' is no less ambiguous.

27. The most attractive spheres are: processing of cotton, sesame, fruits, vegetables, tobacco and concentrated feedstuffs for animals; manufacture of glass, plastic and paper containers; development of thermal and hydro-electric resources. Future regional investments could go to the industrial plant needed to supply machinery and inputs to agriculture.

28. This also assumes, of course, that the diverse popularly-based social forces that supported the revolution have continued to have a decisive voice in government.

29. See IFAD (1980) for a presentation of the dynamics of the Sandinista model.

30. Hydro-electric, geothermal, forestry and marine resources.

REFERENCES

Altimair, O. (1979): 'La dimension de la pobreza en America Latina', *Cuadernos de la CEPAL*, 27 (Santiago).

Balassa, B. (1971): 'Patterns of Economic Structure', in *The Structure of Protection in Developing Countries* (Baltimore: Johns Hopkins).

Banco Central (1982): *Listado Aduana, Importaciónes CIF* (Managua).

Barraclough, S. (1982): *A Preliminary Analysis of Nicaragua's Food System* (Geneva: UNRISD).

Brundenius, C. (1983): 'Algunos Apuntes sobre el Desarrollo Económico de Centro América y del Caribe 1960–1982' (Preliminary draft; Nicaragua: INIES; May).

CEPAL (1982): 'Notas para el Estudio Económico de América Latina. Guatemala, Costa Rica y Nicaragua'.

FAO (1971, 1972, 1980, 1981): *Production Yearbook*.

—— (1971a, 1972a, 1980a, 1981a): *Trade Yearbook*.

Hewitt de Alcantara, C. (1976): *Modernising Mexican Agriculture: Socioeconomic Implications of Technological Change 1940–1970* (Geneva: UNRISD).

IDB (1982): 'Progreso Económico y Social – el Sector Externo', *Informe*.

—— (n.d.): *El Desarrollo Integrado de Centroamerica en la presente década*, Vol. 4, *Desarrollo Industrial*.

IFAD (1980): *Informe de Mision Especial de Programacion* (Rome; October).

Leon, F . (1981): 'Pobreza Rural – Realidades y Perspectivas de Politica', in: *Se Puede Superar la Pobreza? Realidad y Perspectivas en America Latina* (Santiago de Chile: CEPAL-PNUD).

Levy, P. (1976): *Notas Geográficas y Económicas sobre la Republica de Nicaragua* (Managua: Editorial San José).

Lewis, W.A. (1977): *Evolution of the International Economic Order* (Princeton: Princeton University Press).

Maizels, A. (1968): *Exports and Economic Growth of Developing Countries* (Cambridge: Cambridge University Press).

Schejtman, A. (1983): 'Lineamiento para le Análisis Integral de los Problemas Alimentarios Nacionales' (Mexico: CEPAL-FAO; draft).

Selden, M. (1982): 'The Crisis of Collectivisation: Socialist Development and the Peasantry', *IDS Bulletin*, 14, 4 (September).

Steinhart, J. S. & O. E. Steinhart (1974): 'Energy Rise in the American Food System', *Science*, 184, 4134.

UN (Various years): *Statistical Yearbooks*.

UNRISD (1979): *Social Development and the International Development Strategy* (Geneva: UNRISD/79.2).

XI

CENTRAL AMERICAN INTEGRATION, TRADE DIVERSIFICATION AND THE WORLD MARKET

Victor Bulmer-Thomas

I. INTRODUCTION

As far as understanding the dynamics of the Central American economy is concerned, there is no more important question than trade. The region has, for a century at least, had the characteristics of a 'small, open economy' and this openness has increased, not diminished, in recent decades. Instead, as Table I shows, while middle-income oil-importing countries in general have experienced an increase in the ratio of exports to GDP (from 16 per cent in 1960 to almost 20 per cent in 1979), in Central America the ratio rose to nearly 40 per cent in the cases of El Salvador, Honduras and Nicaragua and nearly 30 per cent in the case of Costa Rica. Only in Guatemala, the least trade dependent of the Central American economies, was the share below 25 per cent and even there the ratio rose from 13 per cent in 1960 to 21 per cent in 1979.[1]

This high degree of export specialisation has a number of obvious consequences. Economic growth is in general not only export-led, it is

Table 1 *Ratio of Exports to Gross Domestic Product (%)*

	1960	1979	Notes
(A) Low-income Countries	14	20	Excluding China
(B) Middle-Income Countries	14	18	Oil-Importers Only
(C) Central America			Considered part of (B) by World Bank
1. Costa Rica	21	27	
2. El Salvador	20	36	
3. Guatemala	13	21	
4. Honduras	22	38	
5. Nicaragua	24	37	

Source: World Bank 1983, Table 5.
Note: Although more recent data are available, the year 1979 has been chosen because it is less affected by the regional crisis and world recession.

also export-determined; this has prompted one economist to observe:

A striking feature of econometric models of income determination in the region is the evidence of the continuing dominating effect of terms of trade and other export-related fluctuations on the level of domestic income and product. This is so, despite almost two decades of integration policy designed to diversify these economies to reduce their vulnerability to foreign trade cycles. (Reynolds in Cline & Delgado 1978: 288, n.2).

A further point worth remembering in considering the future of trade to Central America is the region's high degree of commodity and geographic concentration. Coffee and bananas continue to dominate foreign exchange earnings in all republics (see Table 2), while the five principal export crops account for between 50 per cent and 65 per cent of total foreign exchange earnings. At the same time, the three principal export markets — the European Economic Community (EEC), the United States of America (USA) and the Central America Common Market (CACM) — account for over 75 per cent of the value of commodity trade for all republics and over 80 per cent in the case of El Salvador and Honduras.

Table 2 *Proportion of Total Exports Accounted for by Principal Export Crops in 1980 (%)*

Country	Bananas	Coffee	Sugar	Cotton	Beef	Total
Costa Rica	19.8	24.2	4.0	—	7.1	55.1
El Salvador	—	52.8	1.3	8.6	—	62.7
Guatemala	2.9	30.5	4.5	10.9	1.8	50.6
Honduras	27.3	24.4	3.6	1.6	7.3	64.2
Nicaragua	1.8	36.8	4.4	6.7	12.9	62.6

Source: IMF (1982).

The trade structure of Central America has, however, changed considerably in the last two decades. The formation of CACM and the rapid growth of intra-regional trade has brought the CACM share of exports for each republic to some 20 per cent (except in the case of Honduras, where it is below 10 per cent). In addition, there has been a rapid growth in non-traditional exports to third countries. These include cardamon and oil in the case of Guatemala, light manufactures such as clothing and textiles in the case of El Salvador, furniture and soap products from Honduras, chemicals from Nicaragua and simple manufactured goods from Costa Rica.

Despite efforts towards import-substituting industrialisation (ISI) in the 1960s and 1970s and import-substitution in agriculture (ISA) in the 1930s, the dominant economic model followed by Central America since the second half of the 19th century has been that of export-led growth. Within this framework, there have been two key phases: the first running up to the 1929 depression and the second starting after 1945.

Table 3 *Rate of Growth of Gross Domestic Product at 1950 Prices (Rates expressed as geometric annual averages)*

Period	Costa Rica	El Salvador	Guatemala	Honduras	Nicaragua	Central America*
1920–24	3.0	4.3	5.4	0.5	1.9	3.0
1924–29	0.2	2.6	3.8	8.3	6.4	4.3
1929–34	0	− 0.7	− 0.6	− 2.4	− 4.9	− 1.4
1934–39	8.0	3.3	12.5	0.2	2.4	5.3
1939–44	− 2.7	3.5	− 4.7	2.4	4.6	0.6
1944–49	10.9	6.8	6.9	5.3	6.9	7.3
1949–54	5.1	3.8	3.5	2.0	11.3	5.1
1954–59	4.1	3.2	4.9	5.1	3.1	4.0
1959–64	3.9	7.2	5.0	3.9	6.8	5.3
1964–69	7.8	4.7	5.5	4.5	5.5	5.6
1969–74	7.1	4.9	6.4	3.5	5.4	5.5
1974–79	5.4	3.5	5.3	5.2	− 4.7	2.9
1979–82	− 1.2	− 8.1	0.8	0.5	4.9	− 0.6
1920–29	1.4	3.4	4.5	4.8	4.4	3.7
1929–39	3.9	1.3	5.8	− 1.1	− 1.3	1.7
1939–49	3.9	5.1	0.8	3.9	5.8	3.9
1949–59	4.6	3.5	4.2	3.5	7.1	4.6
1959–69	5.8	5.9	5.2	4.2	6.1	5.5
1969–79	6.3	4.2	5.9	4.4	0.2	4.2
1920–50	3.0	3.1	3.8	2.4	3.2	3.1
1950–82	5.0	3.4	4.6	3.7	4.2	4.2

* Figures for Central America are unweighted arithmetic averages of country rates.
Sources: see note 3.

Although the model is now in crisis and has been widely criticised (see, for example, the excellent book by Torres Rivas, 1971), it has not been without its successes. The rate of growth of Gross Domestic Product (GDP) has been quite impressive (see Table 3)[2] while GDP per head has also advanced substantially in all cases except Honduras — at least up to the onset of the present crisis in 1978/9 (see Table 4).[3] Although the

Table 4 *GDP per head. Selected Years, 1950 dollars*

Year	Costa Rica	El Salvador	Guatemala	Honduras	Nicaragua
1920	226	110	166	147	154
1929	212	128	184	184	185
1939	252	128	256	129	132
1949	286	185	220	152	182
1959	309	192	243	158	262
1969	390	256	300	175	363
1979	558	289	377	193	251
1982	493	196	353	177	263

Source: see note 4.

commodity concentration of exports is still high, diversification since 1945 has considerably reduced it compared with the 1920s, for example, when coffee and bananas accounted for over 90 per cent of export earnings in Costa Rica, El Salvador and Guatemala and over 70 per cent in Honduras and Nicaragua.[4]

In recent years, however, the model's failures have been more apparent than its successes. Export-led growth has failed to widen the internal market so that industrialisation — once the 'easy' stage of ISI was passed — has not proceeded at a satisfactory pace. The export-led model has contributed to the increase in income inequality and to the structural imbalance between supply and demand in the labour market, one consequence of which has been the rise in rural-urban migration and unemployment rates. Since the value of exports is so closely linked to the level of imports, the level of investment and the level of government revenue and expenditure, fluctuations in export earnings have been reflected in fluctuations in economic activity and the opportunities for counter-cyclical demand management policies have been very limited.

Despite popular belief, the failures of the export-led model can be attributed neither to a secular decline in the net barter terms of trade nor to the degree of instability in export earnings. As Figure I shows[5] the terms of trade show no perceptible tendency to decline over the long run, although there is perhaps a disturbing asymmetry between the periods of sharp, but short, improvements and the periods of slight, but long, deterioration. Similarly, a recent article (Moran 1983) calculates an index of export instability for various LDCs over the period 1959–75, with the Central American republics recording almost the lowest figures.

Where the model has broken down, however, has been in its neglect of agriculture for the home market. In the context of Central America, it is essential to distinguish two branches of agriculture: agriculture for export (EXA) and domestic use agriculture (DUA). As Figure 2 shows,[6] there has been a marked tendency for EXA to increase its share of net output in agriculture since the 1940s at the expense of DUA. This expansion has taken the form of an increase in area cultivated rather than in yields per hectare (see Bulmer-Thomas 1983: Table 5).

If the two branches of agriculture shared the same technology and production characteristics, the switch of resources towards the more profitable activity might be considered socially desirable. Unfortunately, this is not the case; while DUA is small-scale, labour-intensive and makes little use of capital (both real and financial), EXA tends to be large-scale, land-extensive, using hired seasonal labour and making heavy demands on the region's scarce commercial credit. The result has been a tendency towards structural imbalance in the labour market (adding more to supply than demand) and a distortion of the financial capital market in favour of export activities.

Figure 1. *Net Barter Terms of Trade 1920–1980 (1950 = 100)*

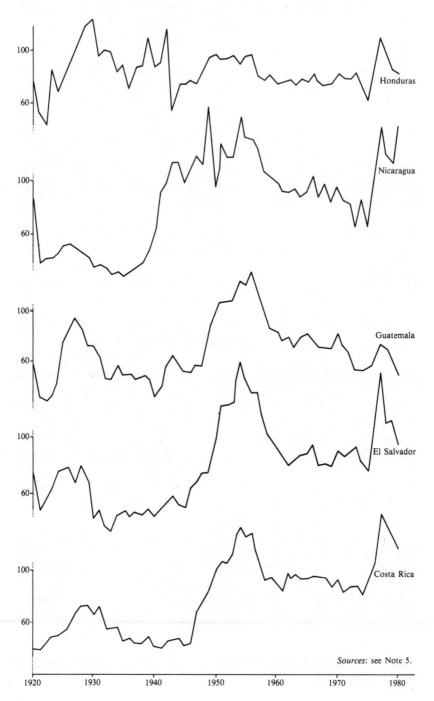

Sources: see Note 5.

Figure 2. *EXA's Share of Net Output in Agriculture (1920–82)*

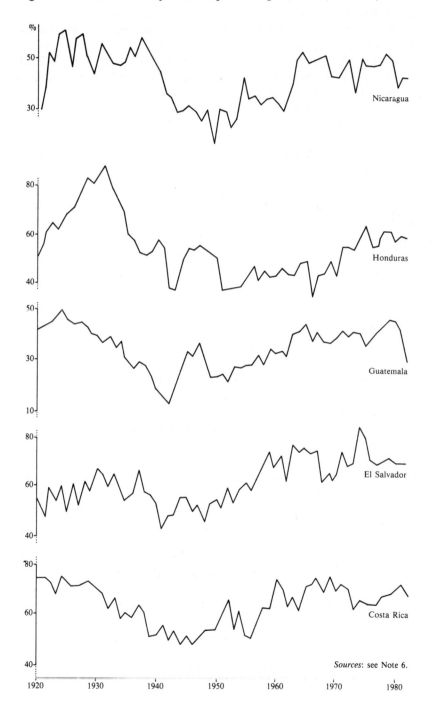

Sources: see Note 6.

The intensification of EXA since 1960 has confounded those who assumed that the additional resources required by ISI would come at the expense of agriculture. While the effect of the common external tariff for industrial products was to shift the internal terms of trade against agriculture, the resource implications of this move in the case of EXA were thwarted by favourable exchange rate, fiscal and credit treatment for the sector. In the final analysis, the extra resources required by ISI came in the main either from DUA (labour) or from abroad (capital).

The fact that EXA not only survived but even prospered during the golden age of CACM (unlike in the rest of Latin America, when industrialisation was first attempted), has contributed to the problem of industrial stagnation.

EXA has not only failed to develop the internal market needed by industry, it has also competed with industry for scarce credit. Furthermore, in periods of declining credit, EXA has been given precedence over industry, as well as paying lower interest charges. The dominance of EXA has also contributed to the inability of industrialists to develop pressure groups capable of pushing their interests with greater effectiveness.

II. THE ROLE OF TRADE IN THE FUTURE ECONOMIC DEVELOPMENT OF CENTRAL AMERICA

The lessons from the export-led model adopted by Central America must be that a concentration on increasing exports is not in itself sufficient. The growth of exports does not necessarily promote the home market through backward linkages nor impove income distribution through its impact on factor markets.

In view of the failures of export-led growth and the depth of the present crisis in the world economy, a retreat into autarky for Central America might appear superficially attractive. This, however, is not a serious option either, as the domestic resource cost of deepening ISI at the national level would soon prove prohibitively high.

It should be clear, however, that in the future, on the assumption of political change in the region, trading patterns will have to change to adapt to the socio-economic objectives set by the region's governments, unlike the reverse as at present. Trade will need to be consistent with income distribution, employment and industrialisation policies rather than simply maximising the rate of growth of real GDP.

Secondly, it is undesirable that trade should occupy such a high proportion of each nation's resources as at present. This is because a high ratio of extra-regional exports to GDP implies in the Central American context, the neglect of DUA and therefore the region's food supplies.[7] Furthermore, the higher the ratio, the more likely it is that fluctuations in export earnings will be translated into fluctuations in real income and the smaller will be the opportunities for counter-cyclical demand management policies. Future governments, assuming political change, will be unable to ignore internal balance (unlike their predecessors), but will have little influence over export earnings (in common with their predecessors). The only solution, therefore, would seem to be a reduction in the export ratio.

If exports decline in relative terms, how will the goods currently imported from outside the region become available? The answer depends critically on the assumption of political change; if this assumption is made, income distribution over the medium term will improve and the internal market of each country will widen; at the same time, political change at the regional level would permit the restructuring of CACM, so that the regional market would also expand. For both reasons, considerable opportunities for further ISI would arise and the extra resources required would come in the main from EXA.

In the absence of political change, the relative decline in exports (i.e. exports growing more slowly than GDP) would probably not occur. Indeed, a more likely scenario is an absolute decline in exports with the released resources left idle or unemployed; this has happened to some extent since 1978 and is conditioned by the difficulty of expanding DUA under the current land tenure system and ISI with the present distribution of income.

A third desirable objective for the future of trade is a reduction in geographic, and to a lesser extent, commodity concentration. The uncertainties in the world economy and the growth of protectionist sentiment in the North make it undesirable for Central America to be so heavily dependent in the case of extra-regional exports on a handful of products and two markets (USA, EEC). Paradoxically, although I believe a reduction in commodity concentration to be less important as an objective, I believe it will be easier to achieve than a reduction in geographic concentration.

III. THE MAIN TRADING REGIONS

The European Economic Community (EEC)

Until the First World War, with the exception of Honduras, the major market for Central American exports was Western Europe. This market was eclipsed by that of the United States following the outbreak of hostilities. In more recent decades, however, there has been a revival in the importance of the EEC market, so that the US market for Central American exports is now dominant only in the case of Honduras.

Although Latin America's share of total EEC imports has declined since 1960, the importance of the EEC market for Latin American exports has actually increased. This is true of Central America as well, although the share tends to fluctuate dramatically as coffee prices vary.

As far as Central America is concerned, exports to the EEC are virtually confined to agricultural products. Of these by far the most important is coffee, where the market is segmented into four types: unwashed Arabicas (produced mainly by Brazil), Robustas (produced mainly by African growers), Colombian Milds (produced mainly in Colombia) and Other Milds, where Central American producers are dominant.

While world trade in coffee has grown at a comparatively modest rate between 1950 and 1980 (2.5 per cent per annum), most Central American producers have been able to improve on that and the region's share of world exports in volume terms rose from 8.9 per cent in 1950 to 11.9 per cent in 1980. During the same period, there has been a marked shift in the coffee market away from unwashed Arabicas to Robustas and Other Milds, while at the same time the EEC's share of world imports of 'green' coffee has gone from 18.9 per cent to 36.2 per cent. Thus, Central America's growing trade with the EEC has been based essentially on a decline in Brazil's market share and a change in tastes in favour of the higher quality Other Milds.

These long-run favourable trends in the coffee market may be difficult to sustain. First, a continuing decline in Brazil's market share is something which can no longer be assumed; indeed, there are signs that Brazil may be forced to increase its world market share in order to ease its problems of external imbalance. Secondly, the existence of an International Coffee Agreement, of which both the EEC and Central American countries are members, based on exportable quotas, means that a growing proportion of coffee exports have to be sold in non-traditional markets at a heavy discount.

In its trade with the EEC, Central America (like the rest of Latin America) suffers from a number of disadvantages. One of these refers to its exclusion from the group of so-called ACP countries, which enjoy preferential access to the EEC market under the Lomé convention. In 1975, there were 46 ACP countries; by the time of the second agreement in 1980, there were 63.[8] Thus, whatever its shortcomings, Lomé remains popular among LDCs and this suggests that excluded regions are at a serious disadvantage.

The preferential treatment given to ACP countries takes many forms, including duty-free access for many primary products to the EEC on a non-reciprocal basis. Thus, coffee from Latin America must pay a 5 per cent *ad valorem* tariff (7 per cent before the Tokyo round), while coffee from ACP countries pays no tax.

Since coffee from ACP countries (Robustas) is only an imperfect substitute for coffee from Central America (Other Milds), this price advantage has not been too serious. This is not the case for all agricultural commodities, however, and bananas are a case in point. Several EEC countries (Belgium, Netherlands, Luxembourg, Ireland and Denmark) impose a 20 per cent *ad valorem* tariff on banana imports, which is not applicable to ACP countries (Langhammer 1980). So far, ACP countries have been unable to exploit this advantage, but it must put future Central American exports to those countries at risk.

A further impediment to Central America's trade with the EEC is the Common Agricultural Policy (CAP). In order to defend CAP prices, a variable levy is applied to imports into the EEC which eliminates any price advantage an exporter might have. The main affected products which might be of interest to Central America are sugar, beef and maize.

In all three cases, ACP countries enjoy preferential treatment over Latin America. Maize enjoys a reduced variable levy, while beef from Botswana and Swaziland (two ACP countries) is allowed in duty-free up to a pre-fixed maximum amount. In the case of sugar, the EEC operates a system of quotas and guaranteed prices for ACP countries, which does not apply to Latin America.

The inclusion of sugar in the CAP and the preferential treatment given to ACP countries has been particularly serious for Central America. High internal prices for beet sugar had converted the EEC from a net sugar importer to a net exporter by 1977; thus, Central America has lost a profitable market and, in addition, EEC exports dumped on the world market have pushed world prices down to levels below or close to cost of production.

The problem of the world sugar market has been compounded by the reluctance of the EEC to join the International Sugar Agreement (ISA). With EEC support, it is generally assumed that an agreement similar to that applied in the case of coffee could be made operational even without reform of the CAP. Without EEC membership the ISA is unworkable.

There are therefore serious barriers in the way of expanded trade between the EEC and Central America. There are also various opportunities, which should not be overlooked; the most important of these refers to the Generalised System of Preferences (GSP).

The origin of the GSP scheme lies in UNCTAD I, which resulted in 1971 in the establishment of preferential treatment for manufactured goods from most LDCs to most DCs; the scheme was renewed in 1981 with minor modifications and an extensive review of the scheme is planned for 1985 (Weston 1982).

Unlike Lomé I and Lomé II, the GSP puts Latin America and ACP countries on an equal footing as far as access to the EEC market is concerned. Unfortunately, preferential treatment has not always meant preferential access and the EEC has operated the GSP scheme in such a way that only the most aggressive exporters (mainly from Asia) have been able to extract much benefit. In addition, textile exports are already covered by the highly restrictive Multifibre Agreement (MFA) and the GSP comes complete with such an elaborate system of quotas and ceilings that there is little immediate prospect for exporters of manufactured goods from areas such as Central America.

In the medium-term, however, the prospects are better. The present GSP distinguishes between four categories of industrial products: textiles, very sensitive products, less sensitive products and non-sensitive products, and the degree of restriction applied to LDC exports is in descending order. Thus, some 1700 non-sensitive products face unrestricted duty-free entry, although this can still be withdrawn at any time at the request of an EEC state after ten days' notice.

In the medium-term, the enlargement of the EEC to include Spain and Portugal can be anticipated. This could have an important bearing on EEC relations with Latin America in general and Central America in particular for several reasons.

First, the enlargement of the EEC must surely lead to the breakdown of the CAP. The entry of Spain alone would add substantially to the arable land of the Community, many of the products from which would qualify for CAP status. The breakdown of CAP, however, would represent important new trading possibilities for Central America not only in maize, beef and sugar, but also in seasonal fruits and vegetables.

Second, as the Lomé Conventions have shown, trade agreements and patterns are not unaffected by colonial experience and history and Spain's membership could prove interesting in this respect. In addition, Spain is one of that growing number of countries which wish to see Western Europe exercise a relationship with Latin America independent of US policy towards the region.

Central America could prove a testing ground for these ideas. Although there are agreements between the two regions, they are of negligible commercial importance (Herrera Caceres 1982). The EEC, however, has signed bilateral trade agreements with various Latin American countries (Argentina in 1971, Brazil in 1979, Uruguay in 1973 and Mexico in 1975) (Muniz 1980) and is currently negotiating with the Andean Pact. On the assumption of political change in the region, an agreement between the EEC and Central America covering, among other things, commercial relations might be reached, which would help to reduce the disadvantage of Central America vis-à-vis the ACP countries.

Realistically, however, not a great deal can be expected in the medium term. The EEC market for Central American coffee is unlikely to expand rapidly, while the sugar market will continue to suffer from the consequences of EEC policy. Banana exports could be threatened by the preferential treatment given to ACP countries, while manufactured exports (even if they grew rapidly) would make little absolute impression.

The United States Market

Although the US market has declined in importance since 1945, both in terms of the destination of exports and as a source of imports, it remains the largest single market for the region as a whole. Almost irrespective of the pace of political change in the region, this is likely to remain true for many years to come.[9]

Unlike the case of the EEC, Central American exports to the USA do not face discrimination vis-à-vis other LDCs with the exception of Puerto Rico, whose products have unrestricted entry. The USA is also a signatory to the GSP, the ICA and the ISA.

Despite this, Central America faces various non-tariff barriers particularly in the markets for its traditional exports. Sugar is a good illustration; although the USA has ratified the ISA, domestic interests forced the US Administration to impose sugar import quotas country by country in 1982; in 1983, furthermore, Nicaragua's sugar quota was reduced virtually to zero for obviously political reasons.

The present US Administration is also anxious to create its own version of the Lomé Convention for the countries of Central America and the Caribbean. Known as the Caribbean Basin Initiative (CBI), this scheme offers a variety of aid and trade measures to all Central American countries except Nicaragua. The CBI is very similar to Lomé II, except that no provision is made for compensating countries for fluctuations in export earnings (the so-called STABEX and SYSMIN provisions of Lomé II).

Although nearly 90 per cent of the Caribbean Basin's exports to the USA already enjoy duty-free access, the CBI is intended to apply for twelve years and this might encourage a shift of resources into activities which previously faced tariff barriers. Non-tariff barriers are likely to be less severe than those facing ACP countries in the EEC market or those facing all LDCs under the GSP scheme. The CBI may therefore offer in the medium-term an avenue for the above proportionate expansion of certain manufacturing activities.

One of those activities is likely to be food-processing. Indeed, the export from Central to North America of fresh and canned fruits and vegetables is likely to grow rapidly. This is because the traditional Latin American supplier of this market (Mexico) is shifting fruit and vegetable production from exports to the home market.[10]

Under the circumstances, the US market must be considered slightly more promising than the EEC in the medium term. This is particularly true of non-traditional exports, where distance from the EEC is a serious non-tariff barrier to the growth of trade. In the case of traditional exports, trade expansion will be hampered by the quotas which apply to beef, sugar and coffee.

The Central American Common Market

The CACM in its first decade (1960–70) took Central America on its first step towards industrial maturity. The share of industry in GDP rose rapidly, an urban industrial proletariat came into being and intra-regional trade increased at an astonishing speed.

The crisis which affected CACM after the war between El Salvador and Honduras in 1969 and the withdrawal of Honduras in 1970 has frequently been analysed (see Delgado in Cline & Delgado 1978). The result of the crisis has been a slight relative decline in the importance of intra-regional trade up to 1980 followed by an absolute decline up to the present.

The crisis has a large number of dimensions. On the technical front, the mechanisms for settling imbalances between member countries have proved inadequate; on the institutional side, national governments have been unwilling to delegate any part of their sovereignty to supra-national organisations; in the field of economics, CACM has run into problems created by the structure of protection and income inequality, while at the political level the pressure groups needed to revive and restructure the CACM have not come into existence.

In the medium-term, the opportunities presented by CACM must depend critically on the assumption of political change. Central America is large enough to justify import substitution in intermediate and capital goods (negligible at present) only at the regional level. This requires a degree of inter-governmental cooperation which is unthinkable at present. Politics accounts for changes in the membership of the EEC, the East African Community and the Andean Pact. The CACM is no exception to the need for some degree of political harmony among participants in a regional integration scheme.

Although inter-governmental cooperation is a necessary condition for the revival of intra-regional trade, it is not sufficient. The next stage of ISI will of necessity require a higher degree of industrial planning if wasteful competition is to be avoided; this will help also to solve the problem of distribution of net benefits among member countries, which proved so awkward in CACM's first decade (Bulmer-Thomas 1982).

The assumption of political change, however, also carries consequences for income redistribution and the market in consumer goods. There are likely to be many new opportunities for ISI in consumer goods if income distribution changes.

The revival of CACM will also require a great deal of attention to institutional arrangements, which at present are inadequate. Existing organisations covering finance and credit need to be strengthened and new organisations are needed to cover research and development, the transfer of technology and labour migration. Above all, CACM needs new machinery for settling disputes quickly and with authority as and when they arise.

IV. MINOR TRADING REGIONS

Eastern Europe and China

Historically, the importance of markets in communist countries has been limited to occasional purchases of traditional exports, the most important being Chinese imports of Central American cotton. In the 1970s efforts were made to increase commercial relations, but these were not noticeably successful. Costa Rica signed a trade agreement with Rumania, for example, but after several years had still not succeeded in exporting any goods at all. Nicaragua has signed several agreements with Eastern Europe, but it is too early to say what the impact on trade flows and resource reallocation will be. Presumably, the main change will be to help Nicaragua compensate for the decline in the importance of the US market.

The best prospect offered by the communist countries is that of a non-traditional market for Central America's traditional exports. Most communist countries are members of the ICA and are therefore bound by quota agreements; Hungary, however, recently left the ICA and is therefore free to buy coffee below ICA prices in the cheapest market.

Another good example is provided by bananas. After the formation of the *Union de Paises Exportadores de Bananos* (UPEB), several Latin American countries came together to form a trading arm (COMUNBANA) to challenge the hegemony of the three leading multinational fruit companies. So far, COMUNBANA's impact has been negligible, with Panama alone making a serious attempt to use it as a marketing agency.

The chief problem has been the vertical integration of the fruit companies, which has made it difficult for COMUNBANA to break into traditional markets. Eastern Europe, however, is a non-traditional market, which has a very low banana consumption per head and thus offers considerable opportunities for an aggressive marketing strategy by COMUNBANA.

In addition to providing a non-traditional market for traditional exports, the economy of the Soviet Union offers other possibilities. The theory of two world markets developed by Stalin has broken down, as

the Soviet Union has come to recognise the importance of the international division of labour. This means that trade with and aid to LDCs
need no longer be based on purely political considerations (Kruschev
once said 'we value trade least for economic reasons and most for
political reasons as a means of promoting better relations between our
countries') (Guan-Fu 1983).

As a consequence of this change in policy, the import of foodstuffs
and raw materials for manufacturing foodstuffs grew from 15.6 per cent
of the Soviet total in 1970 to 24.2 per cent in 1980. In addition, the Soviet
Union has shown itself keen to finance the development of mineral
resources in the Third World even among anti-communist countries (e.g.
the phosphate agreement with Morocco). The USSR is also anxious to
sell turnkey projects and to set up joint business enterprises with LDCs.

Abstracting therefore from the international political environment,
there are reasonable prospects for promoting trade with communist
countries in general and the Soviet Union in particular. Nevertheless, the
political situation is likely to prove decisive; as long as Central America
continues to be regarded as an extension of East-West confrontation, the
Soviet Union and its allies will be anxious to avoid upgrading their degree
of commercial commitment until they have to; if and when they have
to, political considerations (as in the case of Cuba) are likely to be
paramount.

Latin America (other than CACM)

Historically, trade with Latin America has been of trivial proportions
and dominated by imports of oil from Venezuela and, more recently,
Mexico. This was underlined dramatically by the now defunct San José
agreement, under which Mexico and Venezuela supplied Central
America with its oil on preferential terms.

Since Central America has dedicated itself, with some success, towards
self-sufficiency in energy requirements (through hydro-electric and geo-
thermal projects, as well as exploration for and production of oil), trade
with the rest of Latin America, *ceteris paribus*, is likely to shrink even
further.

Recent changes in the character of Latin American integration, in
particular the shift from the Latin American Free Trade Association
(LAFTA) to the Latin American Integration Association (LAIA) (Tussie
1982) suggest that Latin America may become the cheapest market for
certain manufactured products and Central America may be encouraged
to buy from these sources; the countries of LAIA, however, or for that
matter members of the Andean Pact, are unlikely to be in a position to
reciprocate, since both Central America's traditional and non-traditional
exports are competitive with their own.

Nor is it realistic to believe that CACM can form an association with LAIA or the Andean Pact. A non-preferential trade agreement would prove disastrous for Central America's embryonic industrial base (at a level comparable with that in Argentina before 1930)[11] and a preferential trade agreement along the lines of Lomé II would be politically unacceptable.

V. CONCLUSIONS

The fallacy of composition is an argument often applied to the error involved in assuming that what is possible for one LDC is possible for all. There is a symmetrical error, however, in assuming that what is true for all LDCs ('The South') necessarily applies to any single LDC or group of LDCs.

Research on global trade prospects and the future of the world economy tends to be conducted by institutions which have a global perspective. UNCTAD, for example, has in mind the interests of the South, while OECD looks after those of the North. Other institutions with a research interest (e.g. the World Bank) are expected, at least in theory, to consider the needs of all countries.

The overwhelming evidence presented by research of this nature suggests a very uncertain future for the world economy and international trade. In addition, the growth of international commodity agreements based on exportable quotas can be expected to restrict the increase in the quantum of the South's traditional exports.

Individual LDCs must by and large take this research on trust. It does not follow, however, that the gloomy prognostications at the global level apply at the national level. A good example is provided by world trade in coffee and bananas, both traditional exports from Central America. Since 1950, world trade in bananas has grown much more rapidly than in coffee, yet exports of coffee from Central America have grown much more rapidly than exports of bananas.

Despite the gloomy prospects for the world economy, there are still opportunities for both traditional and non-traditional exports in extra-regional markets. In the case of traditional exports, the least favourable markets are the EEC and the rest of Latin America, while the prospects in the US market (abstracting from the international political situation) must be considered fair and those in non-traditional markets (such as Eastern Europe) quite good.

In the case of non-traditional exports, both agricultural and industrial, the best prospects lie with the US market followed (at some distance) by the EEC. Prospects elsewhere must be considered poor.

Despite this moderately optimistic appraisal, what was said earlier about the need for a reduction in the relative importance of extra-regional exports still applies. In the agricultural sphere, a shift of resources towards agriculture for the home market remains imperative; the market for this extra output will come partly from import substitution, but mainly from income redistribution. Eventually, the prospect of extra-regional exports may open up, although this is not likely to happen in the medium-term except in the case of fresh fruits and vegetables.

In the industrial field, the emphasis must be on deepening ISI at the regional level. This, however, is the aspect of trade policy which depends above all on the assumption of political change. Without the latter, industrial policy will be limited to export promotion in light manufactures for which prospects are not brilliant.

With ISI carried out successfully at the regional level, the importance of intra-regional trade will grow in both absolute and relative terms. This, however, should not present a problem and does not in any sense contradict the need for a reduction in the relative importance of extra-regional exports.

So far, little attention has been paid to minerals, exports of which consist mainly of oil from Guatemala, gold from Nicaragua and silver, lead and zinc from Honduras. The conditions for the exploitation of minerals have become more favourable for LDCs in recent years and Central America is no exception. One suspects that the mineral potential of Central America has yet to be tapped, but caution is called for as the same claim has been made repeatedly for nearly 500 years!

Another aspect of international trade so far ignored is the export of services. The case of Panama, for example, shows that a small Latin American country can achieve a dominant position in the export of services. While Central America cannot hope to emulate Panama's pre-eminent position in shipping, finance and insurance, it does have a considerable tourist potential and may yet be able to provide an alternative route for the inter-oceanic transport of cargo including oil.

NOTES

(1) Even if one considers only extra-regional exports (i.e. ignoring intra-regional trade), the figures are still much higher in Central America (except Guatemala) than for the average of middle-income countries.
(2) The basic data for the figures in Table 3 come from a number of sources. For years before 1950, I have used my own estimates of the national accounts (see Bulmer-Thomas 1984) with the exception of Honduras from 1925 to 1950 for which official figures exist (see CEPAL 1978). For the period after 1950, I have used official sources (see Bulmer-Thomas 1983).
(3) The figures have been obtained by dividing GDP figures by population. See also note 2.

(4) Mining exports account for the lower figures for Nicaragua and Honduras in the 1920s.

(5) The barter terms of trade have been constructed as follows: unit values for both imports and exports were obtained for the period before 1950 by dividing the nominal value of the imports and exports by their real values, the latter being obtained as a byproduct of my work on the national accounts before 1950 (see note 2). After 1950, unit values have been taken from official sources.

(6) Data for Figure 2 were obtained as follows: a time series for real value added in each of the four principal export crops (bananas, coffee, cotton, sugar) was constructed using production indices. The sum thus gave EXA, which was then divided by value added in agriculture (see also note 2).

(7) A good example of this is provided by the case study of Nicaragua carried out by UNRISD (see Barraclough 1982).

(8) For a good description of the Lomé Convention, see Hewitt & Stevens (l981).

(9) Although the US Administration resists political change in the region, its strategic interests in the area would virtually force it to continue trading with Central America if political change is achieved.

(10) See *This Week, Central America and Panama* (1983), Vol. VI, No.12 p.95 (Guatemala).

(11) Between 1960 and 1976, the sectoral contribution to the increase in industrial value added in Central America was similar to that in Argentina between 1920 and 1929. See Perez Brignoli (1983).

REFERENCES

Barraclough, S. (1982): *A Preliminary Analysis of the Nicaraguan Food System* (Geneva: UNRISD).
Bulmer-Thomas, V. (1982): 'The Central American Common Market', in A. El-Agraa (ed.): *International Economic Integration* (London: Macmillan).
—— (1983): 'Economic Development over the Long Run — Central America since 1920', *Journal of Latin American Studies* (November).
—— (1984): 'Central America in the Inter-War Years', in R. Thorpe (ed.): *The Periphery in World Crisis: Latin America in the 1930s* (London: Macmillan).
CEPAL (1978): *Series Historicas del Crecimiento Económico de America Latina* (Santiago).
Cline, W. & E. Delgado (eds): *Economic Integration in Central America* (Washington: Brookings Institution).
Guan-Fu, G. (1983): 'Soviet Aid to the Third World; An Analysis of the Strategy', *Soviet Studies* (January).
Herrera Caceres, H. (1982): 'Les relations entre l'Amérique Centrale et la Communauté Européenne', *Revue du Marche Comun*.
Hewitt, A. & C. Stevens (1981): 'The Second Lomé Convention', in C. Stevens (ed.): *EEC and the Third World: A Survey* (London: ODI/IDS).
International Monetary Fund (1982): *International Financial Statistics, Yearbook* (Washington DC).
Langhammer, R. (1980): 'EEC Trade Policies and Latin American Export Performance', *Intereconomics* (September/October).
Moran, C. (1983): 'Export Instability and Economic Growth', *Journal of Development Economics* (April).
Muniz, B. (1980): 'EEC-Latin America: A Relationship to be Defined', *Journal of Common Market Studies* (September).
Perez Brignoli, H. (1983): 'Growth and Crisis in the Central American Economies 1950–1980', *Journal of Latin American Studies* (November).
Torres Rivas, E. (1971): *Interpretación del Desarrollo Social Centro-americano* (San José: EDUCA).

Tussie, D. (1982): 'Latin American Integration: From LAFTA to LAIA' *Journal of World Trade Law*.

Weston, A. (1982): 'Who is More Preferred? An Analysis of the New Generalised System of Preferences', in: C. Stevens (ed.): *EEC and the Third World: A Survey 2* (London: ODI/IDS).

World Bank (1983): *World Development Report* (Washington DC).

PART THREE

TOWARDS A NEW POLITICAL AND SOCIAL ORDER

XII

THE ROLE OF THE CHURCH IN THE CENTRAL AMERICAN REVOLUTIONARY PROCESS

Pablo Richard

I. INTRODUCTION

At the heart of the ecclesiastical debate currently taking place in Latin America are two quite different concepts of the role of the Church: that of traditional Christianity (*Cristiandad*) and that of the Popular Church (*Iglesia Popular*). The issues joined in debate are not about dogma, nor even about some abstract model of what the Church should or should not be. Rather, the debate counterposes distinct historical models of the Church, of its internal structure and its relationship with society. Although this debate generally addresses itself to the Catholic Church, it is equally applicable to the more structured forms of traditional Protestantism.

Traditional Christianity offers a historical model of the Church in which the ecclesiastical authority, or the Church hierarchy, ensures the continuity of the Church institutions through its close relationship with the ruling classes. In turn, the ecclesiastical hierarchy reflects existing structures of class domination. In traditional Christianity, it is the relationship between ecclesiastical and secular power structures which defines how the Church is articulated to society at large. In contrast, the Popular Church offers a quite different historical model in which the relationship between Church and Society is derived in the first instance from the Church's relationship with the oppressed, in turn leading to a non-hierarchical internal organisational structure based on principles of service and fraternal solidarity.

In the present paper, it will be argued that Latin America is at present experiencing a crisis of traditional Christianity and that favourable conditions exist for the emergence of a new Popular Church. However, to analyse such a crisis in abstract theological terms has little meaning; what is at issue is an inherited historical model of Christianity. Admittedly, the emergence of a Popular Church is a recent phenomenon and one which has aroused widespread criticism. But, unlike traditional Christianity, the new Church is not in crisis. On the contrary, it possesses an increasingly well developed theology (the theology of liberation) and enjoys a clear sense of identity and mission. By contrast, the theology of traditional Christianity is in tatters and the Church, in seeking to contain the crisis by invoking hierarchical authority, merely aggravates the crisis further.

From a sociological point of view, the transition from the old model to the new involves breaking traditional ties with the Latin American ruling classes and establishing different relations with the mass of the poor and the oppressed. This in turn means restructuring relations of power within the Church. The need for change is expressed not merely as a debate between protagonists of alternative institutional arrangements but has a strong theological dimension, juxtaposing alternative concepts of faith, of community, of litany, of pastoral mission, and of life style.

At the same time it is important to note that traditional Christianity is itself divided over the relationship between Church and State and, more generally, over the Church's role in supporting and legitimising existing political structures of domination. For Church conservatives, the role of the ecclesiastical hierarchy is to lend unconditional support to the State and the existing system of domination, be it explicitly in its declarations or implicitly in everyday practice. For the reformist current within the Church, which may include Populist, Christian Democratic, and even Social Democratic elements, the degree of support and legitimacy granted to existing political institutions is contingent on how far such institutions conform to norms laid down by the ecclesiastical authorities themselves. But although 'reformist' Christianity may sometimes call upon the church critically to distance itself from the State, the legitimacy of the State *per se* is never called into question.

Within the conservative current, it is useful to make a further distinction between 'traditional' and 'neo-conservative' positions. The strict conservative bases his argument for the legitimation of political structures on the simple tenet that 'all authority derives from God', no distinction being made between different manners in which authority is exercised. In contrast, neo-conservative doctrine is more explicitly ideological and includes a 'theology of politics' which mirrors right-wing ideology. In this sense, the neo-conservative position is symptomatic of the growing politicisation of the Church and, as it gradually displaces traditional conservatism (dominant in Latin America until the Second World War), it constitutes one possible response to the crisis of Christianity.

Equally, there are distinct positions within Christian reformism. At times, reformist currents make the legitimation of existing political institutions conditional upon meeting criteria derived from the somewhat abstract 'Social Doctrine of the Church' (abstract in the sense that it confines itself to general pronouncements about 'the dignity of man and the common good' without specifying how such principles are to be implemented in practice). Where such is the case, reformism is largely 'cosmetic' and ultimately functional to the maintenance of the political system. In certain cases, however, ecclesiastical authority conditions its support for the State on the implementation of specific (and verifiable) reforms in the field of social policy and human rights; viz. the right to work, to education, to health, to basic housing provision, etc. In this view, the Church must distance itself from the State and the Church hierarchy must actively mediate between the State and the common people. But while the Church may defend the legitimate grievances of its flock, it continues to recognise the legitimacy of State power. Occasionally, such as in the extreme case of military dictatorship where political parties have been abolished, the hierarchy may refuse to recognise the legitimacy of the State until a political programme of re-democratisation is announced. In such cases, the Church acts as a quasi-party of the opposition but, where repression continues to take place, the contradictions inherent in the reformist position become more manifest and the ground is laid for clergy and laity to rally to the Popular Church.

The model proposed by Liberation Theology is not simply a 'radical' variant of Christian reformism but, on the contrary, constitutes a decisive break with all forms of traditional Christianity. The role of the Popular Church is not to mediate between the State and the people; rather it is to build the Church on new foundations, a mass base, genuinely reflecting majority aspirations. Irrespective of the image projected by the media, the Popular Church is neither clandestine, anti-institutional, nor anti-hierarchical. It is simply a different model, an alternative way of thinking about, organising and living Christianity, one which implies a fundamental change in the concept of Church. The Popular Church is not in the business of granting or withholding legitimacy, whether conditionally or unconditionally. Nor is it concerned with performing any other sort of mediating role since this in itself would merely constitute a form of legitimation. The aims of the new Church are defined from the point of view of the majority and are based on the fundamental affirmation of a people's right to full economic and social citizenship. The Popular Church considers any political system which threatens this right as illegitimate. Even where the State authentically reflects the interests of the majority, the role of the new Church is not to confer legitimacy on the State for, in doing so, it would be returning to the traditional model of Christianity, albeit a form of Popular Christianity.

It is particularly important to grasp this point if one is to understand the role of the Popular Church in Nicaragua. In Nicaragua, the legitimacy of the revolutionary process and of its institutions is determined by the extent to which the revolution provides jobs, food, shelter, health, education, participation, liberty and dignity to ordinary working people. It is not the function of the Popular Church to legitimise the revolution since the revolution will legitimise itself with or without the Church. The new Church participates in the revolutionary process but continues to preserve its ecclesiastical identity, an identity which does not depend upon any form of political mediation. Moreover, if the Popular Church's mode of insertion into social life no longer depends on its role within the political power structure, the new Church no longer has need of internal hierarchical structures. Political power is replaced by the power of faith and, especially, of hope and charity.

In concluding this review of basic concepts and definitions, it will be useful to refer to the relationship between the Popular Church and the (much discussed) Basic Ecclesiastical Communities (*Comunidades Eclesiáles de Base*). The Basic Community is an ecclesiastical unit constructed, as the name suggests, at grass-roots level; i.e. the urban neighbourhood, the village, a particular farm or school, or within a particular ethnic community or social movement. The 'base' is not defined with respect to Church structure but with respect to particular geographical, social or political entities. Christians adhere to such a Community in order to live, confess, communicate, reflect and celebrate their faith together as part of a commitment to sharing the life of the common people and participating in their activities and projects. The Popular Church is a model of the Church within which this form of Christian witness can be organised and strengthened. Equally, it is from such Basic Communities that the Popular Church can be built, though it is important to note that such a Church is more than merely the sum of its Basic Communities. It is qualitative change, rather than quantitative change, which distinguishes the growth of the new Church, since what matters in the final analysis is the impact of Basic Communities in liberating and transforming the religious consciousness of ordinary people and of society as a whole. Hence, the number of Basic Communities required for the Popular Church to realise its mission will vary according to political circumstances. Under conditions of extreme oppression, a great many Basic Communities may be required whereas, under revolutionary conditions, a small number of Basic Communities committed to the people's liberation struggle can have tremendous impact. In Nicaragua, Basic Communities have probably diminished in number, but the Popular Church has grown enormously. This point is examined in more detail below in reviewing the different experiences of the Central American countries.

II. HISTORICAL ROOTS OF THE 'CHURCH OF THE POOR' IN CENTRAL AMERICA

The rise of the Church of the Poor, or Popular Church, has deep historical roots in Central America. Over the past fifty years one can speak of an historical evolution from 'conservative Christianity' to 'reformist Christianity' and , more recently, to 'revolutionary Christianity'. Such an evolution can be conveniently periodicised in the following manner. The zenith of conservative Christianity occurred between the 1880s and the 1930s and followed a long and mounting crisis of 'colonial' Christianity dating from the early settlements in the 16th century to the end of the Spanish empire in the early 19th century. Thereafter, until the 1880s the conservative Christian model enabled the Church to re-establish itself within a framework of independent nation states. The Church in this period thrived on its continuous struggle against Liberal governments and against the rise of the Positivist movement in Latin America. One consequence is that during this period the Church was forced to seek a stronger base in civil society, particularly in the spheres of family life and education. Nevertheless, the style of Christian doctrine to which this gave rise was above all defensive and dogmatic, implicitly stressing a European rather than local character, as befitted a Church closely allied to the oligarchy and with little concern for the common people other than at times of religious festival.

The process of economic and social change which began to affect Latin America in the 1930s gave rise to a reformist current which lasted until the 1960s, though with significant Latin American regional differences. Industrialisation and urbanisation, the emergence of a new middle class, of populist movements and national-development ideologies, and the transition from oligarchic rule to a more 'democratic' state: all these forces gradually shifted the ecclesiastical hierarchy towards taking advantage of the new social space opening-up within the indigenous (*criolla*) bourgeoisie and new middle class. Hence, the Church could now escape its traditional polarisation between liberal and conservatives and move towards the middle class and more popular sectors. Obviously enough, such a change in no way implied breaking its links with the ruling class and the State, still less (with the exception of a few diehard conservatives) questioning the ascendancy of capitalism as a social formation. But it is this shift in social base which underlies the emergence of reformist Christianity, though with significant ideological variations depending on time and place. Unlike its apologetic predecessor, the new reformist current was conscious of social problems, was open to the middle and lower classes, and was distinctly nationalist and Latin American. On balance, the accomplishments of this period are significant and include institutional reforms within the Church itself.

Nevertheless, the limits of reform began to be reached in the 1960s giving rise, in turn, to a new structural crisis and creating new space for the emergence of the Popular Church.

By the late 1960s, the import substitution model of industrialisation which had been adopted nearly everywhere in Latin America was running out of steam and, at the international level, the developed capitalist countries were showing the first signs of crisis. Against this backdrop, three types of socio-political change can be identified which bear upon the crisis of reformist Christianity. The first is the movement towards new models of political subordination as reflected in the rise of authoritarian military regimes under the ideological banner of National Security. This phenomenon is in part linked to the growing trans-nationalisation of capital and, in particular, to the dominant role of US firms in the Latin American economy whose alliance with local capital depended on reversing a democratic current increasingly receptive to socialist and Marxist ideas. The second is the fatal weakening of those sectors which had been the main actors in popular-democratic movements of the previous decades; i.e. the indigenous bourgeoisie and middle class. These 'middle sectors' were either incorporated into the new political model of domination, or else marginalised and proletarian-ised, thus losing their traditional function as 'buffer' between the ruling class and the popular masses. Thirdly, the breadth and autonomy of mass movements grew (albeit unevenly) in this period displacing, both ideologically and in numbers, the populist and bourgeois-nationalist movements of earlier decades. Moreover, the ideological space for mass politics widened to incorporate new groups such as ethnic minorities, the women's movement, radical Christians, etc., while at the same time, the concept of 'oppression' began to acquire a wider definition, going beyond traditional notions of class position. Nowadays, one can speak of a veritable 'eruption of the oppressed' over the whole of the Latin American continent. Politics has ceased to be an arena reserved ex-clusively for contending fractions of the oligarchy and bourgeoisie; the rise of authoritarian regimes has narrowed the space for party politics and sharpened the dividing line between the small minority in power and the increasingly well-organised majority of ordinary people.

The above phenomena have a direct bearing on the crisis of reformist Christianity and have created new political space within which the Popular Church has grown. There are at least two reasons why an authoritarian political model should give rise to contradictions within the Church. On the one hand, the Church has assumed a more progressive stance on a number of social issues as shown by the Second Vatican Council, the Medellin Conference, and various papal encyclicals which have redefined the role of man in society. On the other hand, authoritarian regimes are inspired by new ideological doctrines, such as that of National Security, which are, by and large, unacceptable to the Church. This strains the relationship between Church and State, a relationship which is indispensable for the continued functioning of the reformist model of Christianity. The Church must openly criticise the State and court the risk of total breakdown in its relations with the State. As the relationship between the ecclesiastical hierarchy and the ruling classes becomes more fraught, so is more space available for the rise of a Popular Church.

A further contradiction within reformist Christianity arises from the gradual erosion of its social and political base, a base which is indispensable if reformist currents are to build bridges towards the oppressed within the framework of the existing system. The economic squeeze on the middle and lower-middle class, whose support traditionally underpinned the populist and national-democratic movements, has left the reformist current increasingly isolated within the Church. Today, it is questionable whether the middle class (in particular the Christian Democratic movement under the banner of the 'third way') has sufficient numerical strength to force through its own political project. Finally, the rise of mass organisations under popular leadership is co-opting the potential social base of reformism. In earlier eras the occasional surge of mass protest had little effect on a Church largely uninterested in the lower orders of society. But during the populist-reformist period the Church made significant gains amongst the lower-middle class and working classes. Today, as popular movements gain strength and autonomy and come to incorporate new groups, reformist Christians are increasingly attracted towards new and non-reformist forms of politics.

In short, the crisis of reformist Christianity arises from the fact that it must simultaneously confront a new authoritarianism which threatens Church–State relations, deal with the erosion of its middle-class social base, and see its project for the wider masses increasingly challenged (if not rendered altogether irrelevant) by the rise of autonomous popular organisations with a different project. The combined force of these factors is such that, throughout Latin America, Christianity is undergoing a profound structural crisis and the Church faces the choice of either renovating the traditional Christian model or abandoning the model altogether. It is the latter option which the Popular Church has clearly chosen. As we argue above, this is not to say that the Popular Church wishes to break its ties with all Church institutions; rather it is to affirm that the Theology of Liberation seeks to emancipate Christianity from *any* mediating function between the state and civil society.

It is true that some sectors of the traditional Church are seeking to refurbish the Christian model. Their problem, in concrete terms, is to come to some form of understanding with new authoritarian regimes, an understanding which would implicitly negate such previous advances as have been made in social doctrine. It would also mean creating social and political space within these political systems, or gaining a foothold which is indispensable to the new project they propose. Not only is this difficult but, if successful, the Church would forego much of its support amongst the people. In this sense, the institutional Church is trapped since to go back on the many ecclesiastical and theological reforms effected in the last twenty-five years would itself provoke an enormous crisis within the Church. In short, the crisis of the Church is structural. By contrast, the Popular Church offers a new model of Christianity which is viable, a model of a Church rooted in the new social space opening up within mass movements.

While the above arguments hold for Latin America as a whole, it is important to emphasise the peculiarities of the Central American region. Perhaps the most distinctive feature of the region is the continued presence of a powerful local oligarchy which, having successfully defended its position in the 1930s, subsequently was able to arrest the growth of a local bourgeoisie and of national-democratic and populist projects. The survival of the oligarchy is in part explained by repeated US intervention in the politics of the region. Also, unlike the rest of Latin America, industrialisation in Central America did not fully get underway until the 1960s, by which time multinational capital had appeared on the scene. Such factors have impeded the democratisation of the State and help to explain why the national bourgeoisie has remained relatively small and why the social and economic base of traditional populism has generally been narrow. An illustrative example is that of Guatemala where the attempt at democratisation in the Arevalo-Arbenz period (1944—54) was cut short by the US with the support of the region's oligarchies. In Honduras and El Salvador, attempts at populist reform have also been few and shortlived. Only in Costa Rica and Panama has a limited process of democratisation taken place though its social and political base has remained weak. In general, since the 1930s, Central America has known little else but repressive regimes representing the interests of the all-powerful landowning class. In the absence of a successful reformist project led by the middle class, popular mass-movements have developed, largely outside the narrow space afforded for parliamentary politics, and a tradition of direct struggle has grown, a tradition unmediated by the reformist currents to be found in the rest of Latin America.

It is little wonder, therefore, that the transition from conservative to reformist Christianity has been so difficult in Central America. Indeed, the Latin American reformist tradition, unable to find political and social space for its project in Central America, has found the Popular Church the only available vehicle for change, thus transforming reformist ideology itself. In this sense, the collapse of the conservative Church

in Central America leads directly to revolutionary Christianity. If the rise
of the reformist movement is rooted in the experience of the Southern
Cone countries in the 1950s and 1960s, the rise of the Popular Church
belongs to Central America of the 1970s and 1980s.

A further peculiarity of the Central American Church is the extreme
polarisation of base and hierarchy. The growth of the Popular Church,
we have argued, is intimately connected with the growth of popular
movements and unmediated by attempts at a 'reformist synthesis'
normally associated with middle class intellectual currents. In other parts
of Latin America, a synthesis between politics and faith has matured
over several decades within the context of reformist Christianity and has
profoundly affected ecclesiastical structures. In Central America, while
a new synthesis between religious faith and politics has grown at the grass
roots, no corresponding change has taken place within existing ecclesiastical structures. The new theology has deep popular roots but changes
in the ecclesiastical structure of the traditional Church have been slow
and largely superficial; hence, the confrontation between the Popular
Church and traditional Christianity has been more intense than in other
parts of the continent. In those Latin American countries which have a
long reformist tradition, the hierarchy has generally been more receptive
to the new theology, even where its impact at the grass roots has been
less extensive.

Three further points are relevant to distinguishing the experience of
the Popular Church in Central America from that of the rest of the
continent. Firstly, in terms of numbers, the new Church has spread more
rapidly. This is because, in the absence of a strong clerical reformist
current, no 'brake' (in the form of mediation between laity and ecclesiastical authority) has been applied to the spread of revolutionary practice
at the grass roots. Revolutionary Christians have also enjoyed greater
access to secular political movements since the vast majority of the poor
consider themselves Christian. Secondly, in Central America, the social
composition of the Popular Church more closely resembles that of
society as a whole. In other parts of Latin America, the new Church
consists by and large of radicalised elements of the middle class. Finally,
the Central American Popular Church speaks a language which more
authentically reflects the everyday concerns of ordinary people. More
emphasis is given, for example, to the 'theology of life' where by 'life'
is meant one's work, land and daily bread. By contrast, in Latin America
as a whole, revolutionary Christianity has normally had to confront
Christian reformism at a level of discourse which is abstract and
theoretical. In short, the growth of the new Church in Central America
has been conditioned by the peculiarities of Central American social
structure and political history. It speaks a language that is born of
the everyday experience of confrontation with the oligarchy and its

conservative Church allies, and it is this, above all, which explains its autonomous character.

III. CHRISTIANS AND THE 'LOGIC OF THE MAJORITIES' IN CENTRAL AMERICA

A particular feature of the Popular Church in Central America which merits more detailed analysis is direct Christian participation in revolutionary processes and its implications for the theory and practice of democracy. Although this phenonemon is typically Central American, its importance transcends regional boundaries and bears upon the relationship between Christianity and politics in Latin America as a whole. To understand this phenomenon, one must appreciate the importance of Christian participation in revolutionary processes throughout Central America and particularly in those of Nicaragua, El Salvador and Guatemala. Here one must distinguish between four types of participants. Firstly, there are what might be called Christian militants; i.e. revolutionary laics who are active in the Church and conversant with theological discourse. This sector of the laity — normally composed of young militants within the apostolic movement — was, historically speaking, the first to be affected by revolutionary Christian currents in the Latin American Church: i.e. the Theology of Liberation, the 1968 Conference in Medellin, the Movement of Christians for Socialism (1970–73) and other Christian revolutionary movements. Although originally a small minority, their impact at the base of the Church has been considerable, particularly on those who work amongst the urban and rural poor. Such Christians were the first to set up Basic Communities, in part to give more valid expression to their principles, but also to bridge the gap between their own typically petty-bourgeois origins and the popular masses. From these Basic Communities it was but a small step to direct involvement in popular political organisations and in mass movements of the Left.

A second set of actors is to be found at the pastoral level; i.e. priests, nuns, and those laics performing pastoral duties. As in the rest of Latin America, some individual members of the clergy have opted for full-time work in revolutionary organisations, typically after years of pastoral work at the grass roots when all avenues of non-violent political change seemed closed and their own flocks had turned to armed struggle. But for the majority of the pastorate an alternative style of work has developed, one which has become increasingly influential and constitutes a new and original element in the Central American equation. This style is no less political in that it recognises the need for revolutionary struggle, but it sees the role of the pastorate as one of 'accompanying' the people in their struggle while continuing to perform a pastoral function within the parish and the community. It is this role of 'pastoral solidarity', so to speak, which has become a decisive element in the politicisation of large numbers of ordinary men and women. For the majority, pastoral solidarity with the revolution has served to legitimise everyday revolutionary political activity and has been a key element in raising popular consciousness. Pastoral solidarity with the revolution has also enabled common people to understand the point of convergence between Christian faith, religious practice, and political practice.

The third key actor is the Basic Community, again a typically Central American phenomenon. Here we are speaking of Christians who have opted collectively, rather than individually, for the revolutionary process. These Communities participate fully in revolutionary work while at the same time sharing their way of life with the common people. Their revolutionary work thus reinforces the lesson of 'pastoral solidarity' and provides an organic link between the pastorate and the people. Such communities are open to common people who find there not only the opportunity of sharing in revolutionary work, but also a refuge, a place for reflection and meditation where one can celebrate the sacraments within the revolution itself. Hence, Basic Communities have been transformed into a focus for evangelical and educational work and have become an organic expression of the link between the Popular Church and mass revolutionary mobilisation.

The fourth and most important actor is, of course, the people. In Central America, ordinary working people are profoundly religious and religious practice in all its forms (official and non-official) has played a key role in building a common culture, in some cases serving as the only means for expressing popular resistance. Traditionally, religious festivals have provided the rare occasion for individuals to re-discover and affirm their common identity, constituting an implicit demonstration of solidarity against oligarchic rule. But these same cultural and religious traditions also testify to the alienation of the masses given that, for centuries, traditional religion has been used to manipulate popular consciousness. Traditional religious practice is, in short, more functional to a strategy of cultural survival than one of political transformation. It is for this reason that the influx of revolutionary Christians, whether pastorate or laity, has played so important a role, for it is the example of revolutionary Christian practice which serves to overcome the alienation induced by a traditional religion of resistance, transforming it into a religion of struggle. Such changes, however, do not take place spontaneously. Nor can they take place merely as a result of the work of revolutionary parties and organisations. A fundamental and necessary element of revolutionary transformation is the mediating role of pastoral and ecclesiastical work carried out amongst the people as part of the mobilisation process.

In speaking of the role of Christians in revolutionary movements, one normally refers to the first two or three actors mentioned above (Christian militants, pastoral agents, Basic Community members). The fourth level is the most important because it is at this level that ordinary people become the active subject of their own revolutionary process, a process which in turn transforms their religious consciousness. For the Popular Church, it is this phenomenon of conscious choice and of self-liberation which gives meaning to the principle of active popular participation in the revolutionary process. In turn, it is the active participation of ordinary people which gives new meaning to the concept of democracy in Central America, a meaning summarised in the phrase 'the logic of the majorities'. No strategy of popular mobilisation can be based exclusively on the concept of class struggle. Class analysis is certainly important to any political project since one must be able to speak of social classes, levels of consciousness, and contradictions within and between classes in order to define a political programme and to build alliances. But this is not enough. In order for social and political mobilisation to take place, it is insufficient that the 'masses' merely 'understand' a project to be in their interests. Individual men and women must consciously decide to fight for their own interests and be prepared to suffer, and possibly to die, for revolutionary objectives. This decision is fundamental to the meaning of the phrase 'class consciousness'.

While it is true that Christians, as members of one or another social class, will mobilise themselves in defence of their class interest, it is also true (particularly in Central America) that the decision to sacrifice one's life in defence of class interest invokes a more fundamental dimension of ideology, or what we have called the Christian identity. The Christian identity is particularly decisive with respect to two tasks: in the struggle for power itself and in fomenting a vision of what sort of new society is to be constructed. A Christian will participate in the revolution when it offers him both the possibility of fulfilling his personal ideals as a Christian and when he believes that the new society he seeks to build is more truly Christian than the present one. While many Christian beliefs and ideals are harshly tested, and in some cases transformed, by the process of revolutionary struggle, the basic Christian identity is not lost — if anything it is strengthened.

One cannot over-stress the importance of these two aspects: the revolutionary struggle and the nature of the society to be built. Political parties normally emphasise the revolutionary struggle at the expense of defining (in other than very general terms) the nature of alternative social arrangements. Christians, by contrast, tend to dwell on a vision of the future, avoiding the problem of political power and instrumentality. A strong Christian presence in secular revolutionary politics thus enriches both Christian and non-Christian alike. Christians are challenged to be more realistic about instrumentalities of social change while secular political parties are forced to think more critically about new societal models. It is in both tasks, of course, that the religious identity of a people must find full expression. Where revolutionary aims and instrumentalities are not perceived as consistent with norms of popular Christian culture, mass mobilisation will be difficult and a danger will exist that the revolution will be 'imposed' by a minority. Hence, it is of vital importance that political parties and revolutionary movements understand Christianity as a fundamental dimension of popular consciousness, one indispensable to the construction of forms of democracy and participation which authentically reflect the 'logic of the majorities'. While revolution in Central America can transform Christianity, it cannot destroy it, and it is a continuing Christian identity which makes for active, conscious and creative participation of the majority in the revolutionary process.

There is a useful analogy here with the problem of indigenous peoples. Individual members of indigenous minorities also belong to one or another social class but, at the same time, feel themselves to be oppressed or exploited as a group. Moreover, they possess a distinct ethnic and cultural identity which is of decisive importance in mobilising themselves as a social force. Indigenous minorities will participate in revolutionary movements where such movements express (rather than deny) their ethnic identity and provide them with a clear role in the construction of a new society. Where a revolutionary movement speaks for their interests as a class while at the same time denying their ethnic and cultural identity, indigenous minorities will not be drawn to the revolution. Equally, if such peoples see the type of new society proposed as one which negates their aspiration to genuine ethnic identity, they will reject it. Exactly the same holds true for the question of women's participation in the revolution. Women, just like men, wish to fulfill their own identity within the revolutionary process and make their own specific contribution to the construction of post-revolutionary society. However much a revolutionary movement may claim to represent women's interests as members of a particular class, unless it expresses the interests of women *per se*, it will fail.

Traditionally, the Left in Latin America has confined itself to the notion of class interests and largely excluded other dimensions of popular culture. The language of the Left has traditionally had little to say about religious, ethnic and gender relationships, all of which are part of the identity of the majority. Socially and culturally, the traditional Left typically belongs to the secularised petty bourgeoisie, is ethnically white and socially *machista*. This is one of the reasons why the traditional Left has remained isolated and has shown little capacity to effect mass mobilisation. Members of the traditional Left have been content to form small parties dedicated to interminable debate over the correctness of this or that position and little concerned with who, if anyone, is listening . (Such parties, one might argue, are the very embodiment of the 'logic of the minorities'.) But this situation has changed significantly in Central America and it is this new-found 'logic of the majorities' which, perhaps more than any other single factor, has contributed to the success of the Central American revolutionary process.

The case of Nicaragua is exemplary in this respect. In Nicaragua, Christians have identified massively with the revolution and, in the process, have found their Christian identity reinforced in each of the various aspects mentioned above. This explains much of the success of the revolution in mobilising ordinary people and in extending democracy in ways that are immediately meaningful and comprehensible. Today in Nicaragua, not only is one free to practise religion but one has a unique opportunity to serve the people, to show pastoral solidarity in the construction of a new society and to participate fully in the work of education for faith and evangelical liberation. In Nicaragua, today's Church expresses the identity of ordinary people in the everyday task of construction and not merely as some abstraction. There is no contradiction between the Church and the revolution. Tensions will only arise between the Church and the revolution to the extent that one or the other party distances itself from the aspirations of the people. If counter-revolutionaries are particularly active in attempting to use the religious and ethnic questions to sow disaccord, it is because they understand the importance of religious and ethnic factors. But to the extent that the revolution is faithful to its own religious and cultural identity, counter-revolutionary tactics will fail. What we have called the logic of the majorities, which is no more than democracy itself, is an integral part of the revolution's own logic. Within this logic, Christians have found new space to incorporate themselves into the revolutionary process of renovation, one which is transforming the Church from the base upwards and turning it into a genuinely Popular Church. It is within such a project that all workers, whether by hand or by brain, can fully realise their Christian identity.

Alas, Higinio: *El Salvador: Por que la insurrección?* (San José, Secretariado Permanente de la Comisión para la Defensa de los Derechos Humanos en Centroamerica), 1982.
Apuntes para una Teologia Nicaraguense. Encuentro de Teologia, 8–14 de setiembre de 1980, Managua, Nicaragua (San José CAV-IHCA-DEI, 1981).
Bermudez, L., T. Castro, & A. Cavalla: 'Cristianismo y Revolución en Centroamerica' (Mexico, Facultad de Ciencias Politicas y Sociales, UNAM, Serie: Análisis de Coyuntura, Cuaderno 4), 1980.

Borge, Tomas: *La revolución combate contra la teologia de la muerte. Discursos 'cristianos' de un Comandante Sandinista* (Bilbao: Desclee de Brouwer), 1983.

Cabestrero, Teofilo: *Ministros de Dios, Ministros del Pueblo. Testimonio des tres sacerdotes en el Gobierno Revolucionario de Nicaragua* (Bilbao: Desclee de Brouwer), 1983.

Cabestrero, Teofilo: *Revolucionarios por el Evangelio. Testimonio de 15 cristianos en el gobierno revolucionario de Nicaragua.* Prologo de Pedro Casaldaliga (Bilbao: Desclee de Brouwer),1983.

Caceres, Jorge et al.: *Iglesia, Politica y Profecia. Juan Pablo II en Centroamerica* (San José EDUCA),1983.

Centroamerica: Cristianismo y Revolución. Documentos de algunas organizaciónes populares centroamericanas acerca de la participatión de los cristianos en la revolución (San José Ediciones DEI), 1980.

Dussel, Enrique, 'Encuentro de cristianos y marxistas en America Latina' en *Cristianismo y Sociedad* (República Dominicana),74 (1982 — Cuarta Entrega).

Dussel, Enrique: 'La Iglesia en Nicaragua (1979–1983)' (Managua: IHCA, mimeo), 1983.

Ellacuria, Ignacio: 'Luces y Sombras de la Iglesia en Centroamerica', *Diakonia*, No.26 (Abril–Junio 1983).

El papa en Nicaragua. Análisis de su visita (Madrid: IEPALA Editorial), 1983.

Estudios Sociales Centroamericanos (San José, Costa Rica) 33 (Setiembre–Diciembre, 1982).

Ezcurra, Ana Maria: *La ofensiva neoconservadora. Las Iglesias de U.S.A. y la lucha ideologica hacia America Latina* (Madrid: IEPALA Editorial), 1982.

Fe Cristiana y Revolución Sandinista en Nicaragua (Managua: IHCA), 1979.

Girardi, Giulio: *Fe en la Revolución, Revolución en la Cultura* (Managua: Editorial Nueva Nicaragua), 1983.

Hynds, Patricia: 'La lucha ideologica dentro de la Iglesia Católica Nicaraguense' (Managua: IHCA, mimeo), 1982.

Hynds, Patricia: 'La lucha ideologica en las Iglesias Evangélicas Nicaraguenses' (Managua: IHCA, mimeo), 1982.

Houtart, F. & G. Lemercinier: *Conciencia religiosa y conciencia colectiva en America Central* (Louvain-la-Neuve: Centro Tricontinental), 1982.

Informe de la Mision de Pax Christi Internacional en America Central, 1981 (4 tomos).

Juan Pablo II en Centroamerica ECA (El Salvador), Numero Especial (Marzo–Abril, 1982).

La fe de un pueblo. Historia de una comunidad cristiana en El Salvador (1970–1980) (El Salvador: UCA Editores), 1983.

La Iglesia Católica en la Revolución Popular Sandinista (1979–1982) (Documentacion) (Managua: IHCA), 1983.

La Iglesia salvadorena lucha, reflexiona y canta (Nicaragua: Ediciónes Secretariado Cristiano de Solidaridad 'Monseñor Oscar Arnulfo Romero'), 1983.

Las relaciónes entre cristianismo y revolución. En: Cuba,Tanzania, Nicaragua, Mozambique, El Salvador, Sud-africa, Guatemala (Madrid: Editorial IEPALA), 1982.

Los cristianos interpelan a la revolución. Fidelidad critica en el proceso de Nicaragua (Managua: IHCA-CAV), 1981.

Montgomery, Tommie Suc: 'La cruz y el fusil: Iglesia y revolución en El Salvador y Nicaragua', en *Cristianismo y Sociedad* (Republica Dominicana), 74 (1982 — Cuarta Entrega).

Nicaragua. Revista del Ministerio de Cultura de Nicaragua, Numero 5, Año II (Abril–Junio 1981). Numero dedicado al tema: 'Los cristianos y la revolución'.

Richard, Pablo: *La Iglesia Latino-americana entre el temor y la esperanza. Apuntes teologicos para la decada de los años 80* (Tercera edición, San José, Ediciónes DEI), 1982.

Richard, Pablo: 'El neoconservadurismo progresista latinoamericano', en: *Concilium*, No.161 (Enero 1981).

Richard, Pablo: 'Iglesia, Estado Autoritario y Clases Sociales en America Latina. Elaboración de un instrumento de análisis', en: *Capitalismo: Violencia y Anti-Vida* (San José: DEI), 1978, Tomo I.

Richard, P. & D. Irarrazabal: *Religion y politica en America Central* (San José , Ediciones DEI), 1981.

Richard, Pablo & G. Melendes: *La Iglesia de los pobres en America Central. Un análisis socio-politico y teologico de la Iglesia centoamericana (1960–1982)* San José: Ediciones DEI), 1982.

Serra, Luis: *Las instituciónes religiosas y la ideología burguésa en la revolución sandinista* (Managua, mimeo), 1982.

Sobrino, Jon: 'Persecutión a la Iglesia en Centroamerica', en *ECA* (El Salvador), 393 (Julio 1981).

Torres, Anabel, *et al*: 'Lucha ideologica en el campo religioso y su significado politico (En los dos primeros años de la Revolución Sandinista)' (Managua: IHCA, mimeo), 1981.

Vidales, Raul: 'Cristianismo y socialismo. Convergencia en el proceso revolucionario', en *Cristianismo y Sociedad* (República Dominicana), 74 (1982–Cuarta Entrega).

XIII

THE INDIGENOUS QUESTION

Roxanne Dunbar Ortiz

I. INTRODUCTION

Approximately 40 million American Indians live within the juridical boundaries of 21 countries of the Western Hemisphere. Eighty percent of all Indians live within five States: Bolivia, Ecuador, Peru, Guatemala and Mexico, where they form the majority of the rural population in each. The other 20 percent of the hemispheric Indian population appear as national and ethnic minorities within countries that fall into three broad categories: (1) high income capitalist countries — United States and Canada; (2) middle income capitalist countries — Argentina, Brazil, Chile, Colombia, Venezuela and Costa Rica; and (3) small, under-developed countries — Paraguay, Panama, Honduras, El Salvador, Nicaragua, Belize, Surinam and Guyana. In the latter category, the Spanish-speaking countries are overwhelmingly Mestizo/Indian ethni-cally, while British-colonised Belize and Guyana, and Dutch-colonised Surinam are predominantly African.

The remaining states of the hemisphere have no identifiable Indian populations and are all Caribbean island states, except for Uruguay. Only Uruguay, Argentina, Costa Rica, the United States and Canada in the hemisphere have majority populations that are of European descent ('white').

II. PRECOLONIAL AND COLONIAL HISTORY

The Western Hemisphere was densely populated at the time of initial European colonisation. The most recent estimates place the hemispheric population at roughly 100 million with about two-fifths of that total in North America, including Mexico. At the end of the fifteenth century the population of Mexico was 30 million (Dobyns 1966, 1976) while, by con-trast, the population of Europe up to the Ural mountains (that is, Western and Eastern Europe) was some 50 million. It has been observed that Indians achieved relatively high densities of population in precolonial America because they inhabited a relatively disease-free environment and, more importantly, because the overwhelming majority had domesticated high yield cereals and pulses (maize and beans). (Dobyns 1976: 1)

These demographic figures are relatively new. During the 1960s, there was considerable debate among experts over the question of the size of Indian population in the Americas prior to colonisation. Up to 1960, the commonly accepted population figure for the entire hemisphere was 10 million.[1] The principal issue in these debates has to do with a recurrent theme in the colonial interpretation of history. As Woodrow Wilson Borah put it:

The destruction of a large native population and highly organised native political and social structures is held to mean greater European guilt because of conquest and domination; conversely, the existence of a smaller native population which underwent less loss or none at all, and the existence of more primitive social and political structures are held to diminish European guilt. (Borah 1976: 18–19)

Indeed, the traditional *apologia* for colonisation asserts that Europeans encountered only scattered 'hunting and gathering tribes' or primitive farmers, who themselves had only 'recently' migrated from Asia over the Bering Straits, and had, therefore, little more claim than Europeans to the 'new world' and its vast resources. Yet only generations after colonisation European jurists denied such rationalisations. There are few mysteries about pre-colonial America if false assumptions and vested interests are set aside.

In America, as in the three other major continents, civilisation emerged from certain centres which, in turn, created peripheries which the centres tended to incorporate, with periods of florescence and integration, as well as of decline and disintegration. At least a dozen such centres were functioning at the time of European colonisation of America. In this paper, a cross-section of three such centres in Central America is discussed. Though Mexico is not part of the discussion, the Mexican state affected the region of Central America historically and must serve as a backdrop to a discussion of the region in pre-colonial times.

From Aztlan (the North, or what is today the 'Southwest' of the United States) came the people, later known as the Aztecs, who were to dominate Tenochitlan, now a Mexican state. Prior to the arrival of the Aztecs and other Northern invaders, the Anahuac valley ('land of water' in Nahua) of central Mexico had been inhabited by a nation which had appeared some 2000 years ago and had built large cities, the largest of which was Teotihuacan. Huge buildings, sculptures and markets existed in the many cities which, in some cases, also housed vast libraries and universities. The written language was based on the Mayan form, as was the calendar used for scientific research and study.

Astronomy and medicine were particularly advanced under the Toltecs. After flourishing for two centuries, this civilisation was wiped out by the invasions of the Anahuac valley by various northern, Nahua-speaking peoples, now known collectively as 'Aztecs'. These events paralleled those of Europe and Asia during the same period, when Rome and other city-states were demolished and occupied by invading Germanic peoples. As in Europe, the invading peoples assimilated and reproduced similar civilisation. The Culhuas built the city-state of Culhuacan on the southern shore of Lake Texcoco, and the city-state of Texcoco on the eastern shore of the lake. In the late 14th century, the Tepanec people rose and subjugated Culhuacan, Texcoco and all associated states in the valley. They also conquered Tenochtitlan which was located on an island in the middle of the huge Texcoco Lake (upon which the modern city of Mexico is built), and which had been founded around 1325 by the Aztecs who had entered the valley in the 12th century.

By forming alliances, the Aztecs emerged dominant and brought the whole of Mexico under their dominion; their economic base was hydraulic agriculture producing maize, beans, pumpkins, tomatoes and cocoa as food crops, and cotton and tobacco. The crafts of weaving and metalwork flourished, providing useful commodities as well as works of art. Building techniques were such that huge stone dams and canals were constructed, as well as fortress-like castles of brick or stone. Markets flourished, as did a far-flung trade network, using turquoise for exchange (money), which came to symbolise the Aztec state.

At the community level, the Aztecs lived in clans with elected leaders. Land was owned in common and worked by commune members. The principal commander of the army was elected from among commune members and was also the main political leader and carried out key religious functions. The Aztec commander and his council exercised control over all war operations carried out by all members of the alliance. Constant warfare tended to skew the equitable distribution of wealth traditionally associated with the Aztecs since distinguished warriors received rewards in property (booty) and land. War prisoners were turned into slaves. As inequality and stratification increased, some members of the Aztec community themselves became slaves. By the time of the Spanish invasion, slavery had become an essential part of Aztec society. The emergence of a clan nobility also transformed elected offices into hereditary ones. In this manner, the clan structure itself gradually disintegrated and a formal class society emerged, while the state developed along lines not dissimilar to those of parts of Europe at that time.

The Mexican state expanded through a series of wars incorporating the territory from the Gulf of Mexico to the Pacific and northward. All conquered peoples were tributaries and their land was seized and slaves taken. Slavery eventually became a prime motive for wars of conquest as did the human sacrifice that had come to be prevalent with the development of the class-based theocratic state. A religious cult became established which required the daily ritual of human sacrifice to the Sun God.

Aztec society, though apparently flourishing culturally, economically, militarily and politically, was in the process of decay. Peasant uprisings were increasing and intensifying all over Mexico. It is possible that the reforms undertaken by Montezuma II, who came to power in 1503, might have succeeded in reversing this decline had he not been overthrown and the Mexican state crushed in the three-year war led by Cortez.

The early development of the Mexican state was conditioned by that of the Mayan state. Located in the northwest part of Central America, the Mayan State was initially centred on the shores of Lake Peten Itza and in the area to the southeast, along the valley of the river Usumacinta, or what is today northern Guatemala and the modern Mexican state of Tabasco. Later, the Mayan state was shifted to the Yucatan Peninsula where, in the 10th century, the magnificent city-states of Chichen-Itza, Mayapan and Uxmal were built. The Mayan state eventually disappeared as a result of internal factionalisation, Aztec annexation of parts of the country, and Spanish invasion, warfare and colonisation. However, during the five centuries in which the Mayan state flourished, the nobility and priesthood came to constitute the ruling group, the nobility owning cocoa plantations and salt mines. There was a distinct commercial class and the cities were urban rather than simply bureaucratic or religious centres. However, ordinary Mayan people lived in communities which retained fundamental features of the clan structure. They were required to work in the nobles' fields and to pay rent for use of the land, and also to contribute to the building of roads, temples, noblemen's houses and other structures. It is not clear if these relations of production were exploitative or democratically and cooperatively developed. What is clear is that slavery existed as an institution, slaves being drawn from such groups as war prisoners, criminals, debtors and orphans. Though slaves were easily freed and slavery was not hereditary, features of slave-dependency for labour were apparent. The Mayan population at the time of Spanish colonisation numbered around ten million.

Mayan culture is amazing to all who study it and is often compared to Greek (Athenian) culture. At its base was the cultivation of maize; indeed, a religion was constructed around that vital and remarkable food, the wild form of which has never been identified. The Mayans developed art, architecture, sculpture and painting using a variety of materials, including gold and silver. But their most impressive achievements were in mathematics, astronomy and medicine.

The extent of Mayan and Aztec cultural influence is not known but was certainly present as far north as the Pueblo city-states of New

Mexico, from which goods were carried by central Plains traders to the Northeast and Southeast. Tropical bird feathers, for instance, have been found in archeological excavations as far north as New Mexico and are thought to be associated with religious rites derived from Mesoamerica. It does appear that traders from central Mexico were also transmitters of culture, and that the Sun Dance rites of the Great Plains and the cultivation of maize by the peoples of the Iroquois nation may have come from Central America.

Another cultural centre in the pre-colonial Indian world, as varied and decentralised then as today, was the Caribbean Basin which includes not only the many islands and clusters of islands and cays, but also the continental rim stretching across Venezuela, Colombia, Panama, Costa Rica, Nicaragua, Honduras, Guatemala, Mexico, Texas, Louisiana, Mississippi, Alabama and Florida. This region, like the rich and temperate Pacific Northwest, was a paradise where hunger and want were virtually unknown. Connected by cultural, clan and trade bonds, the region may have included states or federations which have not been detected. Pre-colonial cultures have been little studied in the Caribbean and most indigenous inhabitants were annihilated or merged with African populations in slavery. The best-known groups were the Caribs, Arawaks, and the flourishing Chibchin-speaking peoples of the South American rim. The total population of the Caribbean before European colonisation was surely at least several million. The most recent demographic studies, referred to above, suggest that Española (Haiti-Dominican Republic) alone had a population of several million.

Whatever disagreement may exist about the size of the pre-colonial Indian population, nobody doubts that there was a massive and rapid decline in population during the 16th and 17th centuries. Commonly referred to as the most extreme 'demographic disaster' in human history, it is rarely called genocide. The 'decline' is nearly always attributed to the spread of epidemic diseases among non-immunised Indian people. 'Most historians now agree that introduced-disease was the major killer of New World Indians and seems to be the only way to explain the rapidity of decline in many areas. This is confirmed by hundreds of reports in the documentary record' (Denevan 1976: 4–5). Denevan, who has summarised and assessed works on demography updating and upgrading population figures, also emphasises colonial warfare as a major killer of Indian people, which reinforced the lethal impact of disease. There were, of course, military actions by Europeans against Indians, but many more were by Indians allied with Europeans against Indians. Other reasons cited by Denevan include massacres, starvation or malnutrition associated with the breakdown of subsistence food production, and loss of will to live or reproduce, including infanticide, suicide and abortion, and massive deportations as slave labour (Ibidem: 6).

However, another scholar detects a tendency to 'accept uncritically a fatalistic "epidemic plus lack of acquired immunity" explanation for the massive decline of Indian populations without sufficient attention to the socioeconomic factors ... which predisposed the natives to succumb to even slight infections' (Keen 1971: 353).

What is known, however, is that the population of Central Mexico was reduced from thirty million to four million in a few decades, and the Inca state population was reduced to less than a million. The total Indian population of the hemisphere fell from 100 million to ten million between 1492 and 1560.

What made such human destruction possible was the rise of the modern state in Western Europe, based on capital accumulation through the exploitation of human labour on an organised and massive scale and requiring the displacement of subsistence and tribute-paying producers from their lands. These developments combined with technological innovations to develop more effective weapons. All together, these factors constitute the equation that characterises colonialism. The Caribbeans and Central Americans were the first victims.

Colonisation by the various European states had similar goals and used similar methods. What was different about 17th century colonisation, the period during which the strip of 13 small colonies was implanted by the British along the North Atlantic seaboard, was the violent competition between European powers for hegemony on the continent. To a large extent, the battle for colonies and for the wealth they produced was the ultimate battle for state power in Europe. The hardest blow fell on the indigenous nations of North America where competition between France, Spain and Britain eventually gave rise to colonial wars which involved allying with and arming Indian groups and nations to do the actual fighting. The Seven Years War, fought between France and Britain on the continent, was also fought in North America where it is known as the French and Indian War. Britain was the winner but all Indians involved were the losers. Britain's victory paved the way for the appearance of the USA and Canada. The other main area of competition and warfare was the Caribbean, a factor of primary importance when looking at ethnic issues in Central America today.

The main factor underlying present realities in the Americas is the birth of the United States, the first empire born as a state.[2] The French revolution effectively ended with the Napoleonic Wars and with France abandoning its North American investments and the USA inheriting them. The huge Louisiana territory, which the French had never attempted to colonise but rather had used for the extraction of furs, was to be the first territory annexed by the US in its eventual ocean-to-ocean territorial claim ('manifest destiny'). Before moving to the military conquest of the Central Plains, the US consolidated the rich farmland of the southeast, displacing most of the agrarian Indian nations rooted there. Next, the US expanded into the old Northwest and the Ohio valley and laid waste to their peoples, deporting the remnants to the Oklahoma Territory which was to serve as a homeland for the relocated southern nations. By 1840, the US could claim to have pacified and colonised all the territory up to the Mississippi River, less than half its eventual territory.

The next stage was that of territorial annexation through wars against newly-liberated former Spanish colonies in Mexico and Central America. Half the territory of the Republic of Mexico was seized, the plum being California, and Central America was placed under indirect control. Having consolidated the northern Mexican territory, and the Oregon territory, the US moved to connect up the two seaboard territories by railroad. Helped by tremendous capital accumulation in part arising from the boom in slave-labour-powered cotton production, the US Treasury underwrote the building of the railroads by private capital. In this way, the uncolonised portions of the Mexican cession area — New Mexico in particular — and the peoples of the North, Central and Southern Plains (the mounted Algonquin and other bison-hunting peoples) were brought under the dominion of US capital and, in particular, were forced to negotiate over 'right-of-way' for the crossing of the railroads. During the 1870s, following the interruption of the US civil war which overthrew the agrarian planter-class and firmly established the hegemony of finance capital, the US military machine moved into the Great Plains and came close to exterminating the peoples of that region.

Following continental consolidation, the US joined Britain, Germany, France, the Netherlands, Russia and Japan in the competition for overseas investments; that is to say, imperialism. The US first annexed and brought within its sphere of interest the remaining Spanish colonies, Puerto Rico and the Phillipines, which were annexed, and Cuba which was occupied. The US also annexed numerous Pacific territories, incorporating Hawaii and Alaska on a permanent basis. As the European powers competed on the continent, and for territorial power in Africa and Asia, the US focused on the economic control of the Western Hemisphere. Central America and the Caribbean were regarded as strategically pivotal to the maintenance of this hegemony.

III. THE INDIAN SITUATION IN CENTRAL AMERICA

In Central America, there are a myriad of clearly identifiable Indian communities. Half of the ethnically distinct Indians of Central America are those of the Maya nation in Guatemala, where they constitute the majority of the population (four million Maya Quiche people out of seven million Guatemalans). For these people, oral Spanish is either a second language or else they do not speak it at all, and they are rarely literate either in Spanish or in their native language. In other Central American countries, the composition of the peasantry, which forms the overwhelming majority of the Central American population, is mainly Indian. Many of these peoples have assimilated the language and religion of the colony but retain distinct Indian cultural traits, including communal social structures. The majority of the peoples of El Salvador, Honduras, Nicaragua, Costa Rica and Panama are poor Mestizos, discriminated against as a national group. In addition, within each of these small Central American nations, ethnically unassimilated Indians make up between five and fifteen percent of the population.

In El Salvador, the population is four million. Following the 1932 massacres that left over 30,000 Indians dead, the term 'Indian' seems to have fallen into disuse. But prior to that time, government population statistics stated that 20 percent of the total population was Indian (did not speak Spanish at all), and 78 percent was Mestizo. It is estimated that there remain tens of thousands of Pipeles, who are of Aztec-Toltec origin, concentrated in the Department of Sonsonate. There are also surviving Nahua, Quiche, and Cakchiquel communities.

Of the three million people of Honduras, some ten percent are listed as Indian, and seventy percent as Mestizo. The Indian population may in fact be considerably higher since statistics depend on individual declarations and the term 'Indio' has a strongly pejorative connotation. Most of the Indian peoples of Honduras, as well as most Mestizos, are descendents of Aztec and Mayan peoples. In western Honduras, one finds the Chorotega, Miquirano, and Goajiro communities. In the Department of La Paz live the Opatoro people, while a few hundred Jicaque people live in the Department of Yoro. In the northern Olancho department are the Paya, and on the Atlantic or Caribbean coast are the Miskitu and Sumu communities, with the majority of those nations lying within Nicaragua. To the north of the Tinto river, along that coast, live the 'Black' Carib or Garifuna-speaking Afro-Indian people, originally from Saint Vincent in the Caribbean. They speak the indigenous Carib language and retain Carib culture. This group also has established communities in Belize, formerly British Honduras, where there are also numerous Mayan Indian communities.

In Nicaragua, out of a population of 2.5 million, about six percent is Indian, the great majority of whom live in the eastern region of the country. The population base of the western part of Nicaragua is the same as that of El Salvador and Honduras.

Costa Rica, on the other hand, is a settler State with a predominantly European population base. Probably no more than 25 percent of the population is non-European, and that part breaks down into approximately two percent Indian, fifteen percent Mestizo-Indian, and eight percent African and Afro-Indian. The largest Indian groups are the Bribri in the Talamanca region in the southern mountains, and the Boruca in the southwest of the country. There are also several hundred Chortega-Mangue (Nicoya peninsula) and Guatuso (northern and western borders).

In Panama, the total population is less than two million, and Indians make up about ten percent, while Mestizos (mostly Afro-Indian, not Euro-Indian) make up seventy percent of the total population. There are about 100,000 Africans and perhaps the same number of Europeans. Actually, Panama, like El Salvador, Honduras and Nicaragua, is over-whelmingly indigenous in race and culture. The largest ethnic group is the Cuna who are located in the far eastern part of the Isthmus, in the coastal and forest area of the San Blas district, and on the group of islands making up the San Blas archipelago. There are also Cuna com-munities around Northern Darien, particularly around the headwaters of the rivers Chucunaque, Capeti, Pucro and Paya. The Cuna make up about one-third of the Indian population and total perhaps 100,000 people. The next largest ethnic group is the Guaymi, who live in the forests of the inland mountains, valleys and savannas of the regions of Chiriqui, Bocas del Toro and Veraguas. The third major group is the Choco who live in the valley regions of the forests of Darien. Another group, composed in fact of Mestizos but who have taken on the par-ticular ethnic identity of 'Cholo', live in communities near the Isthmus.

In a brief survey of the Indians of Central America, it is most important to focus on the relationship of Indians to the revolutionary processes in the region within an historical context. Up to the 1830s, Central America was a political and multi-cultural unit as well as a geographical region. In 1821, the Central American Republic declared its independence from Spain but Britain and the United States soon exercised pressures which led to the creation of the separate republics that exist today.

Mesoamerica, or Central America, is an ancient unitary region within which both cultural diversity and regional integration were uncontradic-tory. The centre of indigenous culture and development, which stretches from the Panama isthmus to North America (as far as the Great Lakes, Northern California and Florida), was the Valley of Mexico. Even before the trauma of European colonialism, rapid and radical transformation of that centre took place in the 15th century under the theocratic state rule of the Queztlcoatl cultists. This theocracy extended its control far beyond the Valley of Mexico, reducing communal peoples to tribute-paying serfs, and subjecting other peoples as far north as Kansas and as far south as Nicaragua.

Though Spanish conquerers were not welcomed by Meso-americans as 'gods' or 'saviours' as European and American history would have us believe, the conquerers did find an extensive empire of subject peoples, dominant cliques and dissident elements, conditions conducive to colonialist consolidation. Under Spanish colonialism, the region remained essentially undivided. The geopolitical division that did develop was between the Caribbean coast of Central America, dominated by Anglo-imperialism, and the Pacific and central zones dominated by the Spanish. Spain with its far-flung empire and a rapidly declining economic base (and threatened by increasing competition from other European powers, particularly Britain) attempted to centralise its power base in the Valley of Mexico and in the Andes, the sources of gold and silver, effectively reducing other regions under its control to peripheral status. Like other peripheral regions of the Spanish empire, the Central American area was regarded as a source of forced labour to be exported to the more productive regions. One part of the empire, the Pacific zone of Nicaragua, was very nearly depopulated as a result of a century of transporting enslaved Indians to the mining region of Peru and other parts of the empire. Few Spaniards, perhaps 200 at most, ever settled on the Pacific coast of Nicaragua, so that the approximately 80,000 indigenous people who remained from the more than one million Indians deported as slaves formed the base of the present population of the Pacific zone of Nicaragua, which even today remains sparsely populated (13 persons per square kilometer). Population also fell throughout the rest of Central America in the first hundred years of Spanish colonialism (16th century), though far less dramatically than in Nicaragua.

Ethnicity is a more difficult phenomenon to assess than demography.[3] In Central America, two important historical processes provide the context for studying the Indian situation today: the particularities of more than three centuries of Spanish colonialism (and two centuries of competing British colonialism) and 150 years of United States political and economic domination which Central Americans call 'imperialism'. Present ethnic relationships are strongly conditioned by these historical factors.

The revolutionary process in Guatemala, discussed briefly in Part V below, stresses the cultural rights and equality of the dozens of exploited Indian groups who, together, make up more than half the population of Guatemala. The new Guatemala, it is said, will be a complex, multiethnic nation-state. On the other hand, El Salvador has become an ethnical homogeneous nation. But the poverty-stricken population is ruled by a narrow and entrenched oligarchy supported by the United States government. This oligarchy suppressed an earlier revolution in 1932 using exceptionally violent means that amounted to genocide. Indian dress and language were among the criteria for choosing victims.

The massacre in El Salvador effectively suppressed organised resistance for nearly three generations, and also suppressed Indian language and dress. However, El Salvador is essentially an indigenous nation that has developed a unitary national culture.

In fact, thousands of Pipile people have survived as a distinct group in El Salvador, and apparently have preserved more of their language and culture than is generally thought. Ethnic revindications may therefore accompany national liberation. Whether or not Salvadorians in general will choose to revive the Nahuat language and other cultural attributes depends on the extent to which ethnic self realisation becomes an explict goal of national liberation. But 'Indianness' is not simply language and folklore. Reverence for the land and the communal construction of society are equally vital elements of the indigenous heritage in Central America. In this sense, a free El Salvador should emerge as profoundly Indian.

Nicaragua is ethnically both more and less complex as a nation than Guatemala or El Salvador. As the revolutionary process has advanced, liberated culture reflects Indian values. For instance, the response to the withdrawal of wheat aid to Nicaragua by the Reagan Administration in early 1981 was to abandon the assimilated use of imported wheat and to reintroduce maize as the basic staple food item. *Maiz es nuestra raiz* was the slogan for the campaign which was initiated with the Festival of Maize. All nationalised land (former Somoza holdings) that had formerly been planted to wheat was planted to maize.

IV. THE MISKITUS IN NICARAGUA

The Nicaraguan people are composed of indigenous Indians, Indians from other regions, Africans, and Europeans, the majority of the population being ethnically Mestizo (Ladino) and bound by a common language, Spanish, and a common religion, Roman Catholicism. However, about ten percent of the Nicaraguan population is made up of peoples who have maintained or developed specific ethnic identities and who form particular communities and nations within the Nicaraguan state.

There are ethnically distinct communities in all parts of Nicaragua, though those in the western or Pacific zone are only subtly distinguishable from the dominant national group. In the Pacific zone are the Indian communities of Subtiava, Jinotega, Sébaco, Matagalpa, Muy-Muy and Monimbó (Wheelock 1974, CIERA 1980). These communities were deeply involved in the national liberation struggle and the civil war and were particularly ill-treated by Somoza's *Guardia*. These Indian enclaves in the western half of Nicaragua are difficult for the non-Nicaraguan to distinguish from the majority Mestizo, since the people of these Indian communities have lost their indigenous languages. Also, nearly everyone in Nicaragua has more or less Indian physical features. However, these Indian communities identify themselves, and everyone else identifies them, as *Indio*. Since the 1979 victory, they have presented their specific demands regarding land and cultural rights and have struggled within the revolutionary process to win their demands. Consequently, the distinct ethnicity of each of these communities has grown whereas prior to 1979, they were gradually being assimilated into the dominant culture. Significantly, numerous Sandinista commanders and thousands of combatants come from these communities.

The eastern half of Nicaragua, or the Atlantic Coast, has a population of some 300,000 people.[4] The Miskitus number around 75,000, or 25 percent of the population of the eastern half of the country, although they account for nearly the whole of the population of the northeastern region and their homeland extends well into Honduras where some 40,000 Miskitus live. The Sumu Indians mainly live south and west of the Miskitu region and number no more than five thousand. There are also 570 Rama Indians who live in four communities in the southern part of the Atlantic Coast of Nicaragua. The African community around Bluefields in the southeastern part of Nicaragua has a population of about 30,000, some being 20th century Jamaican immigrants, while the majority are descendants of Africans who successfully escaped plantation slavery in the Caribbean. The people call themselves 'Creoles' and speak Caribbean English as their first language. There are also two Garifuna communities totaling about 1,000 persons who speak a distinct American-Indian language. These two communities are the southernmost enclaves of a large population of Garifunas in Honduras, Belize and Guatemala. Also called 'Black Caribs', the Garifunas speak the Carib Indian language and are descendents of African and Carib peoples who were enslaved and then forcibly deported from St Vincent to the Central American Caribbean Coast by the British.

In addition to these distinct non-Ladino national and ethnic groups in the Atlantic Coast region, there are also some 186,000 Mestizo Nicaraguans, constituting 62 percent of the population of the eastern half of the country. They are located almost entirely in the southern and south-central region of the Atlantic Coast, and have been migrating to the region as poor farmers seeking land since World War II (CSUCA 1978).

Even before US intervention in Nicaragua led to the evacuation of the Rio Coco border with Honduras in early 1982, the information and factual base for understanding the contradictions between the Sandinista revolution and the Miskitu people was terribly distorted. One lesson from this is the importance of careful historical analysis. The allegations against the Sandinistas fall into two broad categories which are inter-related: alleged insensitivity of the Sandinistas to Miskitu culture and heritage, and human rights violations against the Miskitu people living in the area of the Coco River border of Nicaragua across from Honduras who were relocated during January and February 1982. It is argued that the relocation was the inevitable and capricious result of the inability of the Sandinistas to win the friendship and cooperation of the Miskitu people and to the government's attempt to assimilate them rapidly into the national culture.

In reference to the allegations of human rights violations, the questions upon which the Miskitu exiles base their charges against the Sandinistas are:

(1) Did the Miskitus wish to be moved?
(2) Was the Miskitu population singled out for punishment?
(3) Was the evacuation a pretext for economically integrating the Miskitus?

In response to the first question, it would appear that the Miskitus in fact requested aid from the Sandinistas. There are no confirmed reports of force being used in the process of relocation. It cannot, however, be maintained that the Miskitus would have been given a choice had they insisted on staying in the villages, for clearly the Sandinistas perceived relocation as a military necessity as well as a way of protecting the civilian population. Associated with this question is an implied one; was the civilian population at risk? The answer is clearly 'yes', though a part of the population might have preferred risk to relocation.

The argument that the Miskitu people were 'singled out for punishment' is clearly false. Only the Miskitu villages on or near to the Coco River border were relocated. There was no military presence in Miskitu villages outside that region even though in some, such as Tasbapauni, the southernmost Miskitu village, Steadman Fagoth had well-organised support and arms had apparently been stored. On the other hand, Mestizos, Creoles, and others living along the Coco River were also evacuated. It was the anti-Sandinista forces, not the Nicaraguan Government, who singled out the Miskitu villages as military targets.

Given that the region was militarily at risk, that no let-up in the attacks appeared imminent and that the Sandinista forces could not guarantee the safety of the population, it seems absurd to suggest that the evacuation was merely a pretext for accelerated economic integration of the Miskitus. A feasibility study on establishing Miskitu settlements in the region of relocation had been completed by the government. Many Miskitus and Sumus wanted to set up agricultural cooperatives on better soil. The relocation area was within the Miskitu region. Sandinista officials have stated repeatedly that once the military threat ceases, the Miskitu people will be free to return to the River Coco, and will be aided in rebuilding their villages. What is encouraging in Nicaragua today is that despite the real threat of intervention, the Sandinista leadership appears genuinely to be pursuing the goal of self-determination for national minorities. Clearly there are different views within the Government, even within the Directorate, about how best to do this. Miskitus also differ in their opinions. All agree on the basic principles and all agree that the principles are no more than a point of departure. But, for once in America, the Indian question is alive and is the subject of debate, research and discussion. In developing new policy on the indigenous question mistakes will undoubtedly be made, but the present climate of discussion suggests that the Sandinistas will also learn from their mistakes and not foreclose on the debate.

V. INDIANS IN THE GUATEMALAN REVOLUTION

Indians in Guatemala comprise the majority of the population, estimates ranging from 55 to 85 percent. In reality, practically the entire population is of Indian racial and cultural heritage, with a ruling oligarchy chiefly comprised of Europeanised families. Indeed, very few Indians ever gain access to the ruling political-military clique. Therefore rural and urban workers as well as small farmers and craftsmen are discriminated against, whether they are Indian or non-Indian.

Class, then, appears to determine social position in Guatemala. But the reality is more complex, since a system very much like apartheid prevails. Furthermore, the Mayan nation has never ceased to exist despite the assaults of colonialism and continued repression since independence. As the ORPA, one of the four political-military organisations which comprise the URNG, states:

> According to official census reports, the Indians make up a little more than half the population of Guatemala. But applying precise cultural criteria, their numbers total, without doubt, around 70 percent of the population. The Indian map of Guatemala shows 22 different languages surviving today which are mutually incomprehensible ... Nevertheless, each of these Indian peoples considers itself to be of a common Indian heritage from the Mayan nation; all have experienced the same exploitation and discrimination; all perceive themselves as poor people. (ORPA: 5)

In reality, Guatemala has continued to be ruled by a small, predominantly European oligarchy despite brief periods of reform, the best known being the Arevalo-Arbenz period of 1944 to 1954 which was crushed by a CIA-directed coup. This was the only period in which limited land reform was attempted and new policies for the Indian peoples had begun to take shape.

Since the 1954 coup, two generations of resistance movements have arisen and sophisticated programmes of counter-insurgency have been used to crush them. (Napalm was used in Guatemala prior to its use in Vietnam.) However, the core of the liberation movement was never crushed, and has acquired new impetus since the early 1970s.

Understandably, Indian communities at first responded cautiously to the call of these movements, not for lack of realisation that they were oppressed but because of deep mistrust for a largely non-Indian leadership. More recently, Indian communities have begun to develop their own leaders who have initiated a variety of peasant and trade union movements. The turning point for Indian participation on a massive scale was the notorious massacre of Indians protesting the loss of their lands at Panzos in May 1978; more than 100 Kekchi Indians were killed by the military in the municipal plaza. Then, in January 1980, a massacre of Indians and their supporters took place in the Spanish Embassy in Guatemala City. This too marked a turning point, in that it was the first occasion since the Spanish conquest that Indians witnessed non-Indians dying with them for an Indian cause. The massacre also drew the attention of the world to the Indian situation in Guatemala.

The mass participation of Indians in the war of liberation since 1980 is an irreversible phenomenon as is the growing unity of Indians with all other sectors of the Guatemalan opposition. The Guatemalan military has responded with a policy of virtual genocide. By 1981, the Indian non-combatant death rate had reached 1000 per month. However, the violence practised by the military regime of General Lucas Romero until the time of his overthrow in March 1982, was generalised and directed at all sectors of the population in a more or less arbitrary fashion.

The emergence of General Rios Montt in March 1982 brought a new strategy: that of killing only Indians. During several months of press blackout, and before the Guatemalan opposition movement had achieved unity (formally announced in January 1982), the Rios Montt regime moved to exterminate as many Indians as possible. Within three months, more than a million Indians had become refugees within Guatemala and more than 100,000 had fled the country. Rios Montt, a born-again evangelical, has stated that: 'If we can do away with communism by doing away with four million Indians in this country, that is what we will do.' Thousands of troops were mobilised in the regions with the largest Indian populations: the Departments of Verapaces, Huehuetenango, El Quiche, San Marcos, Solola, Chimaltenmango and Sacateprequez. The objective was to destroy the traditional organisational basis of the Indian people and, in so doing, to eliminate the basis for armed struggle. In reality, the nearly five million Mayan Indians of Guatemala are threatened with genocide in order to resolve the economic, political and military crises of the Guatemalan state.

A confidential Gautemalan army security document dated 1 April 1982, a week after the 23 March coup, is of interest:

[Our aim is] to structure and define nationalism, promote and encourage it in every organisation of the State and spread it to the rural areas, making sure that it forms part of

the process of education and training of the population, as a doctrine opposed to international Communism . . . make sure that programmes are conducted, designed to reduce the
levels of illiteracy, in order to make the population more receptive to new ideas and
augment the feasibility of actions directed at the molding and maintenance of nationalism.

Clearly, the counter-insurgency programme effected by the Rios-
Montt regime focuses on Indians. Like all counter-insurgency projects of
the late 20th century, it is composed of two equally essential ingredients
— war against the civilian population in order to destroy support for the
liberation forces; and a propaganda campaign directed towards the
urban middle-class, international public opinion, and especially US
public opinion. The effectiveness of the political propaganda element
should not be under-estimated.

The theme of the counter-insurgency propaganda coming from the
Guatemalan regime and the US State Department is deceptively simple
and states that, in reality, all acts of violence are carried out by the liberation forces as a means of intimidating the Indian population. The ethnic
element in the formula is a potent one. No longer is the situation described as one of 'foreign communist elements' intervening in Guatemala;
rather a part of the violence is attributable to 'inter-tribal warfare' and
the rest to small guerilla groups, composed of urban intellectuals, who
are terrorising Indian communities in an effort to force Indians to
support their project.

On 8 August 1983, another military coup ousted Rios Montt and
brought the Defence Minister to power, General Oscar Humberto Mejia
Victores. He is unlikely to alter the counter-insurgency programme
against Indians since he was in charge of military operations as Defence
Minister. A month after his coup, a new massacre of Indians was
reported in Quiche (*Impacto*, 2 September 1983).

VI. CONCLUSION

Any discussion of alternatives in Central America must take into con-
sideration the situation and role of the Indian population. The case of
Nicaragua shows that the Indian population need not be very large for
this question to be important, both as it relates to national development
and to the potential for United States intervention. An historical perspective, which neither romanticises indigenous peoples nor denies them their
full role, is crucial to all discussions of the region.[5]

Current US policy in the region contributes significantly to the
injustice suffered by the Indian populations. An alternative policy must
recognise that it is not in the interests of the people of the USA to
perpetuate this situation. One result of US policies has been the reluctant
involvement of Indian populations in a series of military confrontations

in which they have become the pawns and victims of increasingly vicious counter-revolutionary and counter-insurgency campaigns.

As can be seen most clearly in the case of Guatemala, the repressive regimes of the region have made the systematic ill-treatment of Indian populations an integral part of counter-insurgency strategy. US support for these regimes has encouraged this ill-treatment and has increased the participation of Indian populations in the armed struggle.

Recent US policy has demonstrated an inability to tolerate the emergence of new, popularly-supported leftist governments in the region, especially those of Grenada and Nicaragua. In the latter case, US policy has resulted in a massive covert action programme of arming, training, equipping and supporting the counter-revolutionary efforts of anti-Sandinista forces both within Nicaragua and those based in Honduras and Costa Rica. These counter-revolutionary forces include a significant number of Miskitu Indians. Ethnic and historical differences have been played upon in order to promote anti-Sandinista attitudes as part of ethnic identity. Undoubtedly, the decision to move Miskitu villages, though unavoidable, has intensified these feelings.

US policy since 1945 has failed to solve or even ameliorate the social, economic and political situation of the region and has contributed to a worsening of the condition and status of its Indian populations. Their standard of living has deteriorated, their effective participation in the political life of the region has, if anything, lessened and social and cultural discrimination against their customs and way of life has intensified. Life for all the Indians of Central America is one of marginalisation and poverty. Thousands have been killed and hundreds of thousands of surviving members of their families and communities — dispossessed, under-nourished and disease-ridden — are now living as refugees as a result of US counter-insurgency measures.

For all these reasons, a major re-orientation of US policies in the Central American and Caribbean region is required if any progress is to be made towards improving the condition of the Indian populations of the area.

NOTES

1. Deneven (1976: 2) observes that in recent years numerous discussions have taken place regarding the size of native populations, the most comprehensive in his view being that by Henry Dobyns in his 1966 essay. Dobyns has summarised estimates and methodology for the hemisphere and sub-regions, with the objective of analysing 'some major methodological reasons why estimates of aboriginal American population have yielded a picture of a small scale preconquest human population in the Western Hemisphere' (see Dobyns 1966: 396). Dobyns concludes, and Denevan concurs, that the main reason for the low estimates by Rosenblat and others is the failure to take into account the massive depopulation, which they both attribute mainly to introduced disease from the time of

initial European contact to the time of the first reliable population information, a period amounting to from a few to many decades in most regions. Proceeding from this conclusion, Dobyns presents a new calculation of the hemispheric Indian population by deriving a ratio of the degree of decline from the time of contact to the population nadir (the date of recovery — about 1650 for most regions of Spanish conquest). Then he determines depopulation ratios for smaller peoples or regions for which there is good information, giving a rough overall average of 20 to 1, or a population decline of 95 percent. Applying this to the nadir populations for the major regions, he produces a total aboriginal population at the eve of European contact of 90,043,000, a figure that is enormously larger than earlier estimates. Some of the major studies and their estimates are: Kroeber (1934) estimated 8,400,000; Rosenblat (1954) 13,380,000; Steward (1949) 15,490,000; Sapper (1924) from 37 million to 48.5 million; Morner (1967) 33,300,000; Denevan (1966) and Jacobs (1974) estimated between 50 and 100 million, Chaunu (1969) estimated 80 to 100 million, and Borah (1964) estimated the high 100 million figure.
2. Williams (1980) argues that imperialism is the basis of state power, not its product, in the United States.
3. See Morner (1967) for a good summary of racial and ethnic identity in Latin America. Since Indian-ness is the lowest ethnic category in Latin American societies, and language, dress, custom and community responsibility comprise the definition of 'Indian', any individual who so chooses may, and is encouraged by national society to do so, abandon the culture and 'become' Mestizo or Ladino. This process of 'upward mobility' differs from Anglo-America where physical appearance, particularly skin colour, is a bar to social mobility even if wealth is accumulated. It should be pointed out, however, that the ruling classes of Latin America have long reproduced themselves, and these oligarchies are more or less, as in the United States, hereditary; few among them are dark-skinned with Indian or African features.
4. December 1981 demographic data obtained from the Atlantic Coast Research Center (CIDCA), based on information from the 1980 literacy campaign and other new data. There has never been a formal census in Nicaragua, so all demographic data has been guesswork, including these latest figures, though they are considered more reliable. They differ significantly from the figures that the Nicaraguan government took from ALPROMISU/MISURASATA in Fall 1979. The earlier figures were: Total Atlantic Coast 260,000; Miskitu 120,000; Creole 80,000; Sumu 10,000; Mestizo migrants from the Pacific zone 50,000. The 45,000 gap in the Miskitu population figures is explained by the indefinite border between Honduras and Nicaragua. The total Miskitu population in these two countries combined is said to be around 120,000, while 75,000 Miskitus lived in the Nicaraguan boundaries as at December 1981. However, some 10,000 Miskitus crossed the border into Honduras in early 1982. Actually, the Miskitus give little recognition to the international political boundary that divides their territory. The man-to-land ratio in the eastern region of Nicaragua is 1.6 per square kilometer as compared with 13 per square kilometer in Nicaragua as a whole, which itself is considered a figure indicating under-population. However, the rich and plentiful agricultural land in the western zone can support a larger population than can the fragile rainforest terrain of the Atlantic Coast.
5. This paper draws on the previous publications by the author given in the list of References.

REFERENCES

Borah, W.W. (1964): 'America as Model: The Demographic Impact of European Expansion upon the Non-European World', in *Actas y Memorias XXXV Congreso Internacional de Americanistas, Mexico 1962* (3 volumes; Mexico: Editorial Libros de Mexico).
—— (1976): 'The Historical Demography of Aboriginal and Colonial America: An Attempt at Perspective', in Denevan 1976.
Chaunu, P. (1969): *Conquête et exploitation des Nouveaux Mondes (XVIIe Siécle)* (Paris: Nouvelle Clio, Presses Universitaires de France).

Centro de Investigación y Estudios de la Reforma Agraria (CIERA) (1980): *Elementos Generales Sobre el Problema en Nicaragua. Informe No. 11* (Managua: Ministerio de Desarrollo Agropecuario; Setiembre).

CSUCA/Programa (1978): *Centroamericano de Ciencias Sociales Estructura Demografíca y Migraciones Internas en Centroamerica* (San José, Costa Rica: Editorial Universities Centroamericana).

Denevan, W.W. (1966): 'Comment on Dobyns', in *Current Anthropology*, 7.

—— (ed.) (1976): *The Native Population of the Americas in 1492* (Madison: University of Wisconsin Press).

Dobyns, H.F. (1966): 'Estimating Aboriginal American Population: An Appraisal of Techniques with a New Hemispheric Estimate', in *Current Anthropology*, 7, 395–416; and a 'Reply', *Ibidem*: 440–44.

—— (1976): *Native American Historical Demography : A Critical Bibliography* (Bloomington: University of Indiana Press).

Dunbar Ortiz, R. (1977): *The Great Sioux Nation: Oral History of the Sioux-US Treaty of 1868* (New York: Random House).

—— (1979): 'American Indians and Human Rights', in: L. McDonald (ed.): *Human Rights and Educational Responsibility* (Santa Barbara: ABC Clio Press), 237–250.

—— (ed.) (1980): *Economic Development in American Indian Reservations* (Albuquerque: University of New Mexico, Institute for Native American Development).

—— (1980): 'Wounded Knee 1890 to Wounded Knee 1973: A Study in United States Colonialism', in *Journal of Ethnic Studies*, 8, 2, 1–15.

—— (ed.) (1980): *American Indian Energy Resources and Development* (Albuquerque: University of New Mexico, Institute for Native American Development).

—— (1980): *Roots of Resistance: History of Land Tenure in New Mexico* (Los Angeles: UCLA American Indian Studies Research Center).

—— (1981): 'The Reservation as a Social Enclave', in *Development and Socio-Economic Progress* (Cairo), 1, 14, 89–100.

—— (1981): 'The Context of Colonialism in Writing American Indian History', in *American Indian Issues* (Los Angeles: UCLA American Indian Studies Research Center), 159–166.

—— (1981): 'Introduction', to J.D. Forbes: *Native Americans and Nixon: Presidential Politics and Minority Self-Determination, 1969–1972* (Los Angeles: UCLA American Indian Studies Research Center).

—— (1981): *Informe Sobre la Visita a Zelaya Norte en Mayo de 1981* (Managua: Instituto Nicaraguense de la Costa Atlantica).

—— (1982): 'The Miskitu People, Ethnicity and the Atlantic Coast', in *Nicaraguan Perspectives*, 3, 14–19.

—— (1982): 'Miskitus Victims of US Intervention' (Paper presented to the 2nd Round Table Discussion on Racial Discrimination and the Rights of Indigenous Peoples, 7–8 May; University of Santa Clara, California, organised with the International Institute of Human Rights, Strasbourg).

—— (1982): 'Land and Nationhood: The American Indian Struggle for Self-Determination and Survival', in *Socialist Review*, 12, 3–4, 105–120.

—— (1982): 'The American Indian Nation in the United States', in *Tricontinental*, 84, 100–114.

—— (1983): 'The Miskitu Case', in *Covert Action Information Bulletin*, 18, 21–25.

—— (1983): 'Miskitus in Nicaragua', in Stanford Central American Action Network (ed.): *Revolution in Central America* (Boulder: Westview Press).

—— (1983): *Indians of the Americas: Self-Determination and International Human Rights* (London: Zed Press).

Jacobs, W.R. (1974): 'The Tip of an Iceberg: Pre-Colombian Indian Demography and Some Implications for Revisionalism', in *William and Mary Quarterly*, 31 (3rd series), 123–32.

Keen, B. (1971): 'The White Legend Revisited', in *Hispanic American Historical Review*, 51, 353.

Kroeber, A.L. (1923): 'Native American Population', in *American Anthropologist*, 36, 1–25.

Morner, M. (1967): *Race Mixture in the History of Latin America* (New York: Little, Brown & Co.).

ORPA (n.d.): *Indigenous World/El Mundo Indigena*, Vol. 2, 5.

Rosenblat, A. (1954): *La Población Indigena y el Mestizaje en America* (Buenos Aires: Nova Publishers).

Sapper, K. (1924): 'Die Zahl und die Volksdichte der Indianischen Bevolkerung in Amerika vor Der Conquista und in Der Gegenwart', in *Proceedings of the 21st International Congress of Americanists* (The Hague), 1, 95–104.

Steward, J.H. (1949): 'The Native Population of South America', in J.W. Steward (ed.): *The Handbook of South American Indians* (Washington DC: Smithsonian Institution, Bureau of American Ethnology; 7 vols, 1946–1959).

Wheelock R. J. (1974): *Raices Indigenas de la Lucha Anti-Colonialista en Nicaragua* (Mexico: Siglo XXI)

Williams, W.A. (1980): *Empire as a Way of Life* (New York: Oxford University Press).

XIV

REVOLUTION AND PLURALISM IN NICARAGUA

Jose Luis Coraggio and George Irvin

I. INTRODUCTION

In November 1984 Nicaragua will go to the polls to elect a new President, Vice President and National Assembly. The announcement of General Elections in Nicaragua has attracted considerable international response, ranging from the predictable scepticism of the Reagan Administration to cautious optimism on the part of most European and Latin American leaders and something akin to support from the Socialist International. All see 'free elections' as the touchstone of democratic progress made by the Sandinistas though the rules of evidence concerning what is to count as 'free' will undoubtedly be bent to serve particular interests. Indeed, the US Administration's campaign to discredit the elections, in particular by bringing strong pressure to bear on the Nicaraguan opposition not to stand, is already in full swing.

That such manoeuvres are part of the common currency of international politics is well known and need not detain the argument. What is more worrying is the simple, unproblematic manner in which many sympathetic observers of the Nicaraguan revolution tend to conflate elections with democracy. To be sure, the institutionalisation of democracy, of which elections are one ingredient, raises fundamental (and often highly emotive) issues of theory and practice, most particularly under conditions of Third World revolutionary change. For some, the key to analysing a revolution appears to lie in discovering the 'real' project of revolutionary leaders. Sections of both the Left and the Right share this unproblematic approach. In reality, of course, social projects emerge from the dialectic between revolutionary leaders, the class (or classes) they represent, and external political forces. Indeed, understanding the impact of external forces on internal alliances is often just as important as understanding internal alliances themselves, and certainly more so than looking into revolutionary minds. But if one is to 'test' a revolution for democratic tendencies, the place to begin is by analysing how far it gives rise to autonomous mass organisations representing majority interests and how such organisations mediate between the new institutions of state and civil society. This is not the sort of analysis which will generally appeal to those who believe in 'leader-watching', still less to those who claim that the government of El Salvador is 'democratic' because it has been 'elected' while that in Nicaragua is not.[1]

The present paper is divided into five sections. These deal in turn with: the nature of the social revolution and the meaning of 'pluralism' in Nicaragua; the impact of external threat on revolutionary legitimacy, in particular the centralisation of economic and political life; mobilisation and participation as part of the institutionalisation of democracy within civil society; the 'bourgeois question'; and finally the electoral process itself.

II. THE SOCIAL NATURE OF THE SANDINISTA POPULAR REVOLUTION

Most Third World 'parliamentary democracies' lie within the Western sphere of influence. Historically speaking, the question of whether such democracies offer a viable model for overcoming poverty and oppression is still an open one. So far, the record is not very encouraging. On the other hand, there are only a few examples of successful Third World social revolutions, and even fewer that combine fundamental social and economic transformation with democracy and pluralism. We shall argue that one such case is Nicaragua, a country whose revolution is increasingly perceived as a test case for Latin America.

It is important to stress that the Nicaraguan revolution is social and not merely political. This is because the phrase 'political revolution' carries no necessary connotation of fundamental social change. In socially polarised Third World societies, any revolution that is not both political and social may simply result in the substitution of one form of elitist rule for another. Initially in Nicaragua, all observers agreed that the Sandinista revolution was political and anti-Somocista. What was less clear to observers (including some leftist critics) was whether Nicaragua was also a social revolution, that is to say, one seeking to invert the institutional pyramid of organised class power.

The view of the *Frente Sandinista de Liberación Nacional* (FSLN) was that the prevailing socio-economic system, with or without Somoza, must be thoroughly revamped if majority needs were to be met and national sovereignty to be ensured (Wheelock & Carrion 1980). The FSLN fought a long war against Somoza under the banner of social transformation and national independence. As the war entered its final phase, a broad anti-Somocista front was formed and victory came as a result of a general insurrection under the leadership of the FSLN.[2] One of the underlying internal political tensions of the Sandinista revolution is the different nature of the political constellation of forces which overthrew Somoza (Chamorro 1983) and the forces willing to support genuine social transformation. This does not mean that the Sandinistas wished to jetison the concept of a broad alliance once victory was secured. What was seen as vital was the construction of new institutions (trade unions, defence committees, women's organisations, etc.) giving the majority a decisive voice within the revolutionary alliance.

All social sectors have been given the opportunity to participate in the new project, albeit under popular hegemony. Nicaragua is an example of a genuine social revolution in which the old ruling class, far from being liquidated or sent into exile, has been called upon to co-operate in the process of national reconstruction. Indeed, to maintain national unity, the FSLN has had to restrain some of its own followers and, more generally, to exercise a mediating role between contending social and economic demands in the name of the State. The first months of the revolutionary government involved, *inter alia*, restraining those elements who wished to dispossess the bourgeoisie regardless of whether or not they continued to produce. Private property was given full legal protection on condition that it continued to fulfil its social role in production. The government was engaged in almost continuous dialogue and mediation between different social groups; it encouraged reasoned argument, sought consensus wherever possible, and used minimal coercion (Senese 1981)

While it would be naïve to believe that the bourgeoisie could fully support a project aimed at undercutting its political power as a class (though some elements of the bourgeoisie did support this project), that (majority) fraction of the bourgeoisie which did not attack the project was guaranteed continued economic support. At the same time, a minority fraction, knowing that the United States Administration was 'on its side', withdrew its economic cooperation and engaged the government in a fierce ideological debate which echoed the anti-communist slogans of the Somocista period. Faced with economic sabotage, the principle that scarce productive resources should not be allowed to lie idle was given explicit legal expression.[3]

At this stage, it will be relevant to ask how far the motion of 'popular hegemony' is compatible with 'pluralism'. Firstly, it is clear that under all social systems, there are clearly defined limits to the practice of pluralism (viz , in the United States and in West Germany members of the Communist Party are effectively excluded from government office). The relevant question is who determines these limits and what form these limits take. In Nicaragua, pluralism stops short of including those (mainly ex-Somocista) leaders who are actively engaged in armed counter-revolutionary struggle. But no class or social group is excluded *per se*. Indeed, different classes, social groupings and political parties are represented at every level, be it in the *Junta de Gobierno*, the Cabinet, the Council of State,[4] the judiciary system, the mass media, the popular organisations, the churches, the school system, etc. The FSLN does maintain strict control of the Revolutionary Popular Army but the Popular Militia (which is considerably larger than the army) is open to all, an arrangement conspicuously absent in other Latin American 'democracies'.

Once it is granted that the structural limits set on pluralism in Nicaragua are quite consistent with norms observed in advanced Western democracies (and indeed a considerable improvement on those observed in much of the Third World) it will also be granted that, in any process of societal transformation, some sectors will resist anything that threatens to curtail or abolish their historical prerogatives. How well pluralism accommodates such resistance (always assuming it does not take the form of armed struggle which by definition cannot be accommodated) is an important question. Such a question cannot be answered merely by setting out a formal description of juridical and political structures; one must refer to the historical record in order to determine how accommodation, dialogue and consensus take place in practice. We can best illustrate this by reference to the external and the internal dimensions of recent conflict.

III. THE EXTERNAL DIMENSION: THE THREAT OF INVASION AND ECONOMIC DESTABILISATION

How has the Nicaraguan government reacted to growing armed conflict on the border with Honduras and Costa Rica and the threat of direct invasion by American forces?[5] One might assume that, under growing military pressure, the Sandinistas' response would be to tighten government control over all aspects of civilian life. A brief examination of the record shows this not to be the case. If anything, the response has been to decentralise. The opposition newspaper, *La Prensa*, has continued to function; although both television channels are publicly owned, radio broadcasting is predominantly in private hands. Government has been decentralised through the creation of nine regional authorities, leading to a significant growth in regional autonomy and increased popular participation in Government decision making. Arming the people has been speeded up by expanding the Popular Militias (though compulsory National Service has also been introduced). At the same time, the General Election originally announced (in 1980) for Spring of 1985 has been brought forward to coincide with the US Presidential Elections in November 1984.

In the agrarian sphere, land reform has been speeded up and a larger proportion of state land is being distributed to the peasantry. The rural cooperative movement has grown enormously and ranges from cooperation in marketing to input-provision and production. Rural mass-organisations have also grown; these include the Association of Rural Workers (ATC) and the Association of Farmers and Cattle Producers (UNAG). Within the public sector, State enterprises have been subject to stronger financial discipline in keeping with the principle of equal treatment for State and private enterprise. Despite shortages induced by the unofficial blockade and undeclared war, rationing has been used minimally. Some basic commodities (sugar, edible salt, cooking oil) are rationed, but their distribution is administered by local defence committees (CDS) and not by central government. (Petrol, for a time centrally rationed, is now controlled by a two-tier system using the price mechanism.) No private property has been taken over for national defence purposes and, in general, stronger financial incentives have been granted to private capital.

It is clear that external pressure has not led the Sandinistas to abandon their commitment to political pluralism and a mixed economy. But it is worthwhile examining the economic picture in more detail. The crisis facing Nicaragua is one which affects the whole of the Central American region. A sharp fall in the region's commodity terms-of-trade has, since 1978, resulted in a growing regional trade deficit and this, together with large private capital outflows and rising interest rates, has greatly increased the region's overseas indebtedness. Nicaragua has been subject to an even heavier burden. Both in financial and human terms, the costs of the undeclared war have been high, particularly if one includes production lost as a result of military mobilisation. Supplies of raw materials and spare parts, traditionally purchased in the United States, are no longer available; on the export side, the US sugar quota has been cut off. In 1979 Nicaragua inherited the highest *per capita* foreign debt in Central American countries and its decision to honour that debt has weighed heavily on foreign exchange availability; moreover, those multilateral agencies which had traditionally lent most heavily to Nicaragua have been under increasing US pressure to curtail aid.[6] Despite these pressures, Nicaragua's growth rate since 1979 has been the highest in Central America, reaching 5.5 per cent in 1983.

The main objective of Government's economic strategy for the period 1983–88 is to consolidate its present achievements and lay the groundwork for long-term growth in the 1990s.[7] Hence, the projected share of investment in GDP over the plan period is modest, essentially aiming to maintain urban and increase rural infrastructure and production.[8] While consumption is programmed to keep pace with population growth, any increment in real *per capita* consumption will go to the poorest sections of the population. Given the extreme shortage of foreign exchange and difficulties in obtaining multilateral assistance, it is likely that middle class luxury consumption (which consists largely of imports) will need to be reduced further. Hence, credit and exchange rate incentives to boost private profits can only be made good if realised in the form of higher levels of private investment. In foreign trade, the trend towards market diversification will continue, the aim being to achieve a more equitable balance between Western Europe and Japan, the socialist camp and Third World countries. The salient feature of this strategy is that it takes a realistic view of the inherent tension between productive and distributional objectives in a mixed-economy context. Macro-economic balance is respected and inflationary finance eschewed while, at the same time, IMF-style policies, which would place the economic burden on those least able to pay, have clearly been rejected.

IV. THE INTERNAL DIMENSION: STATE AND CIVIL SOCIETY

Politics is essentially about the complex relation between the state and civil society and how political and social institutions serve to register and regulate social contradictions. A defence of democracy which concentrates exclusively on 'access to government' is unsatisfactory because it fails to examine how the governing elite uses formal democratic institutions to serve its own class interests, and what mechanisms are available to the majority for replacing (rather than merely reshuffling) that elite.[9] Nor does such a view take into account the nature of political relations within civil society;[10] i.e. the political content of particular institutional arrangements which govern the organisation of the work-place, the family, the school, the means of communication, etc. All of these are ways of experiencing power which do not enter into the orthodox definition of 'political society'. Ironically, many of the same people who generally welcome the widening of traditional political definitions in advanced industrial countries apply a very narrow definition of politics to Third World revolutions.

What is fundamental to understanding Nicaraguan democracy is that to make formal representative institutions work, there must be genuine reform of wider political relations within civil society. Hence, the decision taken by the Sandinistas in 1980 to hold elections in five years time was not tactical. If anything, 'tactics' would have called for holding immediate elections. It was a decision of principle which argued that, until ordinary people had been given the opportunity to build *their own* representative institutions and participatory practices within civil society, most particularly in the work-place and in the community, they would have little effective weight within the formal political institutions of the State.

One must remember that the Sandinistas inherited neither a 'strong'

State nor well-articulated institutions of civil society. Forty years of Somocista rule produced an extremely crude apparatus of repression based upon personal authority and patronage. The State exercised little effective economic control beyond its ability to syphon-off a part of economic surplus, often by coercion and fraud. Nor did formal political institutions enhance the legitimacy of the State since these were openly manipulated by the Somoza family. In a very real sense, Somoza could claim that he was the State. Equally, civil society was weak in the sense that the masses lacked institutions capable of articulating and defending their interests. In such a context, the term 'masses' is appropriately suggestive of an unstructured underclass, a majority who are not 'citizens'. Not only was this true of rural and urban workers, it was also true of a significant section of the urban middle and lower-middle classes whose historical incorporation into political life was insignificant compared to, say, Costa Rica. For the Sandinistas, therefore, a central objective of the revolution has been to establish the groundwork necessary to the construction of an 'effective' civil society; i.e. a society in which the majority is able to exercise decisive influence over the State through its own autonomous social and political organisations. In the language of Latin American social theory, it is 'to transform the masses into a People'. The literacy campaign, the enormous extension of basic social provisions, the fundamental changes wrought in the rural sector through land reform, all are part of this process.[11] The growth of popular organisations, including urban and rural trade unions, revolutionary defence committees (CDS), youth organisations, women's organisations, organisations for ethnic minorities, the popular militias, etc. reflects the degree to which popular mobilisation has been given priority.

While it is true that most of these organisations are pro-Sandinista, to argue that this detracts from their popular or autonomous character is a *non sequitur*. One might as well argue that no European trade union affiliated to a left-wing political party can be autonomous. The point is, rather, that the test of autonomy lies in the nature of the dialogue sustained between Government and Parties on the one hand, and popular organisations on the other. No-one familiar with contemporary Nicaragua would argue that there is not such a dialogue, nor that the Sandinista government has been unreceptive to the claims and criticisms of popular organisations. But what is also true is that groups that are most strongly opposed to the revolution, such as the Higher Council of Private Enterprise (COSEP), see their own position threatened by the rise of popular organisations. Hence, the task of the FSLN is not merely to build a modern state but to change the way in which the State is articulated to civil society and to prevent the traditional ruling class and its imperial ally from undermining the project.[12]

V. THE 'BOURGEOIS QUESTION' AND OTHER ISSUES

Just as the 'agrarian question' is central for a society in transition from
pre-capitalist to predominantly capitalist forms of organisation, so too
is the 'bourgeois question' central for a society attempting to emerge
from dependent capitalism (cf Gorostiaga 1983). If the aim of the
Sandinistas' project were to abolish private property, the 'bourgeois
question' would reduce itself to one of organising charter flights to
Miami. Clearly this is not the case; the FSLN has made it clear that
democratic socialism in Nicaragua is to be built around a mixed
economy. The question is what form of mixed economy? The Sandinista
answer is that private capital must be subordinated to 'the logic of the
majorities'; i.e. that a new balance must be established between the
public and private sector which guarantees that the satisfaction of basic
economic and social needs will take precedence over private accumulation. Since a defining feature of the dependent economy is the degree to
which internal capitalist development is conditioned by the international
division of labour, one role of the State must be to regulate the external
sector directly (through control of trade and finance) rather than indirectly (through commercial policies). Similarly, the State must also
'lead' the accumulation process in the sense of undertaking productive
(as opposed to infrastructural) investment and restructuring existing
capital along lines consistent with a new structure of income distribution
and consumption. To act as 'centre of accumulation', the State must
ensure the availability of adequate real and financial resources, relying
on surpluses from productive State enterprise and not merely on its
ability to tax away private surplus or borrow abroad. In short, the
economy will be 'mixed' in the sense that the State will have a decisive
presence in modern production and control key areas of trade and
finance, while within the private and co-operative production spheres,
peasant food production and supporting activities will be given priority.
The market will not be replaced by central planning, but its logic will be
subordinated to that of the Plan and its functioning regulated on a day-
to-day basis by old and new policy instruments. In short, within this
model of the mixed economy, the State (in close alliance with the peasantry) guarantees production and accumulation in key areas, but the
bourgeoisie continues to exercise considerable autonomy and to operate
under market rules.[13]

The political question implied above is whether the bourgeoisie will
accept a project which grants them proportional (i.e. minority) political
representation as a class and which, though allowing them considerable
economic freedom, curtails their economic capacity for extended
reproduction. The evidence so far suggests that the bourgeoisie is
divided, a majority favouring acceptance and a minority committed to

active opposition. This is so because, historically, the Nicaraguan bourgeoisie has been weak, divided and dependent on State patronage. Significantly, important numbers of small capitalist producers (who dominate cotton and coffee production) are finding that their access to credit and other services has increased under the new government.

There are of course other dimensions to this problem. Not all individuals will see their interests as congruent with those of their class, and the matrix of relationships within a given class will be cross-cut by conflicting identities. In Nicaragua today, the parents, sons and daughters of a middle-class household may be drawn to the revolution in different ways, whether as Christians, as members of a women's organisation, as participants in the literacy campaign, etc. Within the reshuffling of class forces implied by the revolution, popular hegemony does not mean that individual members of the bourgeoisie have no access to politics; indeed, in their different roles, individuals may have greater access to politics. But revolution does mean that the bourgeoisie's class-monopoly on politics has been broken.

A revolution transforms the questions that society has to confront. In Nicaragua, the 'national question' is no longer how to build a national bourgeoisie; it is how to build an organised people as the subject (rather than the object) of revolutionary change. The articulation of a popular identity does not subsume traditional identities; if anything, questions of identity and social role become more important. For example, there is the question of ethnic minorities and of building a multi-ethnic society;[14] there is the agrarian question of how to give the peasantry its full role in the economic and political development of the country and how far peasant cooperatives are a viable, non-exploitative form of labour organisation. There is the question of women and of their role, not merely within their own organisations but within other popular organisations, within the family and within the community.[15] Equally, youth as a distinct social force is already, and will continue to be, of key importance (Nuñez Soto 1982).

The timing and rhythm of this process cannot be centrally legislated. Moreover, the restructuring of social relations creates new identities. For example, the revolutionary defence committees (CDS) are an important institutional expression of new social relations at the community level as are the new forms of local government (Downs & Kusnetzoff 1982). In short, a non-rhetorical use of the phrase 'national liberation' implies major changes in the relations of power within civil society as well as the socialisation of state political and economic power. This process may encounter powerful opposing forces, particularly from abroad, which is the one reason why, under Nicaraguan conditions, the construction of civil society must be articulated to a national project, based on the widest possible coalition opposed to the counter-revolution.[16]

VI.   THE INSTITUTIONALISATION OF DEMOCRACY AND ELECTIONS

We have argued that the fundamental objective of the revolution is not to consolidate power in the hands of the State; rather, it is to transform civil society by creating an autonomous institutional base for the majority from which the State derives its legitimacy and political power is mandated. Within this logic, 'revolutionary democracy' is neither first nor foremost about holding general elections, although elections may help to formalise democratic processes once an adequate institutional base exists within civil society for articulating particular interests and identities and expressing majority opinion. By the same token, pluralism is not exclusively about political parties. The essence of pluralism is that it allows for a diversity of views that enriches political and social practice at all levels, not merely at the level of political parties.

In September 1983 the law on political parties was approved after months of debate in the Council of State. This law explicitly states that no political group will be excluded from participation in government (all groups will have 'the option' to political power) except for 'those proposing a return to Somocismo'. The electoral process began in early 1984 with the discussion and approval of a new Electoral Law,[17] the constitution of a Council of Political Parties, and the fixing of the date of elections. The coming months will see the preparation of an electoral register and the launching of party electoral campaigns. A general amnesty has also been announced extending to all counter-revolutionary groups, with the exception of ex-Guardia members whose trials are still pending and the main contra leaders.

Some friends of the revolution see a potential danger in the institutionalisation of an electoral system which gives everyone access to power. It has been argued, for example, that the combined problems of right-wing ideological manipulation, external vulnerability of the economy, and pressure exerted by the US Administration might result in the bourgeoisie regaining power through the ballot box. Such a view, pessimistic as it may appear, does require discussion, particularly in a Latin American context where elections have for so long been manipulated by the Right. The problem with such a view is that it requires one to believe that little has changed in Nicaraguan civil society and in the nature of the State. In this view, the bourgeoisie would be dealing with the traditional 'masses', disorganised, politically inexperienced, alienated from the social process and lacking the most elementary consciousness. Equally, one must assume something like a return to the *status quo ante* under which the masses were confronted by the full force of ideological and repressive State *apparata*. But that is precisely the situation which has been transformed by the long Sandinista struggle, the popular insurrection and the consolidation of revolutionary power.

If our arguments are correct, they should help to dispel some of the criticisms of the Nicaraguan revolution voiced both from the Left and from the Right. Democracy in Nicaragua is not merely a question of elections. It is about a process of building democratic institutions in civil society and the State in order to effect revolutionary social change. Equally, our argument suggests that critical friends of the revolution might more usefully be concerned with the progress of democratisation and maintenance of pluralism within a country at war than with defending the right of a fraction of the bourgeoisie to return to power. It goes without saying that in Nicaragua, a victory by the Somocista right would not simply reverse the revolution but would plunge society into a new round of violent social conflict. On the other hand, international solidarity for the revolutionary process, particularly solidarity which helps to neutralise external military and economic destabilisation, could make a significant contribution towards strengthening the institutionalisation of democracy in all its forms.

In conclusion, we would argue that the Sandinistas have shown remarkable tenacity and vision in building a revolutionary democratic project. Elections in Nicaragua are not a tactical ploy, but they are an important step in a wider process of change. In understanding the logic of the Sandinista political project, it should be apparent why elections cannot be the exclusive test of democracy. Ironically, in holding elections when a majority of the population is now literate and organised, the revolutionary process will have gained legitimacy at the expense of its 'democratic' detractors, particularly those of the new Right in the United States. After all, it is the Right which has the most to fear from the emergence of genuinely democratic revolutionary projects in Latin America and the Third World for which the fate of the Nicaraguan revolution is so important.

NOTES

José Luis Coraggio wishes to express his gratitude to the Guggenheim Foundation for supporting his research in Nicaragua, and to the Centre for Latin American Research and Documentation (CEDLA) in Amsterdam, where he was Visiting Researcher while co-authoring this paper. The paper was originally published in *Millenium Journal of International Studies*, 13, 2 (1984).
1. Compare the recent report of the 'Kissinger Commission' (1984) with Holland & Anderson (1984) and PACCA (1984).
2. See *Nicaragua, La Estrategia de la Victoria* (Mexico: Editorial Nuestro Tiempo , 1980).
3. In 1979 the programme of the new Government of National Reconstruction specifically mentioned that under-utilised land would be included in the agrarian reform. On 29 February 1980 a decree-law on 'decapitalisation' was announced; this was followed by the Agrarian Reform Law of 19 July 1981. These laws constitute, so to speak, the basic 'rules of the game' regulating private property. See *Leyes de la República de Nicaragua*, Vols 1–V (Ministerio de Justicia, 1983).

4. In May 1981 the Council of State consisted of eight political parties, seven trade union organisations, etc. About the 1980 debate related to the change in composition of the Council of State, see Senese (1981).

5. See, for instance, 'Bases juridicas para garantizar la paz y la seguridad internacionales de los Estados de America Central' (Official Proposal of Nicaragua to Contadora; Managua, 15 October 1983).

6. See Morrel & Biddle (1983a) as well as their previous report (1983b).

7. See Nicaraguan Government of National Reconstruction: 'Economic Policy Guidelines 1983-1988' (Managua, 1983).

8. Ministerio de Desarrollo Agropecuario y Reforma Agraria: *Estrategia de desarrollo agropecuario y reforma agraria* (Managua, December 1982).

9. In fact, regular elections were held in Nicaragua under the Somoza regime.

10. For a conceptual framework see Laclau (1983). See also Mouffe (1983). From our point of view, future debates around the concept of hegemony should emphasise 'external political dependence' of Third World countries; i.e. the correlation of forces is not determined exclusively within the national political arena. In the case of Nicaragua the real threat to the Sandinista revolution comes from the Reagan Administration; its dilemma is that it sponsors a fraction of the bourgeoisie which has little real internal weight. Should such an alternative be imposed upon the Nicaraguan people by military means, a long war of popular resistance would be the only outcome because of the strength of the autonomous mass organisations. In this sense, there would be no chance of a repetition of the Grenada tragedy where events occurring within a small vanguard party determined the fate of the revolution.

11. A very important example is the development of the 'popular teacher' in Nicaragua. See Torres (1983).

12. A clear case in which the FSLN was not successful in preventing this manipulation of specific identities in favour of the Reagan Administration's project is the case of the Miskito communities. Although many 'mistakes' have been recognised by the FSLN, the truth of the matter is that the question of integrating minorities while at the same time preserving their autonomy has not been satisfactorily resolved anywhere. In Latin America the Left has oscillated between the extreme positions of identifying these minorities with the proletariat (thereby seeing their complete proletarianisation as the 'solution' to the problem) and proclaiming support for an 'indigenophile' position where complete self-determination is the goal and where all non-Indians are seen as 'white', a highly apolitical view. Under a social revolution, new possibilities present themselves for seeking fresh approaches to this difficult question. But in the case of Nicaragua the fact that the contras had infiltrated the Atlantic Coast zone and that some religious leaders had denounced the revolution as 'evil' produced a situation whose handling by the FSLN cannot simply be seen as a mistake, but reflects real contradiction between the need to defend the revolution against external aggression and the need to allow for self-determination and the articulation of the Miskito community within the national liberation process. A further historical element is the lack of participation of isolated Miskitos in the revolutionary struggle against Somoza. This further illustrates that the direction of the revolution is not unilaterally determined by the 'project' but by the dialectics of struggle.

13. See Irvin (1983). For a discussion of some of the theoretical and ideological difficulties of planning in the first phase of transition, see also Coraggio (1982).

14. Hegemony develops unevenly due to its contradictory character and liberation does also mean transformation. When we speak of transformation, we imply both ideological and behavioural change. Such is the case, for instance, of the Miskito community which had been only marginally active in the revolutionary struggle, and felt that the revolution was the affair of the 'Spaniards'. The problem of the Miskito community is of relating not only to the Sandinista revolution but to the Nicaraguan nation as a whole. A more dialectic approach to this question will become easier once contra activities cease.

15. For a critical assessment of the struggle for women's liberation in Nicaragua, see Molyneux (1983).

16. An analysis of the succession of events before and after the revolutionary triumph in Nicaragua would show: (a) that many who now oppose the Sandinista Revolution and claim that it has betrayed its principles, entered into the massive front against Somoza quite late and, until the final days of Somoza, sought to negotiate with the United States envoys

for a 'Somocismo without Somoza' based on purging the National Guard; (b) that this internal opposition is unable to present any meaningful national project to the people of Nicaragua and for this reason depends on the United States Administration to create a real alternative to popular power in Nicaragua.

17. The main provisions of the Electoral Law (22 February 1984) are: (1) that the President and Vice President of the Republic would be elected by direct ballot and that a legislative body of 90 members would be elected under a system of proportional representation; (2) that the National Assembly, during its first two years, would draft a new Constitution; (3) that the State would finance all political parties wishing to campaign but that other sources could also be used; (4) that only those war criminals serving sentence or whose trials are pending, and those who have appealed for external intervention against the government, would be excluded from the electoral process. Some reactions to these measures show their effectiveness: certain members of the opposition have said — despite claiming that elections are their main objective — that they might not participate 'because they know the elections would not be fair'. Meanwhile, spokesmen for the Reagan Administration have said that they do not trust Sandinista intentions because 'they are acting out of fear', a somewhat ironic situation given that the Reagan Administration has justified its 'covert' action campaign against Nicaragua as a means of forcing the Sandinistas to hold elections. See *Envio*, 3, 33 (Managua, Instituto Historico Centroamericano; March 1984).

REFERENCES

Chamorro, A. (1983): 'Algunos rasgos hegemonicos del somicismo y la revolución sandinista', *Cuadernos de Pensamiento Propio*. INIES, 5 (Managua).

Coraggio, J.L. (1982): 'On the Significance and Possibilities of Territorial Planning for Transition in Latin America', in *Regional Development Dialogue*, 3, 2.

Downs, C. & F. Kusnetzoff (1982): 'The Changing Role of Local Government in the Nicaraguan Revolution' (mimeographed).

Gorostiaga, X. (1983): 'Dilemmas of the Nicaraguan Revolution', in R. Fagen & O. Pellicer: *The Future of Central America: Policy Choices for the US and Mexico* (Stanford).

Holland, S. & D. Anderson (1984): *Kissinger's Kingdom? A Counter-Report on Central America* (Spokesman).

Irvin, G.W. (1983): 'Nicaragua: Establishing the State as Centre of Accumulation', *Cambridge Journal of Economics*, 7.

'Kissinger Commission' (1984): *Report of the National Bipartisan Commission on Central America* (January).

Laclau, E. (1983): 'Socialisme et transformation de logiques hegomoniques', in C.B. Glucksmann (ed.): *La gauche, le pouvoir, le socialisme* (Paris: PUF).

Molyneux, M. (1983): 'Women and Socialism: The Revolution Betrayed? The Case of Nicaragua' (paper presented at a CEDLA Workshop, Amsterdam; October).

Morrel, J. & J. Biddle (1983a): 'Central America: The Financial War', *Report to the Washington Seminar on Policy Alternatives for the Caribbean and Central America* (October).

—— (1983b): contribution to *International Policy Report* (March).

Mouffe, C. (1983): 'Socialisme, democratie et nouveaux mouvements sociaux', in C.B. Glucksmann (ed.): *La gauche, le pouvoir, le socialisme* (Paris: PUF).

Nuñez Soto, O. (1982): 'La ideología como fuerza material y la juventud como fuerza ideológica', in: *Estado y clases sociales en Nicaragua* (Managua: Editorial ANICS).

PACCA (1984): *Changing Course: Blueprint for Peace in Central America and the Caribbean* (Washington: Institute for Policy Studies).

Senese, S. (1981): 'Apetti giuridici del nuovo assetto politico sociale', in *Relazione presentate alle giornate di studio sul Nicaragua* (Rome: Fundacion Lelio Basso).

Torres, R.M. (1983): 'De alfabétizando a maestro popular: la post alfabétizacion en Nicaragua', in INIES: *Cuadernos de Pensamiento Propio* Serie Ensayos No. 4 (Managua).

Wheelock, J. & L. Carrion (1980): *Apuntes Sobre el Desarrollo Económico y Social de Nicaragua* (Managua: Secretaria Nacional del FSLN).

CONTRIBUTORS

Barraclough, Solon: Director, United Nations Research Institute for Social Development (UNRISD), Geneva, Switzerland.

Bernal, Richard: Lecturer, Department of Economics, University of the West Indies, Kingston, Jamaica.

Bulmer-Thomas, Victor: Lecturer, Department of Economics, Queen Mary College, London, England.

Corragio, José Luis: Research Fellow, Coordinadora Regional de Investigaciones Económicas y Sociales (CRIES), Managua, Nicaragua.

Den Uyl, Joop: Leader of the Partij van de Arbeid (Labour Party) and former Prime Minister, The Hague, Netherlands.

Dunbar Ortiz, Roxanne: Professor of Ethnic Studies, California State University, San Francisco, USA.

FitzGerald, Valpy: Professor of Development Economics, Institute of Social Studies, The Hague, Netherlands.

Gorostiaga SJ, Xabier: Director, Instituto Nacional de Investigaciones Económicas y Sociales (INIES), Managua, Nicaragua.

Hertogs, Erik Jan: Research Fellow, Centre for Latin American Research and Documentation (CEDLA), Amsterdam, Netherlands.

Irvin, George: Senior Lecturer in Economics, Institute of Social Studies, The Hague, Netherlands.

Jiminez, Edgar: Professor, Department of Social Sciences, Universidad Iberoamericana, Mexico City, Mexico.

Marchetti SJ, Peter: Research Fellow, Centro de Investigaciones y Estudios de la Reforma Agraria (CIERA), Managua, Nicaragua.

Pellicer, Olga: Former Director, Department of International Politics, Centro de Investigación y Docencia Económicas (CIDE), Mexico City, Mexico.

Richard SJ, Pablo: Research Fellow in Theology, Departamento Ecuménico de Investigaciones, San José, Costa Rica.

Torres Rivas, Edelberto: Professor and Executive Member, Instituto Centroamericano de Documentación e Investigación Social (ICADIS), San José, Costa Rica.

Watson, Hilbourne: Associate Professor, Department of Political Science, Howard University, Washington DC, USA.

INDEX

Page numbers in italics refer to Tables. Figures are indicated by (F) following the page number